With Gen 1978

ANOTHER HOME

*"These are the two great works which we are to do
in this world: first to know that this world is not our
home, and then to provide us another home whilst
we are in this world."*

John Donne: Sermon LXXII

by

RONALD SELBY WRIGHT

WILLIAM BLACKWOOD & SONS LTD., EDINBURGH 1980

FRATRI DILECTISSIMO
D.S.W. 1910-1972

ISBN 0 85158 139 0

Foreword

This short Memoir was written initially at the request of my sister Ray, for her and her family, and was not meant for publication; but since so many friends (neither having seen nor read it!) have asked me to publish it I have finally been persuaded to do so.

It is, of course, a personal record, a "period piece", which I know can be accused of many things—of frequently being dull, of sometimes being indiscreet, of the inevitable "name-dropping", of repetition, of omission and of lack of orderly sequence, to name but a few. But at least I hope that no one will find that I have written anything nasty or unkind about anyone, and no "scandal" (which of course all helps I suppose, alas, in these days to make it rather dull!)

It has been fun for me to remember some of the things that I thought I had long forgotten; and now that I have finished it I find that there are many more things I ought to have remembered. Some people may be annoyed because their names have been mentioned; some others because their names have not been mentioned:

> If I offend it is with my goodwill;
> I come not to offend but with goodwill.

In addition to my sister who started it all, I should like to thank Mrs Taylor, my secretary, for typing and often re-typing these pages, and, too, Harry Richmond and Norman Drummond for urging me on; and with them the other Trustees of the Canongate Boys' Club for all the help they have given me—whose help I hope may be returned in some small way from any profits from this book which will go to help the work of the Church in the Canongate, to Henry Kirk for assisting with the Index, and to Mr J. R. Snowball of William Blackwood, for whose expert advice and encouragement I am so grateful, and who has prevented me from putting the MS.

at times where no doubt some people feel it ought to have been put in the first place—into the waste-paper basket!

If, however, this simple book can in however small and inadequate a way show my gratitude for the very many kindnesses I have had from so very many people, it may have served some little purpose; and I only regret that I have not been more worthy of them.

RONALD SELBY WRIGHT,
Easter 1980.

The Queen's House,
Moray Place,
Edinburgh.

Prologue

THE DEBT TO MY PARENTS

Like most of my immediate contemporaries, I was brought up in what today would be regarded, I suppose, as a rather sheltered atmosphere—though we never regarded it as such! School, homework, school games, the Saturday penny, the garden; and on Sunday, church, walks, the visit to Granny.

Home was the centre and very nearly the circumference. Instead of Sunday School (to which we *never* went) each night my mother would read to us before we went to bed from that lovely book, Robert Bird's *Jesus the Carpenter of Nazareth*, or some similar book of stories. We had, on looking back on it now, the four great needs of every child, affection, security, discipline in the best and fullest meaning of the word, and example. And the realisation still that these are four of the greatest needs for every child is the first great debt I owe to my parents.

Whatever troubles there were, were almost entirely hidden from us; and troubles indeed there were, though we were not to learn of them till much later. My father who had once had what was called "private means" and been an officer in the Argylls, lost his private income but still continued to live as though he hadn't; and even up to his death in 1942, he never quite realised it. The result was that he was continually in debt. Yet he spent little on himself but always for the family, giving us the best education he now couldn't really afford, and every summer that month's holiday in the country or by the sea.

It is true that sometimes we noticed that certain things were no longer in the house, and the cook went, and then one of the maids, and "paying guests" began to arrive, but all this never worried us—and never once did our parents ever say or make us feel that we owed anything to them; indeed one of the lessons our parents taught us was to try never to run into debt or live beyond our means; and they certainly could speak with full knowledge and authority on that subject! Before I went away anywhere even as a very small boy my father always gave me a 10/- note (quite a sum in these days), not to spend, but "in case I got stuck". He lived in constant fear of what he thought was insecurity, terrified that we would take up music at which he and my grandfather were so proficient—he urged us to "go into the Bank or somewhere you get a pension at the end". But when I said I wanted to go to University, he never said that this was going to cost him more, and he gave me all the encouragement he could. When I changed to the church, and saw this would·mean another three years, he still never complained—students got no grants in these days and my pocket-money I now earned by tutoring. Never once did he give me or any member of the family any impression that he was having a hard time to do all this for us; never once that we owed him a debt—and never would he have regarded it as such. Yet how great is the unpaid debt I owe now to him.

Yet how much greater debt I owe to my mother. For she was at the receiving end. If the struggle was unknown to us—for we had all we wanted—school, clothes, a comfortable home, good holidays, the excitement of going to the pantomime at Christmas—the struggle was more than known and borne by my mother. She was a gracious and beautiful person and had known in her young days much gaiety and happiness. If she bore much anxiety and sadness she never showed it to us and remained gay and happy to the end; her love for us all, her courage, her faith and her marvellous sense of humour carried her through. Every night when we were small children she sat beside us as we said our prayers (I remember how we always included in our prayers "the donkeys and ponies and horses and mules") and then she'd tuck us in and we'd go off to sleep surrounded with affection and security, the shadow of the coal fire flickering on the ceiling and the sound of the Water of Leith flowing outside.

She taught us the now old-fashioned but still much-needed virtues of good manners, based on self-respect, and respect for other people, and the need to be kind and how "a gentleman was someone who is at home in any company . . .".

She never lectured to us or got angry with us; when we did something that was wrong she looked sad and disappointed and that to us was sufficient punishment in itself. And she taught us the meaning of trust. She trusted us and somehow that meant that we tried not to let her down, and when we did, well, that again was sufficient punishment. Above all she taught us to trust in God. Here again she showed us by her example. After she died, I found in her small Bible that she carried everywhere with her these words written by her in pencil: "If you pray for your son to be kept safe and he does not return, he is still safe, God has kept hold of him."

Each Christmas dinner from the time I was very small my father made me get up and make a little speech "to thank your mother for all that she does for us all during the year". I think this was the hardest speech I ever had to make, yet surely it was the greatest. "Warm are our hearts, although we do not bare them," wrote Neil Munro. We took it all—the affection, the security, the discipline, the example—so much for granted. How great is my debt—and like so many of my dear father's—alas, how unpaid. I thank God for every remembrance of them.

Acknowledgments

This whole book was written more or less "at a sitting" and was neither revised nor re-written, so that I hope I have not published anything here for which I should first have asked permission, but if I have I apologise sincerely now.

It has not always been possible to trace the sources of some of the illustrations, and here again when I ought to have and have failed to do so, I offer my apology.

After fifty years in one parish as Honorary Warden of the Boys' Club and as Minister, and changing from the Old Town to the New, has meant the inevitable misplacement, loss, or destruction of papers, as well as the necessary disposing of many books, pictures and bits of furniture, and the consequent inability to find or remember some names and sources.

Anyone who has had to move house after many years in one place will, I know, understand; the others I hope will too. And to both I convey my apologies and hope that they will understandingly forgive.

The Prologue on pages vii to ix was first given as a talk on the Home Service of the B.B.C. in a series called "The debt to my parents".

RONALD SELBY WRIGHT

Contents

List of Illustrations

PART I

Chapter 1

When my grandfather died in 1928 the shops were closed during his funeral and crowds lined the treet. I never knew him well and he was regarded as rather an eccentric. I remember he kept a brown hen which he had won in some competition and which laid him at least one brown egg a day. My father always referred to him as "the governor" and often called him "sir", never "dad" as we called our father.

He spent his last years in Helensburgh, known to everyone, liked and probably better loved than by his family, for although respected, they probably had rather a fear of him. He had a large family and treated them, one is led to believe, as so many Victorian fathers did in these days. He lived his latter years in the Bank House at Helensburgh with his second wife. His first wife, my grandmother, was Anna Bennet-Williams of Kynance, Cornwall and of Pyt House, Tidsbury, Wiltshire, whom he married in 1870 and who died in 1891.

My late Aunt Clarice told me that they had the names of her mother's family back to 1414 and that among them the famous Jenevora who lived in the days of George II and was a young lady of the Court and that "George II, then Prince of Wales, fell in love with her and married her. (I have a copy of the original picture belonging to the Wallace Collection.) This state of affairs could not be allowed! So the marriage was pronounced null and void and she was sent off home, but not before an infant was on the way—a boy—who it seems took the name of her late husband Bennet-Williams *but* from that time the family crest had the three Prince of Wales's feathers added to it which rather bears out the story."

I don't know why my grandfather came to live in Helensburgh because he had been brought up in York where as a young man he taught music and was the Assistant Organist of the Minster. He was a brilliant musician and was pitch perfect. When a cock crew he could tell you the note straightaway and, I understand, was always correct—which must have been a comfort to the cock. He was a Bachelor of Music of Oxford where he had been a student at New College. My father told us that after he died he found among his papers an invitation to be an Honorary Doctor of Music of Cambridge. Whether he ever accepted or not that Honour we do not know, but I know that he always wore his Oxford hood when playing the organ at Helensburgh.

. His father, my great-grandfather (1825-1858), was a schoolmaster, having taken an M.A. at Oxford, and had been brought up at Bishopthorpe under the guidance of the Archbishop of York, Vernon Harcourt. The story goes that his father, the 5th and last Duke of Gordon (1770-1836) two years before he became the Duke and while he was still Marquis of Huntly, produced a son by a Campbell of Argyll, though he was himself married, but, as Burke euphemistically puts it, "by *her* had no issue". George, Duke of Gordon had served with the Guards in Flanders in 1793/4 and with his father raised the Regiment now known as the Gordon Highlanders, which he commanded from 1795 to 1799 in Spain, Corsica, Ireland and Holland, where he was badly wounded. He became a full General in 1819. Sir Iain Moncreiffe tells me that he was the origin of "The Bluebells of Scotland"—"Oh where, and Oh where, has your Highland laddie gone?" and was descended through Aberdeen, Atholl, Derby and La Tremoille from William the Silent, Prince of Orange, Founder of the Dutch Republic.

The boy's mother was a friend, and I believe a relative, of the Archbishop of York, Vernon Harcourt, who originally had been known as Vernon but added Harcourt to his name when he inherited some estate. She brought the baby to the Vernon-Harcourt family and asked if they would look after him for her. She was what would be called today "an unmarried mother". The good Archbishop agreed to do this; and since he had a family of his own, some of whom were not yet quite grown up, he offered to adopt the child but to give him in his early years into the foster care of people on the Bishop-thorpe estate, who had no children of their own and who longed for a baby to bring up. Their name was Wright and as the boy grew up he was able to enjoy the loving care of two people who had longed for a child, as well as the influence of Bishopthorpe and the Vernon-Harcourts.

Vernon Harcourt died a very old man in his ninety-first year, soon after a wooden bridge had collapsed and thrown him and his Chaplain into a pool below, at which he said to his Chaplain, "Well Dickson, I think we have frightened the frogs". That was the year 1847, he having been born in 1757. For many years Bishops and Incumbents continued in their Dioceses and Parishes until they sank into senility and expired, since there was no means of providing a pension for them.[1]

The Archbishop had two eccentricities. When he became Archbishop in 1808 he requested that all his clergy should reside in the Diocese—which seems a not unreasonable demand. Sidney Smith happened to be one of them and was very annoyed at having to move to Yorkshire, though not into his own Parish, for he lived twelve miles away at a place called Haslington, near York, and had to drive over to Foston every Sunday. He greatly resented this and complained, "A diner-out, a wit and a popular preacher, I was suddenly caught up by the Archbishop of York and transported to my living in Yorkshire where there had not been a resident clergyman for 150 years. Fresh from London, not knowing a turnip from a carrot, I was compelled to farm 300 acres and without capital to build a parsonage house." Another of the Archbishop's eccentricities which must have cast a doubt on the validity of the Confirmation was that he would appear in the pulpit of York Minster and, extending his hands over the congregation, would pronounce the words of Confirmation once.[2]

Three of the Archbishop's sons must have been too old to have had very much influence on my great-grandfather, though no doubt he met them frequently. Leveson Vernon

[1] *The Parson and the Victorian Parish* by Peter G. Hammond, p. 41.
[2] Ibid, p. 171.

Harcourt (1788-1860) was Chancellor of York; Octavius Vernon Harcourt (1793-1863) was an Admiral and built several churches; William Vernon Harcourt (1789-1871) was General Secretary to the first meeting of the British Association in York in 1831, and was a former student of Christ's Church, Oxford, Canon of York and Fellow of the Royal Society. In 1824 he carried out chemical experiments with Davy and Wallaston and was President of the British Association in Birmingham in 1839.

The greatest influence on his life at that time must have been the Archbishop's grandson, William Vernon Harcourt's son, Sir William Vernon Harcourt (1827-1904), who was a friend and direct contemporary of my great-grandfather. He was educated privately and then had a distinguished scholastic career at Trinity College, Cambridge, and among the offices he held was twice being Chancellor of the Exchequer under Gladstone and Leader of the House of Commons under Rosebery. He declined a peerage in 1892 (though his son accepted a Viscountcy in 1863) and the *Dictionary of National Biography* called him "the last of the old school of parliamentarians".

In Donald Macleod's *Life of Norman Macleod* he tells of his meeting Mr and Mrs Wright in York. My grandfather (1851-1928) was called William Robert, my father Vernon (1879-1942), and I was baptised with the middle names of William Vernon.

Though it began, as it were, on the wrong side, that is the story of the Wright side of the family.

My mother was a Selby—and that was quite a different story! Her great-grandfather was a Selby of Yerle who was to have inherited the estate when his uncle died. Unfortunately for him the uncle married late in life and produced a son who became the heir and so Robert, for that was his name, tactfully withdrew and became factor to the Minto estates, and was succeeded by his son Ephraim, and then by my grandfather, also Robert. Robert married Christian Stuart, aunt of Professor James Stuart Stewart and grand-aunt of the Reid twins, Professor J. K. S. and Dr G. T. H.

My mother's grandmother who has always been referred to in the family as "Granny Rutherford", has too an interesting history. Her father was a courier to the Mintos and was killed out riding and the Mintos took into the family both her and her brother, one of the first pupils at the Edinburgh Academy, who later became an Admiral. She lived as one of the Minto family and kept a very interesting diary which is now in the National Library of Scotland. She travelled everywhere with the Minto family and there are most interesting accounts of when Lord Minto was Ambassador at Berlin, and stories of their travels on the Continent. She was brought up like one of the daughters of the house, one of whom married Lord John Russell, the grandfather of Bertrand Russell, who was a very strict Scottish Presbyterian of the old school, which no doubt accounts for Bertrand Russell's having had "enough of it" when he was a boy—which is a lesson to us all.

My mother took him the diaries which he found most interesting. It was really his grandparents, for whom he had great affection and respect, who brought him up and not his father and mother.

My grandmother was all that a good granny should be—gracious, loving, kind, understanding. We saw a lot of her when we were children because she came to live at 9 Saxe-Coburg Place when later my father took number 12, when I was only three years old, and we visited her every day and each time were the richer for it. Most Sundays we went to church with her and sat beside her when she gave each of us a pan drop during the sermon to keep us from being too bored. The minister was the Rev. Harry Moir of St Bernard's and her Elder was Lord Guthrie who used to visit her in a horse-drawn carriage. One of her daughters, Kathleen, whom we called simply Keeshy, used to help me each night with my homework—dear granny and Keeshy, how we loved them both.

And that is the Selby side of the family.

Chapter 2

All the childhood I can remember was spent at 12 Saxe-Coburg Place with my father and mother, my younger brother Pip and my sister Ray; my youngest brother Bob was sixteen years younger than I and he was hardly able to share in our childhood memories, and he, with my sister, were a great comfort to my father and mother in their latter years. In these days our house stood complete, whereas nowadays the houses are nearly all divided into three or four flats. The back garden led down to the Water of Leith and in the front there was a garden for residents where we used to play cricket and football, not always to the entire pleasure of the older residents, especially when the cricket ball used to reach the road or sometimes the windows—that was known as "six and out or nothing and in". There was a lot of young people living there at that time, mostly from the Academy; No. 3 was indeed an Academy Boarding House, run I remember by a rather fierce Matron called Mrs Menzies, and it was there that I got to know so well John Lowis whom many years later I met when he was a Colonel in the Gurkhas in Italy, when I was Senior Chaplain of the 10th Indian Division. Then there was the Ashcroft family living at No. 11, and the Don-Wauchopes living at No. 13, though the youngest one there, Pat, was certainly a good deal older than the rest of us and didn't join in our games but spent most of his time playing cricket for Grange. His father had been a rugger international along with his father's brother, two of the early famous Fettesian internationals. Colonel Wood lived in No. 14 with his wife and two sons Phil and Bob. Phil became a Colonel later in the R.A.M.C. and won a D.S.O. in the Desert war; and on the other side of the Square for a time lived the Rev. Bruce Nicol and his family. He was a remarkable man and died quite young when minister of Govan, and his wife was a remarkable woman, living in Aberdeen until she was aged 90. The two most connected with us were their sons Bruce and Tommy. Tommy was then aged five but he later became my Senior Chaplain when I was Moderator, after he had been a distinguished Assistant Chaplain-General at Scottish Command, and later still became Domestic Chaplain to the Queen.

We all lived, I suppose, in a very closed and protected community, a world of home and school on weekdays and Church on Sundays. Apart from our cricket and football, the

Square was a quiet, peaceful place, and I still have memories of the Punch and Judy shows, the German Band, the organ-grinder with his poor monkey, and the Russian bear, that used from time to time entertain us. We always felt very sad about the poor monkey and even sadder about the Russian bear. Not so long ago I came across a poem[1] in *Blackwood's Magazine* which reminded me again of this poor bear, especially one verse in particular which expressed then the feelings I must have had as a small boy:

> And bruin lifted up its head
> And lifted up its dusty feet,
> And all the children laughed to see
> It caper in the summer heat.
> They paid a penny for the dance,
> But what they saw was not the show;
> Only, in bruin's aching eyes,
> Far-distant forests, and the snow.

On the whole we made our own entertainments; trains, pet rabbits, guinea pigs and Belgian hares (you never hear of Belgian hares nowadays), and, of course, toy soldiers. I have a vivid memory of Sir Donald Francis Tovey coming into our nursery one day and whistling all the bugle calls for our soldiers! He had a great respect for my father and indeed told my mother once that my father had had the ball at his feet, if only he would kick it, to become a great and outstanding musician. In his early days my father won a gold medal in London and was an Associate of the Royal College of Music, and also studied music at Edinburgh University. I shall never forget hearing him playing "See The Conquering Hero Comes" on the great organ in the Usher Hall, when Admiral Sturdee got the Freedom of Edinburgh. Indeed my father was asked to go with Melba on one of her tours as her accompanist, but he had too many other interests and other responsibilities; and indeed too many other worries, ever to kick the ball or accompany Melba. We read a lot of books—Gunby Hadeth, Percy F. Westerman, John Buchan, G. E. Henty—and papers and magazines like Chums, The Captain, The Boys' Own Paper and the Children's Newspaper.

[1] "My Mother Saw a Dancing Bear" by Charles Causley—*Blackwood's Magazine*.

We had our quota of nurses and servants—some nice and some not so nice—who wore uniform different in the morning from the evening, and "of course" we all went to Church but never to Sunday School. Sundays were different from other days, no games, only books to read, no working in the garden, best clothes. We always said Grace before meals; the one I remember best is "Thank God and the British Navy for our good food, Amen". Each night we said our prayers, usually with our mother beside us—usually lists of people whom we should pray for, occasionally leaving out one or two who had temporarily annoyed us; and of course we prayed for the animals: "The donkeys, the ponies, the horses, and the mules".

As mentioned before, we were constantly in my grandmother's house at No. 9 where two of my aunts lived, and we used to visit the homes of schoolfriends and friends of my father's and mother's. One of the visits I remember most vividly was when my brother Pip and I went to see, on several occasions, old Sir John H. A. Macdonald, Lord Kingsburgh, then Lord Justice Clerk, and he used to tell us stories about some of his cases. I remember him telling us about the Monson case and how Monson could not speak the truth even in his own interest! He was an Archangel in the Catholic Apostolic Church which I sometimes attended. His son was Norman D. Macdonald, an eccentric if ever there was one, but a rather charming eccentric at that. When he was a boy he remembered being sent up by the Rector of the Academy to 17 Heriot Row with a message which he delivered personally to Robert Louis Stevenson. On more than one occasion he and his wife invited my brother and myself to Coll-Earn, Auchterarder, to stay with them. They had a tennis court where A. J. Balfour first learned to play tennis, and even a small golf course in their grounds. It was when staying there on one occasion that my brother and I got into trouble with George Bernard Shaw. He, like a true Fabian Socialist, was staying at the most expensive Gleneagles Hotel, and we decided one day we would stalk him when he was out walking by himself. We managed to dodge behind bush after bush, not realising all the time that he had seen us, and suddenly he turned in great pretended fury and chased us away, and we felt rather pleased that G. B. S. had spoken to us! But we didn't say just quite what he had said. . . .

We had too some very wonderful holidays—North Berwick, Tynron, Balnaguard, and various other places.

North Berwick those days was slightly different from what it is now. For one thing most of the large houses where fairly wealthy people lived have now become hotels. One never sees on the links nowadays prominent politicians as one used to do when I was a boy. It was not an uncommon sight to see A. J. Balfour, Sir John Simon and H. H. Asquith, although political enemies, great personal friends. I remember once as a boy being hit by a golf ball, not at all seriously, by A. J. Balfour, who came over and apologised most profusely to me, to the great amusement and delight of my father. I remember, too, one Sunday morning going to the Episcopal Church with my father, and his nudging me and saying "look", and there in front of me was Mr Asquith entering Church in his carpet slippers.

At Balnaguard, near Grantly Castle, where Admiral Lord Beatty used to come for his holidays, largely for the shooting, my father used often to go and play to them in the evenings, and later sometimes stayed with them. My brother and I could only see them from a distance when they were out shooting, and I have at least on one occasion seen King George V shoot with them as a guest.

There really must have been some very worrying days for my father and more for my mother, but for us children they were very happy days. My brother and I always shared a bedroom and each night we went to sleep with the dancing reflection of the coal or log fire on the ceiling and the sound of the Water of Leith outside, and from my brother's bed "Goodnight, Daw" and from mine, "Goodnight, Pip" and from both "see you in the morning".

I have not said very much about my mother. But she was the one person who kept us all together and looked after us all. It was she who read to us each night from *Jesus the Carpenter of Nazareth* or from some other similar book. It was she who stood by us as we said our prayers. In these days ladies never thought of going out to work, but it did mean that they were always in the home, always waiting for us when we got back, always interested in what we were doing, always understanding and always kind. I am glad to think that before she went South to stay with my sister at Richmond in Surrey, from where she never came back, since she died there of leukaemia, she was able to spend the evening when I was presented with the silver chalice which the Queen had given to Canongate for my 25th Anniversary there as Minister, and was able to receive the various guests as they came in where we met in the Canongate Tolbooth, and hear Dr Warr give his, as usual, charming little Address, and the equally charming Address from Professor J. S. Stewart, which followed. The whole evening gave her great pleasure; and that was her last evening in Edinburgh.

When I went to see her in Richmond as she was dying, indeed on the last evening of her life, I had to get the train back, and when I got to Edinburgh I 'phoned my sister to ask how she was keeping and she told me she had died at the very moment that my train left to go North, as though she wished to go up North again to the places she loved, and the hills of home. Home would never be the same again without her graciousness, her kindness, her faith and her wonderful sense of humour.

Once again it was left to my sister to carry the heaviest part of the burden, as she had done when my father died, and as she has done so often since, with that same graciousness and courage and sense of humour.

Her first marriage was a disaster and she had to divorce her husband because of his cruelty, but it was more than made up for by the happiness of her second marriage to Stanislaw Komorniki, a Polish officer then in the British Army who came from an old and noble family whose land and property was confiscated, first by the Nazis and then by the Russians, but who made his home in this country, and of him and my sister—who changed their name to Kaye since nobody could pronounce or spell the other name—it can truly be said that "they lived happily ever after".

When her grandchildren's home was broken up she and Stanley took them both in as a part of their loving family and both Lila and Gina owe to them a home life they had never experienced before, for she loved them both dearly. Later too when her other daughter, Thelma's home broke up, she had her in a flat beside her, and Thelma and her young daughter were too a great comfort to the family. Most people might well have broken under the strain, but not Ray or Stanley or Thelma—they are made of more cheerful and more courageous stuff.

Chapter 3

I was born in Glasgow on 12th June, 1908 and was baptised Ronald William Vernon; Selby came later (and of that more anon).

I have never regarded myself as a Glasgow citizen since I came at the age of three to Edinburgh where I have had my home for the rest of my life, yet, it was a gracious gesture on the part of the Lord and Lady Provost of Glasgow when they invited me to lunch with them in the City Chambers on my 65th birthday. (As gracious a gesture as when the Lord Provost of Edinburgh invited me to an official lunch at the City Chambers when I retired from the Canongate in September 1977—only I had to reply to his speech then!)

Before I went to the Edinburgh Academy in 1915 I attended a private school in Ann Street, Edinburgh. I do not remember anything about it, except going there and coming back; but I well remember my first year at the Academy under Miss Millar. I once asked the then Head Master of Sedbergh, who had previously been Head Master of Cargilfield in Edinburgh, Mr Bruce-Lockhart, whether if he could afford to send a boy to either a Prep School or a Public School, but not both, which would he choose, and without hesitation he said "the Prep School". And certainly my years at the Edinburgh Academy Prep (and the two Forms in the Upper School) gave me and my brother a classical and cultural foundation for life, for which we were both ever grateful.

The Rector was Dr R. H. Ferard, a classical Oxford Don, whom the small boys never really got to know, but whose influence on the School was great. He was a typical old-

11

fashioned type of Head Master, always immaculately dressed, and my respect for him grew greater when I heard how once passing Inverleith Park on a frosty day when the pond was covered with ice, he saw a dog which had obviously fallen through the ice, struggling in the middle of the pond, and in a second had taken off his bowler hat and overcoat and went into the pond and rescued the dog, and then, donning the bowler hat and coat, walked away as though nothing had happened. It so happened that Arnot Fleming's father had seen him from a window; else nobody would have known anything about it, for he certainly would not have told anyone himself.

Though an Etonian himself, he was a great supporter of the Day School, and it was that which made him apply to be Rector of the Academy: "I applied for the office (of Rector) because I had come to the conclusion that the Day School is a higher as it is certainly a more natural type of institution than the Boarding School. . . . The Public Boarding Schools of the country have done and are doing admirable work . . . but the artificial segregation involved in the system is apt to beget a code of conduct and attitude to life less in contact with reality than will be found where the life of the School is carried on in intimate union with that of the home". And I certainly would agree with that.

He retired to Oxford; and the Academy, and those beyond its walls, recognised how great a Rector he had been; though the Academy has always had good Rectors, all of whom I have known to my lasting benefit since Dr Ferard's day.

My brother and I had many happy memories of the Academy days, and could not be too grateful for all the School did for us. We made many lifelong friendships. Especially do I remember that morning of the 11th of November 1918 when at 11 o'clock we heard the sirens going, and those of us in Miss Wood's class—5A in the Prep—rushed out to join the whole School in the Yards to cheer the Union Jack as it was raised on the mast. The Great War was over and we all got a half-holiday.

The Masters in the Upper School seemed to a young boy rather forbidding characters. There was, for example, B. L. Peel, known as "Billy" Peel, who used to pretend to wonder why parents when writing him a note would address him very often as "W. Peel, Esq."; and there was A. J. Prestland, who, wearing two pairs of glasses, would prowl round the Form Room like a tiger waiting for its prey; and "Beaky" Druitt who always wore his mortar-board cap with or without a gown, stiff and unbending, strictest of all with his own son, who later became Sir Harvey Druitt, and who taught me that it was seldom a good thing for a father to teach his own son in class. And then there was Cabeb Cash with his long black beard who used to rush into the Yards to tell the frightened Prep School boys that if they made any more noise he would put them into his deepest dungeon—and we all believed that he had one! And dear "Jas T"—James Taylor, the "father" of them all and the only real type of old Scottish Dominie, whose funeral I was to take—at his request—many years later.

The tawse was frequently in use—I think, on retrospect— too frequently—and if we were taught that the fear of the Lord, we were certainly aware, too, that the fear of the master, was the beginning to us of wisdom.

Though I have visited, stayed and preached at many schools in England and Scotland, there have been times when I still feel that when the school bell tolls it tolls for me! But they were happy days as a whole. Behind the sternness there was a kindness based on the real vocation that they all had to help us in every way they could.

Both my brother and I were sorry to leave the Academy in 1921, but I am happy to feel that I have retained a close connection with it ever since. In 1953 I was asked to give the Address and dedicate the 1939-45 War Memorial, and dear Ian Gillan said the Prayers, and General Sir Alan Cunningham, deputising for his brother, Admiral-Viscount Cunningham who was ill, read the Lessons.

From 1966 to 1973 I was Hon. Chaplain of the School and in 1973, after my year as Moderator, I was greatly pleased and honoured to be made an Extraordinary Director.

The reason for both my younger brother "Pip" and myself leaving was really twofold. The fees had risen again and had become really too much for a rather extravagant and now not so well-off father; and the desire of my mother and the Selby family that we should go to the school that my grandfather

13

Selby had gone to as a boy in 1857. Children, one sometimes forgets, have no say in where or how they are to be educated, and we found ourselves in the autumn term of 1921 as boys in what was then called the Edinburgh Institution, later called Melville College, and now called Stewart's/Melville College, in a completely new atmosphere and having to make new school friends without giving up the old ones; the fees now not quite so high as the recently increased fees at the Academy.

By this time my father's private income had diminished considerably, though he didn't always seem to realise it. When we ran short of matches he would order twelve dozen boxes; after a meal when we were short of butter he ordered a whole barrel; a whole salmon would arrive for a meal and kept us going in different forms, for several days. My sister remembers a turkey arriving once which was too large to get into the oven. Understandably he was constantly in debt, but always optimistic; and all through his life he was constantly telling us that whatever else we did, never to get into debt. He would quote Mr Micawber "annual income £20, annual expenditure £19.19.6d., result happiness. Annual income £20, annual expenditure £20.0.6d., result misery." Indeed he was in some ways very like Mr Micawber himself. You will remember how David Copperfield describes him, "I have known him (that is, Mr Micawber) come home to supper in a flood of tears and declaring that nothing was now left but the gaol (my father would have said the poorhouse) and go to bed making a calculation of the expense of putting bow windows to the house, 'in case anything turned up'; and the extraordinary thing is that very often something did 'turn up'".

He seldom, if ever, spoke to us about his early days, and I do not think ever about his family. Dr Charles Warr tells in his early schooling how "the advanced pianoforte was looked after by a dashing, stylish, well-favoured young man called Vernon Oswald Wright, a first-class musician. He had just become organist of Rhu Parish Church after having been Assistant Organist at Bangor Cathedral, and most of the senior girls cherished for him a secret but hopeless passion,"[1] and in a letter to my mother extending his sympathy to her on the death of my father, Dr Warr wrote how my father's

[1] *The Glimmering Landscape* by Charles L. Warr, p. 47.

14

"passing has brought back so many memories of my child-hood . . . young and handsome and wonderfully patient with us little boys, who must have caused him excruciating torture from the noises we drew forth from the piano! And then, there were, later, such happy occasions and meetings at Rhu—hardly a soul left there now—of these old days where he was so popular with everyone, and latterly the wheel of life brought him and my brother together at Hillhead . . . he had a great aptitude for friendship and in your loneliness and sorrow you will be supported by the reflection that you are in the thoughts and sympathies of an unusually wide circle."

That letter, written to my mother on the 5th of March 1942, just after my father's death, gives at least some idea of the way he was regarded by those who knew him best.

Occasionally he would come out with some unexpected remark about his early days, for example, in London. Once when he found me engrossed in reading *The Story of San Michele* I said to him, "You really must read this wonderful book", he looked over my shoulder and saw the photograph of Axel Munthe, the author. "That is Dr Munthe," he said to me, "an unpleasant man; I met him several times in London and didn't like him at all." He knew Fr Stanton of Holborn who has always been one of my heroes, and talked about him with great love and affection. He told me once how when staying with the very wealthy Sir William Orr-Ewing, he had asked if he could get him anything when he was out, and the reply was "there is one thing you could get me and no money could buy that—peace of mind".

My father also held a commission in the Argyll and Suther-land Highlanders but in the early years of the War he was invalided out and decided, though completely untrained, to go into business, and became first a temporary Manager of the Edinburgh Eagle Star and British Dominions Insurance Company, and when the War was over and the Manager himself returned, an Inspector in the Scottish Life Insurance, where by his playing he wooed many people to take policies, to the mutual benefit of himself and the Company.

Though his private income continued to diminish, his extravagances remained the same. If missing the Sunday morning train to Glasgow to play on his beloved Willis organ

15

in Hillhead, he thought nothing of taking a taxi the whole way there rather than be late. Later he took a small flat in Glasgow so that there would not be the same weekend rush, and spent most of the Saturday afternoons in the Western Baths, of which he was a life member, and in the evening frequently playing to the down and outs in the Salvation Army. He dearly loved Hillhead, not just for its organ, but because of his friendship with the Rev. Alfred Ernest Warr, and later Dr W. D. Maxwell. Most Sunday afternoons he spent with the Warrs' uncle and aunt, Mr and Mrs J. F. White.

He, as mentioned, could sometimes be an embarrassment to the family and not least to my mother. I remember setting off on our annual holiday (and wonderful holidays they gave us) and my mother saying as we entered the station, "are you sure you have got the tickets, Vernon": to which he replied, "of course I have, they are in my waistcoat pocket where I always keep them": the trouble was that he was not wearing a waistcoat on that particular day!

He had a great sense of humour and a fund of stories, but sometimes his humour could be rather misplaced. Once when rebuked by a very pompous hospital matron who obviously didn't like him and rebuked him in front of the other nurses by way of trying to humiliate him, he looked at her solemnly and sadly and said "Dear me, that means our weekend in Paris is off"—to the added fury of the matron and the obvious joy of the nurses.

He loved us all dearly and did all he could to help us, and we loved him too, though perhaps we didn't always appreciate "poor old Dad" as much as we should have. He was by no means perfect and perhaps we should not have loved him so much if he had been.

Chapter 4

My brother and I felt pretty strange at first in our new school which was then housed in Melville Street; but from it we both received great kindness, from Masters and boys alike. It was much smaller than the Academy and we were rather older

16

"new boys" than usual. I was the odd man out in my Form because of this and so I feel got rather preferential treatment. By this time too Selby had been added to my name, since my mother always felt that the mother's name should be added to the surname. Here was her chance now that I was going to her father's old school. (My younger brother and later my youngest brother had already been baptised Derek Selby and Robert Ashcroft Selby.)

I soon found myself the youngest N.C.O. and Tent Leader at the Corps Camp, with older boys than myself under me. My classical background at the Academy was a great help and stood me in good stead, since I was at least two years ahead of the other boys in that department, and was indeed the only boy then who took Greek. What I owed to the classics at the Academy I now equally owed a tremendous debt to the teaching of English, which was quite outstanding, and received a knowledge and love of the English classics, and not least of poetry, which has never left me.

As at the Academy, teaching was in the hands of dedicated and devoted Masters who didn't know the meaning of "overtime" or "extra-curriculum activities", though none was very highly paid. Today I think with gratitude of men like John Henderson who ran the games, was P.T. instructor, acted as School Secretary and Bursar, Captained the Corps, was everyone's friend, and often had boys to tea at his home. How he did it all so willingly and so cheerfully I don't know. When I left school in 1927 he asked me to help him as a Royal Scot Cadet Officer in the Corps Camps; and I was the last to see him leave with his wife for Australia—an old man now—to stay with his only daughter, and there he died soon after. "Johnny" was the most-loved, respected and dedicated schoolmaster you could ever meet.

Then there was Robert Rose who taught classics with the drive and ferocity and dedication that made even the poorest scholars pass exams. His voice could be heard sometimes throughout the whole school, shouting at his class and calling some of the boys "dolts" and "duffers", throwing chalk at them and making frequent use of the tawse. Yet when off parade he was the kindest and quietest of men, greatly loved and respected.

17

Many years later when Tony Chenevix-Trench gave me Ian Maclaren's wonderful schoolboy story *Young Barbarians* to read, surely one of the best school stories ever written, I was reminded of Robert Rose when I read of Dugald Mackinnon, or as he was called "Bulldog".

The General Strike of 1926 took place during my last year at school and in common with nearly everybody, we all tried to do something to help our country. I enrolled as a Special Constable and though I was never called upon to take any active part, and I suppose in any case was under age, along with all the others after the Strike was over, I received a certificate of thanks from the Prime Minister, Stanley Baldwin. My father and many of his friends did all kinds of odd things to help, like driving trains, 'buses, etc. It was quite amazing the way everyone rallied to help the country at a time when strikers were trying to do, as they tried again to do in the winter of 1979, what even Hitler had not been able to accomplish—bring our country to a standstill. As usual, it was the ordinary folk, who had nothing to do with it all, that suffered.

I greatly enjoyed my last years at school where for my final three years I played for the School First XI at cricket and for the First XV at rugger, of which I was Captain for the last two years. As our school was small in numbers we didn't win very many of our matches, although we set out in anticipation each week; and we learned to play just for the enjoyment of the game, to take our defeat cheerfully (as indeed we had to!) with all the more satisfaction of sometimes even winning. I don't think I would really have enjoyed playing for a team that "won all its matches". I won the Directors' Prize for the best "All-rounder".

No one could have been happier than I was during these last years at school and I felt the Edinburgh University very dull in comparison. It may have been largely my own fault, since I found my chief interests outside the academic life. In these days, of course, there were no students' grants, and for pocket money I tutored between lectures and in the early evenings, and even taught for a time at Craigflower Prep School. Of course the University was much smaller in these days—there would be round about 2,000 there—and was chiefly concerned as far as it affected me, with attending lectures, tutorials, and sitting exams. We had none of this desire that so many seem to have today, of wanting to run the University as students; we left that to older and wiser people.

I had intended reading Honours History which I greatly enjoyed, but, over half-way through, the History Professor, Basil Williams, said that I would have to give up the Boys' Club, and having refused to do this, I then went on to take an ordinary degree, which meant almost going back to the beginning and staying longer than I had expected or desired for my degree, and it meant I spent six years in the Arts Faculty before becoming an M.A. In retrospect I do not really regret this since it gave me a wider sense of study. I would have missed English under Sir H. J. C. Grierson, whom later I got to know well, Economics under Professor Ogilvie, always courteous and gentlemanly; Professor Baldwin Brown, so much loved by us all and so kind and generous in his marking (he once gave me 100+ out of 100!) and the great Professor A. E. Taylor, to whom I owe so much, whose Moral Philosophy classes were so outstanding, for he was one of the greatest scholars of his time. I was present in his class when the tassel of his mortar-board went on fire. He used to raise his mortar-board every morning when he came in, with his gown flowing, doffing it to the class and saying "Good morning ladies and gentlemen" and for a while he appeared with a gown over his overcoat and an umbrella over his arm while he lectured. I remember once when the rude habit of students shuffling their feet towards the end of a lecture particularly annoyed him and he looked up and said "just allow me to cast one more pearl". He had his obvious likes and dislikes: "a comic clown or ignorant buffoon-like Mr Chesterton". He was a great Churchman—an Anglo-Catholic who for a time had been an agnostic. His Gifford Lectures "The Faith of a Moralist" is surely one of the most outstanding of contributions to that famous lectureship. He was probably the greatest living authority on Plato, and there are endless stories about him. He was always very kind to me, though I was far from being one of his best students. Once when I failed in one of his exams I went round to his house to ask him why, and he could not have been more kind. He said that he "felt like a doctor who

19

had failed with his patient", got out my paper and went through it with me, and said he didn't know why I had failed but that it had probably been an external examiner, and that I should be all right next time. When I published *Asking Why* he kindly wrote the Foreword to the book and he was one of the first contributors to *Asking Them Questions*. In fact had it not been for him and H. R. Mackintosh I doubt if the book would have been started at all and become what it became—a bestseller, at the time when I was still a student at New College where I went after leaving the University. I specially remember H. R. Mackintosh's kindness to me. Knowing as he did, that I was night after night running the Boys' Club in the Canongate, he would sometimes allow me off some essay that he had told us to write and give me a good mark in compensation for it. On one occasion when I was ill and confined to my bed, he walked all the way down to Saxe-Coburg Place to give my mother a bunch of grapes for me. He was a living example of the Gospel he taught and preached.

I remember New College better not for what I was taught there, but for the people who taught me. They were great and good men. There was the Principal, Alexander Martin, and Professors like H. R. Mackintosh, William Manson, Adam Welch and John Baillie (who twenty years later was to present me for my Hon. D.D.)—great names and great people. Once again my chief interests were outside the walls of the College.

During my student days there at least two events stand out in my memory. I shall never forget the night that Earl Haig's body was brought home to Edinburgh—or rather the early hours of that morning of 4th February 1928. It was a bleak night, as bleak as a February night in Edinburgh can be, and the hour was that when normally most folk are asleep in bed; but it seemed as though the whole of Edinburgh had turned out to pay their respects and show their affection for their own great citizen of whom it has been written that, though it may be in history easy to find a more brilliant man, it would be hard to find a better man. How silent the tremendous crowd that lined the street was, so that you could hear the clatter of the horses' hooves coming nearer and nearer as hats were raised and heads were bowed. His mortal remains were borne into St Giles' and thousands passed by his covered coffin four deep on that cold,

20

wet February day, to pay their last tribute. And the next day the body of him who could have been buried in St Paul's Cathedral, was borne on a simple farm cart from the little border town of St Boswells to Dryburgh—a journey of five miles in the country of the Tweed, sheltered by the Eildon Hills. So was the great cavalry officer laid to rest beside the man who once said of himself he had always "a troop of horses galloping through his brain"—Walter Scott.

And the other outstanding memory was a year later when with an equally great crowd I stood watching the Moderator of the Church of Scotland and the Moderator of the United Free Church of Scotland greeting each other and leading a long procession of the two Assemblies numbering over 2,000 ministers and elders, to be greeted by Dr (then Mr) Warr on the steps of the West door of St Giles' Cathedral, with the words "Now is the Son of Man glorified. Peace be unto you". The whole of the High Street and Lawnmarket and the Mound as far as New College were both packed with people and we all sang psalms and paraphrases—the "Auld Hundreth", "O God of Bethel", "The Lord's my Shepherd" quite spontaneously; it was a thrilling and uplifting experience. And on the afternoon of that same day, 26th May 1929, I attended the great service of Union in the Industrial Hall in Annandale Street. As Dr Warr was later to write, "There has never been an indoor meeting like it in the long history of Edinburgh". In the presence of the Duke and Duchess of York (later King George VI and Queen Elizabeth) and amidst great enthusiasm, Dr John White was elected Moderator of the United Church. It seemed as though half of Scotland was there that day; even the Church of England was represented by two Scotsmen—Lord Davidson of Lambeth and his successor as Archbishop of Canterbury, Dr Cosmo Lang. But what I remember most and what most moved me was the singing by 12,000 voices of the second version of Psalm 102 to "Duke Street"—"Thou shalt arise and mercy yet . . .":

> "Thy saints take pleasure in her stones
> The very dust to them is dear . . .
> And generations yet unborn
> Shall praise and magnify the Lord."

Chapter 5

After leaving school I continued my interests there as I have mentioned as an Officer under John Henderson in the School Corps, and also in running a cricket team for the Prep; but my main outside interests I owe to two great and good men in particular—Dr Charles Warr of St Giles' and Dr George MacLeod of St Cuthbert's.

Dr Warr—or as he then was, Mr Warr—came to St Giles' in my last year at school and in the year that I joined St Giles'. He had known my father years before, and it was through my father that I met him. I had previously gone to Broughton Place Church because my mother knew the Minister there, Dr Fairweather, who had been an Assistant Minister when she lived in Crieff. But I found St Giles' very much more congenial and Dr Warr from then to the day of his death became one of my great guides and friends.

From the time I entered the University until the time that I was licensed, that is from 1927-36, I was the Reader at St Giles' and what I suppose today would be called "Student Attached", and it was Dr Warr who challenged me by saying, "Look, you spend your evenings playing cricket in the nets; what about helping young boys who have little or no chance in this life?"

St Giles' at that time had a Boys' Brigade Company run by a respected Edinburgh W.S. called F. P. Milligan; and so it was that I set to work to try and help him with his Company. I knew nothing about The Boys' Brigade, or Scouts, or Boys' Clubs, but I soon realised that if one was going to do anything at all one would need to start from scratch.

Mr Milligan always seemed to have a cold and when I went up each evening he always asked if I would carry on since he was not feeling very well! When he gave up The Boys' Brigade Company I then decided it would be better if we started something quite new, especially for boys who didn't like uniformed organisations like The Boys' Brigade or the Scouts. And so in a room in Fisher's Close which belonged to St Giles', I started in 1927 what became the St Giles' Cathedral Boys' Club, and later the Canongate Boys' Club. I have told the story of that Club in a book I have written about it,[1] and therefore I will not enlarge on it here, except to say that the premises were so small—just really one room—and belonged to the Church and so we didn't really have it for ourselves. When at last we managed to get a place in the Canongate in Gullan's Close, we were able to call ourselves in very truth a Club, and it became indeed one of the very best-known Clubs in the country.

As for Dr George MacLeod—or as he then was, Mr MacLeod, Minister of St Cuthbert's—I can never forget, too, my first meeting with him in my last year at school. He had just come to St Cuthbert's which he filled to capacity each time he preached, and continued to do so until he went to Govan some years later. My brother and I decided we would go to hear him preach one Sunday in the morning at St Cuthbert's and he preached on the text "If I had not come, you would not have had sin". We were both so thrilled with the sermon that we decided we would both go and hear him again that evening when he happened to be preaching in Inverleith. Much to our surprise and I must admit, our pleasure, we heard him preach again from the same text. It so happened that I had arranged to have tea with him and meet him personally for the first time that coming week. He had a beautiful double flat in Eglinton Crescent and he was looked after by Mr Fallon and his wife. Fallon to those who didn't know him well was at first rather a forbidding figure, and he ushered me into his study since his master had not yet appeared. When the master did appear he looked at me and said, "Ah, if you had not come I would not have had sin, because nobody would have known that I had preached the same sermon twice on the same Sunday!" As I say, we had never really met before and yet he had noticed in two packed Churches individual people in them. I don't need to say any more about George MacLeod and the great influence he was and has been on so many young people in Scotland. It was he who got so many of us interested in Toc H, and as Dr Roy Sanderson and so many others could tell you too, the impact of Toc H in Edinburgh in these days was really quite tremendous. As an example, eight of the first twelve Boys' Clubs in Edinburgh came about through Toc H.

[1] *Our Club* (Oliver & Boyd: 2nd Edition, 1969).

George MacLeod had gathered a wonderful team around him, including the beloved Canon Laurie of Old St Paul's who twice refused a Bishopric; P. H. B. Lyon, the Rector of the Edinburgh Academy and later Headmaster of Rugby, and General Dudgeon, Inspector of Constabulary—all incidentally holding the M.C.

Toc H, for those of you who do not know, is based on remembrance of the Elder Brethren who gave their unselfish sacrifice that we might give our unselfish service. We met every Monday night to, as we put it, "re-charge our batteries"; and what wonderful meetings they were! Perhaps it is summed up best in the ceremony of light we had at each meeting or in the Toc H prayer that we repeated together each time we met: "O God who has so wonderfully made Toc H and set men in it to see our duty as Thy will, teach us to live together in love and joy and peace, to check all bitterness, to disown discouragement, to practise thanksgiving and to leap with joy to any task for others. Strengthen the good thing thus begun that with gallant and high-hearted happiness we may work for Thy Kingdom in the wills of men through Jesus Christ Our Lord." And if sometimes the high-hearted happiness turned into what "Nunky" Brown sometimes called "high-handed heartiness" it nevertheless showed us young people that Christianity was a joyful thing and something that meant doing a kind of a service for others in comradeship and friendship.

There were some books at that time that especially moved and influenced me: one was Shackleton's *South* and another H. F. B. Mackay's *Message of St Francis of Assisi* and too the writings of Studdert-Kennedy. In the name of Toc H for two winters at Christmas holiday time some of us set off on what we called "Franciscan Treks", tramping the roads and taking with us not more than one shilling a day; sleeping where we could and trying to meet people on the road to help them. We wanted to see what it was like to be a tramp and to meet and get to know the "down and outs" and to see how people would receive us. The first trek we did we had with us a fine American called Phil Giles and Harry Whitley—full of life and fun—was also with us then. We tramped the North roads in the snow and sunlight and met some of the roadmen at Struan, among many of the others we met, who were men sometimes of remarkable backgrounds—schoolmasters, lawyers, etc. who had come down in the world through drink or who were escaping from the realities of life. We were able to talk to them and indeed sent Christmas cards to their families from them, families from whom they had been cut off deliberately, or who had cut them off themselves.

On the second trek Kenneth Strachan came with us and we did a similar journey, this time to the Aberfoyle area. I remember one cold night when we were sleeping in a hay-barn Kenneth calling out that he "felt nature very near!" I don't know if these treks did anyone much good; but they certainly did us good because we were able to learn through them what it was like, however temporary, to be on the road and be sustained with the "spirit of the Troubadours".

Then there were the Scottish Schoolboy Club Camps run by Stanley Nairne, Neil Campbell, Roy Hogg and Jack Tait, and other kindred spirits. Some of us went as Tent Leaders and had there a wonderful experience of the joy and purpose of the Christian faith, based on friendship.

All these helped to guide me in my vocation to become a Minister. What decided it was on a certain wet November night walking down below the Castle at Johnston Terrace. It was a very cold night and the rain was coming down very hard, and two of the Club boys were walking beside me; they had no overcoats, only ragged clothes, and I looked round at one whose gym shoes were open and letting in all the rain. That pair of gym shoes was my Damascus road and decided me then what my vocation was to be. The boy on that "Damascus road" was Jimmie Dalgleish who was eventually killed beside me during the War about ten years later.

Just at the time when my studies came to an end and I was to be licensed, there was one Church that I wanted more than any other in the Parish that I had got to know better than any other, with the young people there whom I had made friends, with whom I had walked and talked and camped, and that Church suddenly became vacant. Mr White the Minister of Canongate for nearly fifty years retired and indeed shortly afterwards died, and so after my licensing I went through for a short time to Glasgow where I became Assistant Minister of the Cathedral under the beloved Dr Nevile Davidson, who had then only been there for a year. I had hardly been there for more than two months before, to my great joy, I was called to be Minister of Canongate. I stayed at the Cathedral until after Christmas so as not to leave them shorthanded over that period, and was Ordained and Inducted to Canongate on the 7th of January 1937—and so another dream was realised.

Chapter 6

So many of my dreams have come true but none more than when I was called to be Minister of the Canongate in Edinburgh. For nearly ten years I had got to know the Canongate boys through the Boys' Club, which I had started, as mentioned before, in that small room in the then St Giles' Hall in Fisher's Close, for the boys who came to our Club nearly all came from the Canongate, or from the lower part of the High Street. This was because the Fettesian-Lorettonian Boys' Club under the beloved "Nunky" Brown had for some years before taken most of the boys from the Lawnmarket and the upper part of the High Street, and there had been nothing really for the Canongate boys except a rather limited Boys' Brigade. Some years before, I had told George MacLeod that if ever I became a Minister I would like to become Minister of Canongate—and now here I was! I knew I was succeeding my dear predecessor Thomas White who had laboured first for two years as Assistant and then for forty-eight years as Minister in Canongate—and "laboured" is the right word for it—and had died in that summer of 1936, shortly after his retirement.

The Church, like the Parish, was very poor. Many people lived there with families of sometimes as many as seven in one room, and indeed in No. 1 St John Street, two doors from the Manse in No. 3, 157 people lived up one stair. That Manse where he had lived for so long, was in a very poor condition—although they put in electricity for me when I went there, but he had had to make do with gas-lighting;

26

however the people did their best in his time, and they were all good, kind people, and Thomas White surely the best of them all. As that other fine man, Cecil Thornton, who was then Minister of St Margaret's and was later, on retirement, to become one of our own members, said of him when we dedicated a door in the Church to his memory, "When we honour Thomas White we come more into line with Heaven's judgments than we usually are. He was one of those who made little impression on the world, not very wise, or brilliant, or strong, or anything that is commonly held in esteem . . . he had chosen to confound the false values of the world for God had real work for him to do and, unsung of men, he did that work faithfully."

One could not have had more loyal or faithful friends than John Inglis, the Session Clerk, and John Sellers, the Treasurer, and at my first Kirk Session Meeting when there were only five Elders able to be present, one of the Elders said to me, "Tell us what you want us to do and we will do all we can to help you". And they certainly did, both then and until the end of my Ministry of forty years there.

I had met Mr White on only one occasion—when I went to ask him if he would mind if I started a Boys' Club in the Canongate from St Giles' Cathedral. We had had an offer of some old halls in Gullan's Close belonging to Thomas's Episcopal Church, which had been unused for some time. He said he would be delighted to see the Club there, so I went to see the lawyer, Mr John F. Falconer, later to become the famous Lord Provost Sir John Falconer, founder of the Edinburgh Festival, and offered him £10 a year for the hall. I remember his look of surprise at the smallness of the offer and so I suggested £20 (since we didn't have any money and it didn't really matter!) Well he smiled and said he would agree to that.

As mentioned, I have already written the story of the Boys' Club[1] so I won't go into all that again, but sufficient to say that we now had a building of our very own—a large hall for games, a room for billiards and a canteen, an office and a reading-room, half of which we soon turned into a Chapel— and a beautiful Chapel at that. The whole place was lit by

[1] *Our Club*: 1954: New edition 1969 (Oliver & Boyd).

ancient gas jets when we first entered it, some of which leaked rather badly, rats abounded, and in order to add to our "comfort", the back door led into the Close where Burke and Hare had murdered Bonny Mary Paterson.

But perhaps here I could repeat one of the several "Miracles" which I have experienced during my life. Not long after we had got into the building there arrived one November evening an old lady whom I had never seen before. She had come up the dark Gullan's Close and heard the noise of the boys and had come in to see how we were. She looked round and spoke to us for a while and as she left she handed me an envelope. I asked her who she was and she said it didn't matter, but after some pressure she told me she was living in a certain hotel in Edinburgh, but just for the night. I said goodnight to her and saw her going up the dark Close again into the Canongate and eagerly opened the envelope to see what she had put into it, and there were twenty one pound notes, the rent for the year. I 'phoned the hotel the next morning but was told she had been staying there for only one night and had gone early that morning and left no address.

Then a short time later one evening a man came in with his young son. He had been taking him round to see the old Closes of the Royal Mile and noticing the Club he came in and spoke to me, and though delighted to see so many happy boys, was horrified at the poor light given by the gas jets. He turned out to be the head of a big electrical firm and there and then decided that we must have at least good lighting in the place, and so he arranged to give us electricity. He had just been passing by . . .

When the electricity came it showed up, after much neglect of years, the gloom and dirtiness of the walls and ceiling and the need for them to be cleaned; and as people gradually came down to see us, mostly from St Giles', they realised that the place would need to be cleaned up. And so gradually the place was painted from top to bottom; and then one day Dr Douglas Strachan—the stained-glass window artist—probably the greatest of his time—he did the stained-glass windows for the National War Memorial at Edinburgh Castle—came down to see our Chapel and decided he would like to do something to help, and so he put into the Chapel five beautiful stained-glass

My Father, 1927

My mother with myself and Pip, c 1913

Pip, *c* 1968

Ray and Stanley, 1979

3

1st XV, 1926-27
Mr John Henderson and Self—centre of front row

Melville Dinwiddie, Self, Ronnie Falconer, Roy Hogg, Nevile Davidson
Dunkeld, Easter 1957

JOHN KNOX AND SAINT GILES SHAKE HANDS
OVER THE GOOD WORK IN GULLAN'S CLOSE
1933

5

Club Group, 1935: the 13th Earl of Home, K. T. centre with Dr Warr

The Boys' Club Activities, 1955

The Canongate Choir, 1957
Middle Row—The Rev. Hugh Mackay (Assistant), K. MacLennan, E. Elliot,
R. Long, R. Rooney, N. Black, J. P. Fisher (Head Boy), The Duke of Hamilton,
R.S.W., Gen. Sir Horatius Murray (Governor of the Castle), S. McFarlane,
I. Mackellar, I. Wood, I. Mackenzie, J. Cuthbert, A. Wright, Mr Laidlaw

Skateraw in winter

Skateraw in summer

windows of his own.[1] I remember going down late one evening and seeing him painting above the reredos of the Holy Table in gold letters the words: "God is Love".

Of course we got some help from Dr Warr and from the folk at St Giles' but the boys and myself took it in turns to keep the place clean; and we all soon realised that knees were meant for scrubbing floors as well as for kneeling in prayer, and more of the meaning of the words "orare est laborare".

We owed a great deal to Miss M. R. MacLeod, the beloved "Aunt Polly", the daughter of the "great Norman", who acted as "cleaner-in-chief" and brought down ladies to help, and also a character, an unemployed night-watchman, about whom I have written in the Club book, called Dodd, one of the most devoted and dedicated of men one could meet.

Soon more Leaders came to help us, notably an Edinburgh lawyer, James P. Shaw, so beloved of so many boys, who died quite young, his last words to me being, "I don't think I have done these boys any good, but O the good they have done me"; which of course was quite untrue, because he had done them more good than he could ever have imagined. Then there was Cyril Jones and George Thomson and Alastair Blair and my brother.

In its early days we ran for a time a Scout Troop in the Club. Our first Club-Scout Camp was at a place called Spott near Dunbar, where after many adventures we ended up being flooded out. Previously we had had one or two trial weekend Camps at Pinkie before Loretto School took it over from Lady Hope. At that first Camp we had the greatest of help from Kenneth Strathan and my brother. Kenneth, who became later a Canon in the Episcopal Church, and I had to go up on the Sunday to read the lessons in our respective Churches and we left the boys in the care of my brother, whose knowledge of Scouting was slightly less than mine, which though I was meant to be Group Scoutmaster, was slightly less than normal. It so happened that the Commissioner arrived that day and found the Union Jack flying upside down, and the Scout Commissioner's greeting to my brother was met by a sort of Nazi "heil" salute! The boys all arrived late—in the middle of

---

[1] Four are now at Rannoch School Chapel and one at Nunraw—given by the Club Trustees.

29

the Minister's sermon—at the Parish Church for the Morning service, to the consternation of the Minister and the small congregation!

Later we had some glorious Camps at Mallaig by the Lake of Menteith under the auspices of that great Leader of youth—Major F. M. Crum. On arrival at the Waverley Station Alfred Armour found a free fight going on, attracting quite an audience, among one or two of the boys, and when we got to Stirling the guard said to me, "I went through the Battle of Loos but I would not like to fight that lot"; but they really turned out to be a fine crowd of fellows.

Camps at Pease Bay and at Reed's Point followed, where the sun seemed to shine all the time, except for that last Camp at Reed's Point when it rained for a fortnight; and that decided me that we would need to see if we could not find somewhere in the nature of a hutted Camp. And so we came to Skateraw where we built our Camp, laid the pathways, planted our trees, laid on water, and where we remained for forty years, and which has to this day become a legend to so many old boys; where stood, and now re-stands—for we had to leave the Camp in 1977 when the Electricity Board bought up the shore for Torness Power Station—a memorial "for those who loved to camp here and gave their lives that others too might love it", a memorial of a large wooden Cross, around which each boy put the number of stones of his years of age. And, since the cairn faces the East where the sun rises and is by the shore, these words were added: "And when the morning was come they saw Jesus standing on the shore". Of these great days at Camp we too could sing:

"O the great days in the distance enchanted
Days of fresh air in the rain and the sun."

Camp was always the best room in the Club.

When the war came, and we had to give up the building in Gullan's Close and move into the old Manse in St John's Street, the Club was looked after by the good James Shaw. We moved after the war to places like Brown's Close and Playhouse Close for a time, until eventually we got Panmure House, which had been practically a ruin, as a gift from Roy Thomson, later Lord Thomson of Fleet, the fine house which had belonged to Adam Smith of *The Wealth of Nations*, a not inappropriate house to have for a Boys' Club, for surely the wealth of any nation lies in its youth.

After a brilliant sermon—as was to be expected—by George MacLeod who was the Moderator at that time, Panmure House was opened on 6th October 1957 by the Princess Royal accompanied by the Duke of Hamilton, the Club's Honorary President, and less than a year later, on 1st July 1958, the Club was again greatly honoured by the visit of the Duke of Edinburgh who stayed some time in the Club, presented personally the first winners of his Award with their badges, and unveiled the War Memorial and sent a message later to say how impressed he had been "by the happy atmosphere of the Club and the well-being and liveliness of the boys".

Later still, a new Hall was built as an Annexe, the foundation stone of which was laid by Lord Home on 3rd March 1967 and dedicated by Dr Warr. There could have been no one more suitable to do this than Sir Alec, as, having renounced his peerage to become Prime Minister, he was known at that time, for no Scotsman was more loved and respected than he, and indeed on more than one occasion the boys of the Club had been invited to visit the Hirsel by both his father and himself. In 1931 his father, the beloved old Earl, who has become even better known now through three of his sons' books, came to visit the Club in its Gullan's Close days and later spoke in the Chapel; and I shall never forget the visit paid by the Club to the Hirsel in July 1951 when he was so kind to us and having that last sight of him waving us all "goodbye" from his door with "Come back and see us again soon!" Alas, all too soon some of the boys were to return but this time to sing at his funeral service in the same Chapel in the Hirsel where we had sung at prayers before we left not so many days before. He was a very great Christian gentleman and everyone loved him.

We were to return again more than once to the Hirsel. On one memorable occasion when Henry Douglas-Home—the "Bird Man" of the B.B.C.—told the boys about the birds of the countryside and showed them some of their nests. Another well-remembered time was when Lady Caroline Douglas-Home acted as our very kindly hostess since

31

her father, who had invited us and who had meant to be present, had been suddenly called away on Prime Minister duties.

As a Boys' Club Panmure House could not have been better except for one thing. It lacked a large recreation hall where boys could kick a football about and play basketball, and take part in general exercise, and when a large block of slum dwellings beside the Manse was demolished it left a large space vacant and I had had my eye on that as a prospective site for a hall. I told the boys that one day there would be a hall there as an annexe to the Club and I was quite determined that there would be. I approached the various authorities and learned that if we could raise half the money the other half would probably be granted us by the Government. But unfortunately this was the time when there was quite a tight squeeze on public funds. The Russell Trust came to our help and gave us a good donation and it looked as though the Town might come to our aid too. But there was so much putting off and putting off that we began to feel we would never reach all the money we required for the hall. Sir Basil Spence had drawn up a very fine design for us with a changing room, showers, and the hall itself, to fit into the site that was available, which was not quite as large as we would have liked, but certainly large enough for a badminton court with a little over, and with a platform that could be used for any theatricals or the equivalent.

Then one day something quite extraordinary happened. I was coming down from the early morning service that we had in the Church in these days at 8.30 a.m. and I said to, I think it was Jim Colquhoun, "I am going to go back now and write to as many sources as I can find and to as many people whom I think might help, to see if we cannot raise the money for this new hall". I opened the third letter of the post that had come that morning and it turned out to be a letter from a lady whom I didn't know who lived in Bridge of Weir. It was a note to say that her father had left some money some years ago and she would like to give it for something that might be of some help, and could I suggest anything suitable. I immediately wrote to her and told her that we needed another £14,000 for the new hall we were contemplating putting up in connection with our

Boys' Club. I realised that this was a lot of money to ask, but perhaps she might be able to help towards it. At the end of the week I got a reply to say that she and her family would be very glad to give this money, and so to my great joy I saw the fulfilment of another dream coming true.

The lady turned out to be the daughter of the late Lt.-Col. Harry Younger and so I thought it would be an appropriate thing to call the new hall after him—the Harry Younger Hall; his family after all had for a hundred years been one of the main sources of employment in the Canongate and he himself had been a man who was held in tremendous respect by everybody. He had been at Winchester with George MacLeod and that was why I asked George MacLeod to officially open the new hall after Lord Home had the year before laid the Foundation Stone for it. And so another miracle came true.

The new hall was opened the following year, on 24th November 1968. Messages of goodwill were received from H.M. the Queen, the Duke of Edinburgh, the Prince of Wales, and from many former Club boys at home and overseas. At the service in the Church preceding the opening, almost twenty former Leaders—thirteen of them now ordained—attended, while nine others who were ordained, sent their apologies.

In May 1974 a small annexe was added which we called "The Stag's Head" and which was opened by the young Earl of Cassillis who was one of our outstanding Club leaders during the time he stayed with me at the Manse.

Although I was, of course, Minister of the Canongate, I was equally Honorary Warden of the Club, which I remained until the Club closed in March 1978, over fifty years since I first started it.

The Trustees of the Canongate Boys' Club still remain; and though we no longer have a building in Edinburgh or the Camp at Skateraw, we have now Whiteside Cottage in the Peeblesshire hills—the "friendly hills that are green to the top" as Colonel Freddie Johnston used to say—through the kindness of the Earl of Wemyss and splendidly restored by the South of Scotland Electricity Board, with electricity throughout—a change from Tilly lamps and Calor gas—and which, as I write, we are handing over largely to the boys

33

of Fettes College to be used by them and Loretto and Clifton Hall Schools.

Chapter 7

I shall never forget my opening Social in the Canongate. It was held most inappropriately in the Church—and a pretty full Church too. People sat with buns in the pews and on the floor of the Church and in the then vast gallery, and cups of tea were handed round—not always very successfully. Songs and recitations were given—some of rather doubtful quality! Dr Warr to whom I have always owed so much, kindly came and introduced me, and the much-beloved Canon Laurie of Old St Paul's came too and spoke, and was greeted with loud applause when he came through the Church. Professor Fulton of Glasgow University brought good wishes from Glasgow Cathedral and some others spoke too. The Communion Table, on which sat an ancient aspidistra in a hideous red bowl, was moved to the side to hold the platform party's hats and coats, and trestle tables set up in its place on which we could have our tea and buns with a little more dignity than those in the pews. It was all so welcomingly and kindly meant, although it was so out of place in the building.

On the Sunday following Professor John Baillie "preached me in" taking as his text "a pearl of great price"; and from the beginning no one could have had a more friendly or, in spite of the obvious difficulties, a more encouraging welcome than I had. In contrast to my predecessor's experience in his early days, the Kirk Session did everything possible to help me, whether in the much-needed change of Order Form in worship, in the restoration of the fuller observance of the Christian Year, in the starting of the Watchnight Service on Christmas in 1937, or in the almost total renovation of the Church itself. Christmas Eve Watchnight Service indeed came in for quite a lot of criticism, not least from some other Ministers; it was regarded as rather "popish", but it was not long before many other Churches were following our example, and indeed now the Service on Christmas Eve is almost universally held within the Presbytery of Edinburgh. In my Pastoral Letter of February 1938 I wrote:

"None of those who were present is likely to forget the first Watchnight Service to be held in the Canongate for centuries. It was a moving and wonderful experience to see the body of the Church filled to overflowing at that hour of the night. Young and old alike—some had come from their own firesides, some from their work, tired from the Christmas 'rush', some from theatres and dances, in party frocks and 'evening dress', and one in the proud uniform of the Scots Guards. All had come to the Father's House to celebrate in the best way the birthday of the Son who is the Saviour of the world. And as we passed out, shaking each other by the hand and wishing each other 'A Happy Christmas', into the crisp December air, past the beautifully-lit Christmas Tree that the King had given us, I'm sure we must all have felt that there was no better way of bringing in Christmas Day than this."

The Canongate Kirk has, of course, a great history dating back to the foundation of the Abbey of the Holy Rood by King David I in 1128.[1]

As is generally known, the Abbey Nave became the Parish Church at the Reformation and remained so until first Charles II and then James VII decided that they wished the building to be used as the Chapel Royal and for the Knights of the Thistle; and so the present building was started in 1688.

It was first known as the Kirk of Holyroodhouse (Canongate) and later as Canongate Kirk (the Kirk of Holyroodhouse). Its first Reformed Minister in the old Abbey building was the great John Craig, and among its subsequent Ministers could be found names famous in Scottish history,

[1] See my *The Kirk in the Canongate*, Oliver & Boyd 1956: 2nd impression 1956: 2nd edition 1958. *An Illustrated Guide to the Canongate Kirk, Parish and Courtyard*, 1956. *A Short Guide to the Canongate Kirk (The Kirk of Holyroodhouse)*, Edinburgh, 1974.

not least Thomas Hannay who later became Dean of St Giles' and at whose head Jenny Geddes is reputed to have thrown a stool; the great Dr Hugh Blair to whom crowds came to hear preach what seems today to be the most boring sermons, and who was a friend of Dr Johnson to whom he had been introduced by Boswell who was actually a member of the Church. "Though the dog is a Scotsman and Presbyterian, and everything he should not be," said Samuel Johnson of Blair, "I was the first to praise him." Then there was Dr Mitchell who was five times Moderator, and Dr John Lee, later Principal of the University of Edinburgh.

The Church has some of the most priceless Communion and Baptismal silver plate, most of which had been used in the old Abbey Kirk at Holyrood before moving to the present building, and is still in use. But, as mentioned, the Church was in a poor state of repair inside and out, and since much had been done to spoil the interior during the early part of the 19th century, one of the first things I decided to do was to try to repair and restore it. I invited Ian Lindsay to be our architect and he drew up plans which he discussed with me and which were put before the congregation, who gave their wholehearted agreement, though I know they thought it was really all a wild dream because we had no money to pay for it.

Then the War came and all had to be shelved, but during the War I sent out an Appeal for £20,000 in one pound notes to every person I could think of, from the Royal Family downwards, and donations came from the King and Queen, from Queen Mary and the Princess Royal, and all the rest of the Royal Family, and all through the War money continued to come in—even from Harry Lauder and Dr Cosmo Lang, the Archbishop of Canterbury! We owed a great debt to men like Robbie Fulton and Duncan McNeil, later too to John Summers and George Wilkie, and of course to George MacLeod who took over Acheson House when I was called up, and which at the time I had obtained as a Manse by the good grace of the Marquis of Bute who had just restored it and which was to be the Manse of the Canongate for the next ten years, since I had had to leave 3 St John Street which had now become quite impossible to live in as a residence with its leaking nailsick roof, damp walls, and innumerable swimming galas by the rats in the oft-flooded basement.[1]

Canongate Parish and its Kirk is on some ways unique, for not only does the Parish comprise part of Edinburgh's Royal Mile steeped in the history of Scotland and includes Arthur's Seat and the Royal Park, and also the Palace of Holyroodhouse, but by a strange chance of history, Edinburgh Castle. As Sir Walter Scott put it: "It bears, or rather once bore, the same relation to the Good Town that Westminster does to London, being still possessed by the Palace of the Sovereign, as it formerly was dignified by the residence of the principal nobility and gentry." And later he said, "We will not match ourselves except with our equals, and with our equals in age only, for in dignity we admit of none". It was Lord Cockburn who said, "The very Canongate has a sort of sacredness in it"; and Sir J. M. Barrie, "Who could ever hope to tell all its story or the story of a single Wynd in it?"

When I knew it first it was, as mentioned before, in a deplorable state of bad housing—often at least seven in a room—appalling sanitary conditions, also an example of a real poverty unknown today, mass unemployment and deprivation which however bred with it a spirit of courage and neighbourliness, of trust and kindliness and of a cheerfulness born of adversity. In many ways the people of Canongate were examples of the survival of the fittest.

I told the congregation that our (and by "our" I meant not just mine but their's too) first duty was to the Parish and that with their help I intended to concentrate on that. This quite frankly didn't go down too well at first even though I did try to explain that it was those who didn't go to Church who should be our main concern and the main concern of those who did, and I quoted William Temple's remark that "the Church exists primarily for those who never go near it". I

[1] Owing to the expense of the upkeep we later had to move after the War to 17 Regent Terrace which overlooked the Parish and that remained the Manse for another ten years; but our eyes were ever fixed on Reid's Court, the old Manse of the Canongate, where the good Dr Buchanan lived through all his Ministry, and where he died in 1832, and which I had hoped to get back eventually and indeed got back again as the Manse in 1958—but that is anticipating.

explained that I was the Parish Minister as well as the congregational Minister and to me the Parish must come first since I relied on them to help me.

There was a teeming un–Churched population in the Parish with 3,000 school–children alone, and though many actually didn't attend the Church, the organisations were on the whole well–attended. There was a large Men's Club, a large Youth Fellowship as well as the Boys' Club, and the various Church organisations lke the Sunday School.

The Evening Service in these days was, curiously enough, better attended than the Morning Service—the Morning Service being chiefly for those who lived outside the Parish—and it was not until the blackout nights and later television gradually extinguished the Evening Service.

The inside of the Church was still very primitive and heating at times was almost non–existent and had to be kept going by an ancient coal–boiler; a rather grim erection dominated the front of the interior of the Church to which the pulpit was attached, and in the pulpit itself there still remain the brass gas jets—though no longer in use—a rather dim light over the pulpit having now taken their place. From the pulpit the whole Service had been taken and conducted. There was no centre aisle so that wedding couples had to part almost immediately after their marriage at the first pillar. Half the cloth on the Communion Table was torn, as indeed was the carpet under it, and, as I have already mentioned, the aspidistra which at first I could not get rid of since it was given by some member of the congregation, I at last caused its demise by the crime of poisoning!

But they were all great people—and after all it is people who matter—who had a vision of what we would like to see one day and it kept us going. I was young and enthusiastic and my waking dreams were of what would be, and my vision what it all became.

Although many of the people of the Parish didn't go to Church very much, at least the Church always went to them and was always welcomed with kindly affection, and there was never a dull moment; and though one was often tired in the work, one was never tired of it.

Chapter 8

"The magic word has come padre—mobilisation"—that was the message I got from Walter Scott in the early evening of 1st September 1939, when I was having my bath. During the Territorial Summer Camp at Strathpeffer we all felt that war could not be too far away; now it looked as though it were in very truth upon us. I went to the Drill Hall in East Claremont Street to find what looked like the whole of the Territorial Battalion of the 7/9th (Highlanders) Battalion, the Royal Scots, reporting for duty. Most had come from their offices and works after hearing the news on the wireless and had come even before going home. The M.O.—Jimmie Mason-Brown—was there giving injections and I was there at his request to help with the needle. It was Friday night and we were due to move to our posts on the Monday, so I still had a short time to do what was possible to clear up at Acheson House, and prepare to preach in the Canongate on Sunday.

Before the Service in the Church I had spoken at an early Service for a group of Gunners in Leith, and it was during that Church Service I had placed a wireless set so that we could hear what the Prime Minister had to say at 11 o'clock, and it was there that we heard Mr Chamberlain announce that we were now at war with Germany. Hardly had he spoken before the siren sounded throughout the Church, and indeed throughout the whole country, an anxious and rather frightening moment; but it turned out, as we all know now, to be a false alarm.

On the Monday morning we marched from East Claremont Street with the pipes playing and kilts proudly swinging, to the Waverley Station, where crowds gathered at the side of the road to wave us farewell. The train was waiting for us but we had no idea where we were going—rumour had it that we were all going to Egypt—but we landed at Kinghorn where we could see Edinburgh across the Forth but were not allowed to tell anyone, and with the address "c/o Army P.O."! We were there for three months before we went for another three months to Dumfries.

The Kinghorn days were great days—days of getting to

know each other better than we had before the first intake arrived. We were all volunteers, proud of our Battalion and ready for anything. Indeed it was more like a larger edition of the Boys' Club. The fact that this was the only Edinburgh Territorial Infantry Regiment made it all the easier. Some of the Club boys had already joined us and most of the others I had already got to know in the Drill Hall and at the Strathpeffer Camp. Under the Command of Iver Salvesen we had a really good team of officers, including John Chiene, John Gray Newton, Graeme Warrack, Hugh Rose, Ian Crawford, Walter Scott; and the N.C.O's, and indeed all the Battalion, were a really great crowd of fellows. Iver was the most generous of men, but people didn't realise this, as everything he did was anonymous; we were, for example, the first Army unit to have a Church of Scotland Canteen, set up at Kinghorn, because of his generosity.

We were in these days still a singing Army with "Roll out the Barrel"; "We'll hang out the washing on the Siegfried Line"; "Run rabbit run" and all the rest of it. Sometimes one would hear breaking out:

> "Why did I join the Dandy Ninth
> Why did I join the Army
> Why did I join the Dandy Ninth
> I must have been . . . barmy."

We were at heart all glad that we did, and thought that the War would probably be over before the end of the year. We didn't realise that it was the "phoney" war that had started and was to go on for many months yet—indeed, after the "phoney war"—years!

Our first intake came to us at Kinghorn, a very fine crowd of young fellows, mostly from Yorkshire, who were by no means averse to wearing the kilt and seemed greatly to enjoy being "adopted" Scotsmen.

Our next intake came when we arrived three months later at Dumfries, also a good crowd of fellows. Dumfries itself was a very different proposition. For one thing we ran into one of the severest winters in living memory, deep snow and ice— even trains had to be dug out—and our premises were far from satisfactory—largely old disused mills, very often with little glass in the windows, sometimes with the snow driving on to the bunks which were largely mattresses on the floor. Many went down with 'flu. For more reasons than one I shall never forget my first Christmas. Quite a number went home on leave to recover from 'flu and about half the Battalion was left.

As a Padre I had received a very large quantity of what were known as "comforts for the troops"—socks and Balaclava helmets, scarves, etc, and along with those, what were known at the time as "Jocks' boxes" containing such things as sweets and chocolates and tobacco; and so late on Christmas Eve 1939 some of the officers, including Dick Normand and Charlie Herriot, joined me as I went round all the beds when everyone was asleep, and at the foot of each bed we filled Christmas stockings with the contents of the Jocks' boxes, so that when each woke up in the morning he found on the floor at his feet that he had a Christmas stocking waiting for him, filled with an orange, sweets and tobacco and other things that had come out of the Jocks' boxes, and everyone began to feel there must be some truth in Father Christmas after all!

On Christmas morning we had a voluntary Service and at least 90 per cent of the available troops turned up.

After the severe winter in Dumfries we were next posted to the South, round about Yeovil and Sherborne.

By this time I was beginning to realise all the more what I had always felt—the value of compulsory Church parades. A great number of the troops in our Battalions had seldom, if ever, been to Church since perhaps their Sunday School days, and I found to my surprise that when I held Confirmation Classes, whether for the Royal Scots or the 4th Battalion of the K.O.S.B., with whom I was also attached, the numbers coming forward quite astonished me. The Battalions were becoming a "family", and soon the troops were beginning to realise that part of a family was sitting round the family table. I was quite amazed how many came to the classes—sometimes as many as forty from one Company, and what a high percentage came to the Services of Holy Communion.

These early summer days in Somerset and Dorset were never to be forgotten. Sometimes on Sundays I would take as many as six or seven Services, talking to small groups, but sometimes in some of the glorious Churches in that part of the

41

country. We filled Yeovil Parish Church and lovely Parish Churches like Crewkerne, and sometimes held small Services in the open air to meet the needs of smaller and scattered units, though then, of course, we had no organ to lead us and not even a Regimental band and I frequently had to be the Precentor; and I shall always remember a Service taken at eight in the morning in a field near Montacute for a Company of the 155 Field Ambulance. My precenting was even worse, and I started in a low key which got lower and lower as the hymn went on, until in a soft voice, but loud enough to be heard by me, I heard the Officer Commanding the Unit, Major, later Sir John, Halliday Croom, saying to himself in desperation: "Hell, I cannot get any lower."

One of the most enjoyable visits that I paid whilst we were stationed at Yeovil was to the Franciscan Friars at Cerne Abbas, and I specially remember one weekend there when Hugh Walpole was staying with them, and the discussions we had at night. At this time his views about the Church were changing and he was becoming more friendly and no longer cynical towards it; indeed one could say that he had become almost totally back to his early days; and here he was clearly "at home", staying with these delightful Franciscans—men like Br Douglas whom I remember taking, years later, round Edinburgh, truly one of our real and living saints of our time. I remember Hugh Walpole telling me then that when he wrote *Mr Perrin and Mr Traill* he was thinking of himself as he was and as he might become as a schoolmaster.

I got to know Cerne Abbas itself a little better after the war too, when Cyril Taylor was Rector there before he went as Precentor to Salisbury; and it was there I, for the first time, heard him play on his piano that lovely tune of his called "Abbots Leigh", truly one of the best among the better tunes in our hymn books.

Then we went on to Newbury—we were now getting ready for action. We were staying at Burley House near Newbury at the time and it was from there that we left to go to embark at Southampton. I remember Burley House particularly well because it was there for the first and only time that I met General Sir W. Carton de Wiart, the famous V.C. He walked one day into the hall and I thought I was facing a

42

pirate chief. I think they were going to take over our billet after we left, but I cannot remember that, though I immediately knew who he was. He was quite unique, having a black patch over one eye and one arm. Later on during the war he and the beloved General Richard O'Connor escaped together and were quite understandably captured, as they must have been a very obvious pair. Each in his own way was a remarkable man.

Nor shall I ever forget at Burley House hearing and seeing Drummer Reid blowing the Last Post on the night before we left to go to France. I saw him silhouetted against the evening sky and have seldom been so moved, wondering for how many other people that last night would have an even greater significance. As it turned out, on that particular expedition we lost none of our Battalion, but before the war had finished the Last Post had sounded in a different context for quite a number.

The "phoney" war had finished, Dunkirk was over, and we were sent out as the Secondary Expeditionary Force. The 155th Infantry Brigade consisting of the 7/9th Royal Scots and the 4th and 5th King's Own Scottish Borderers and supporting troops, set off on what happened to be my birthday—12th June 1940—sailing from Southampton and disembarking at St Malo. Little did we know how soon we would be back again in the U.K. We had hardly got into France before we heard of the disastrous fate of the 51st Highland Division at St Valery. We took the train to a place called Silde le Guillaume (which the troops immediately christened "silly billy") crowded together with our vehicles and our kit.

We soon realised that as the Germans were advancing so France was disintegrating, and Walter McLean, my ever-faithful batman and driver, confided in me that he thought that the French liaison officer who had gone round with us in the Padre's car, was a fifth columnist. In a couple of days he had disappeared and the wood in which we had been resting was shelled shortly afterwards.

By this time we had a new Battalion Commander, Lt.-Col. F. L. Johnston, who had taken over from Iver Salvesen when we were stationed at Yeovil, Iver gallantly stepping down to

43

Second-in-Command. Freddie Johnston was a Regular soldier and one of the finest men you could ever meet. We—he and I—had a very strange experience in a wood at this particular time. We were settling down to sleep beneath some bushes when he said to me, "I have got a strange feeling, padre, about what we are going to see when we go up this avenue of trees here tomorrow morning. I have never been in this part of France in my life before and yet I am sure we are going to see a house there with a green door. . . ." And he began to describe what was waiting for us. Sure enough we went up the avenue of trees and there was the house he had described and yet he himself had never seen it until we saw it together then!

As we were lying under the bushes trying to sleep in the early hours of the following morning, a despatch rider arrived and told us that we had to make straight for Cherbourg. It was Sunday and we had little or no time to arrange any Church parades, but the Medical Officer, Hilary Dorman, and myself, with his batman and my Walter McLean, decided to have a short Service on behalf of all the troops; and so under a greenwood tree we had our short form of prayer on behalf of all the others. Just as we were beginning a young despatch rider drove up on his motor bicycle and asked if he could join us. His name was Pinchbeck and I had met him quite often before. He said to me, "I don't think we need to worry about ourselves too much, sir, do you? It's the folk at home I am worrying about, can we specially remember the folk at home?" And so on behalf of all the Battalion we remembered the folk at home especially in our prayers that day. Shortly afterwards Pinchbeck, a very fine young fellow, was killed. When we got back eventually I was able to tell his people that his last thoughts were for them.

Most of the Battalion embarked for Cherbourg, but there was a rear party left and I felt I should stay with them. German 'planes were overhead and the German armoured cars and tanks were very near. We sat in a field destroying everything we could, throwing new blankets into the river, burning cars and other vehicles; and in the middle of all this sat Billy Gray-Muir who had been left in charge, having his hair cut! "Do you remember, sir," said a Corporal, "telling us about

Pont's drawings in *Punch* on the British character? Well, there is a very good example of it now" and he pointed to Billy.

Eventually our rear party split up and I found myself, quite by chance, leading a group of about fifty to sixty troops, all of different Regiments, on to the pier at Cherbourg, where under constant fire from enemy 'planes we managed to get across the Channel just before Rommel arrived, and—very tired and with only the uniforms we wore—arrived at last at St Neots. The whole expedition had taken less than a fortnight, and it must have been a very difficult decision for General Sir Allan Brooke to make to withdraw the troops, because the original idea had been to at least hold Britanny; but it would have been quite impossible to have done so.

I will never forget the Service we held when we got back to England and the singing of the 124th Psalm.[1] Surely it can never have been sung with more feeling or with more vigour.

It was strawberry time at Wisbech and at March and St Neots, and there was no one to pick the strawberries, and so the troops obliged and gorged themselves until even they got tired of them.

At last we arrived at Houghton Hall in Norfolk as our H.Q., with its considerable grounds and its Jacob flock of sheep, its roe deer and beautiful gardens, and our Church Services were held within the beautiful little Church in the grounds, the Church that brought to Goldsmith's mind his *Deserted Village*. We had to have two Services there each Sunday morning, since the Church was not large enough to hold us all, and several other Services for Brigade and Battalion Companies. We were warned about fifth columnists and spies in the district and had to be very much on our guard. Most of our equipment had already been lost or destroyed in France and private cars had to be requisitioned. I was given a beautiful Armstrong-Siddeley for the padre's car by Lady Galloway, who was then living at Cambridge, much to the envy of the others and to the joy of Walter McLean.

They were good days at Houghton and the sun shone there

---

[1] Even as a bird out of the fowler's snare
Escapes away, so is our soul set free;
Broke are their nets and thus escaped we
Therefore our help is in the Lord's great name . . .

45

and we were still free men, and the comradeship and good spirits of everyone was just out of this world. It was there that Freddie Johnston used to say to me, "How is the temperature, today padre? How do you find the troops?" And I would say, "I haven't had a grouse all week"; and he would say, "What's wrong with them padre, what's wrong with them?"

It was a time when we were all expecting at any moment there might be an invasion from across the Channel, and indeed there were many rumours of invading forces landing in the South of England, and we met some people who had actually "seen it"! It was now the time when "Dad's Army" was at its brightest and best, and "Captain Mainwaring's" men were seeing to it that no enemy forces ever arrived here; or that if they did they would have wished they hadn't!

Of the many memories I have of Houghton there are two that stand out, one I have already written about of the old Rector at Massingham,[1] the other I have mentioned in other places. We found a great many old Army bicycles and we decided we would have a cycling club, and so I led the club out along the Norfolk roads where our good Colonel took the salute as we marched past. We cycled to many places in the country and on one occasion after a very hot and rather longer run than usual I gave the young corporal who was with us, a pound note to buy some tea and buns. He came back with the tea and buns and also the change in silver. I never counted my change, for the club boys knew that I trusted them. However on this particular occasion I felt that there was rather more than there should have been and so I counted the change and it came to exactly one pound. So I called the corporal over and said, "Look here, I gave you a pound note and you have given me a pound in silver back, how do you make that out?" and he said, "We knew you never counted your change, but we wanted to pay for our own and we wanted you to think you had paid for us".

From the great days at Norfolk we were posted back to Scotland where we had great days too at Gullane; the men too were nearer their own home ground and were able to get a little more leave. At Gullane the Battalion was much

[1] See, e.g., *Seven Sevens*, pp. 45-47.

more compact and we were able to do far more things as a Battalion.

I started a branch of Toc H, helped by John McVie, Joe Cameron, and some others, and David St Clair-Erskine from his contacts and experience was able to invite some distinguished people along to speak to us—distinguished, that is, in their own line of country—people like Judy Campbell and Binnie Hale, and others like Beverley Nicholls, and actors like Cyril Richard and the Crazy Gang.

At Gullane we spent some wonderful months and like so many things at that time, never to be forgotten; and we were sad when we had to move up to our new station at Bridge of Allan; and somehow it was not quite the same there. It was at Bridge of Allan that I had to leave the Brigade to become Radio Padre. I didn't want to become Radio Padre; I wanted to stay with my Unit.

The whole idea of the Radio Padre originated through General Sir Frederick Pile, Dr James W. Welch, the Director of Religious Broadcasting, and Melville Dinwiddie, Director of Scottish B.B.C., who between them felt that something should be done for the Forces who didn't have padres. I had already done a series of broadcasts with my Boys' Club before the War—a series of ten discussions which was later published by the Oxford University Press under the title of *Asking Why*, and I was asked to do a similar shorter series with some of our troops in our Division in 1941. Partly as a result of this James Welch and Melville Dinwiddie met me in the then University Club to discuss the whole idea of having a Radio Padre, though at the time I had no idea that I was the person they had in mind. When I got a letter from James Welch in June 1941 asking me if I would try out a new job (which some of the men of Ack Ack Command had asked for, and which the producer of "Ack Ack, Beer Beer" had also said was needed) though feeling honoured at being asked, I had very mixed feelings about it. What he wanted me to do was this. He wanted me, with the Army's permission, to get around as many of those, at that time very many, lonely posts dotted all over the country and meet as many of the men as I could, and every week talk to them over the air, taking the place in some sort of way of their own padres who, because of the extent of ground they had to cover, could seldom see their men; and also "to link up the homes". I really didn't feel able to do this at first, for various reasons. In the first place I didn't know anything about Ack Ack (though that turned out to be irrelevant since all the Forces and indeed the "Home" was covered); in the second place if I broadcast every week, and sometimes more than once a week, I doubted whether I could get it across or have enough to say; and in the third place, possibly my strongest reason of all, I didn't want to leave my old Division, and especially my old Battalion, not only all of whose names, but also, in most cases, whose nicknames I knew. I had wanted to see the War out with them, as I had seen it in with them, and was very reluctant at the thought of leaving. But anyone who knew Dr Welch knew that he was a very difficult person to whom to say "no" and get off with it!

James Welch was a distinguished Director of Religious Broadcasting with the B.B.C. from 1939 until 1947. Among his previous appointments he had been Principal of St John's College, York. From 1942 until 1947 he was a Prebendary of St Paul's Cathedral and Hon. Chaplain to Dr William Temple when the latter was Archbishop of York and later of Canterbury. He resigned his Orders in 1947.

He told me a most interesting ghost story that he had been told by Archbishop William Temple concerning his father when he was Bishop of Exeter before becoming himself Archbishop of Canterbury. As Bishop he was visiting on one occasion a large house in his Diocese and was spending the night there. On arriving at the house and going upstairs to his room he passed a priest coming downstairs and wished him good evening. Before dinner that night he asked his host if that would be his Chaplain that he met on the stairs and would he be joining them at dinner? His host looked at his wife in a rather startled fashion and then said, "Have you seen him? We haven't got a Chaplain and no priest lives in this house except, well except, the one you met on the stairs tonight." Bishop Temple looked rather worried and then after dinner said to his host: "Could you leave me in your study for a while—I think that that priest may come to me." And so, late in the evening, he sat in the study before a good fire reading, when suddenly he looked up and there was the priest standing by the bookshelves! The Bishop put down the paper and asked if there was anything he could do, any way he could help him. The priest pointed to a bookshelf and shook his head as the Bishop pointed to the books on the shelf in turn, until he came to one when he nodded his head. The Bishop removed the book in question from the shelf and as he did so a sealed envelope fell out. The priest pointed to the fire and the Bishop, sorely tempted to open it and read its contents, placed the envelope in the midst of the flames. The priest bowed and disappeared and was never seen again in that house.

This was the story that Archbishop Temple told his son who was later to follow his footsteps to Canterbury, and William Temple told it to his Chaplain James Welch, who in turn told me. Make of it what you will!

And so I went down to Bedford, which was then the Religious H.Q. of the B.B.C., to discuss it with him. He was very keen about my accepting the appointment but gave no reason why he had asked me, a Minister from the Church of Scotland. My own suspicions were aroused, and I could not help feeling that Melville Dinwiddie had more than a lot to do with it, which was later confirmed. The upshot of it was that I agreed to do a series of four discussions with troops from my Division, and this came off in November of that year under the title of "Let's Ask the Padre". It seemed to have gone off fairly well, but I still had not agreed to go on with the idea of regular broadcasting, and in any case I didn't think the Army would agree to release me on secondment. And then eventually something decided me that made me feel quite emphatically that it might be the right thing to do; at the same time I believe the Chaplain-General felt that this opened the way for him to release me on secondment. The other Churches, the Church of England, the Church of Rome, and the Free Churches, had all agreed that if I did this job they would raise no objection from a denominational angle, but would support me. The support I had from these Churches was all along quite excellent, not least from the Roman Catholic Church.

Indeed it was the Roman Catholic member of the B.B.C. team, Professor A. C. F. Beales, who was later to write most generously in *The Universe*: "The Radio Padre is recognised all over the country as easily the finest thing religious broad-casting has ever done for us . . . here is a man who really knows the people he is talking to; he knows their lives and really understands their difficulties."

Even the Rationalist paper *The Free Thinker* later had kind words to say: "Many people in these grim days must have drawn comfort both from the manly yet gentle appeal this man made."

And so it was that, frankly at first rather sadly, I went down South to join the Staff of the B.B.C. in 1942 with a secondment to them for six months, which later turned out to be seven, and later still, though not now as a secondment, for at least a couple of years.

For the first month I remained at H.Q. in Broadcasting House, now, as mentioned, in Bedford, because of the bombing in London, and I was immediately struck by the hard way they worked, by their unselfish co-operation, and their friendship. I found in James Welch, Eric Fenn, Cyril Taylor, A. C. F. Beales, and John G. Williams, people who immediately became, and ever remained, my friends. No one could have had a better start or a more friendly and encouraging support to a new venture.

When I first arrived at the B.B.C. in Bedford, Dr Welch was having a battle with some of the leading Churchmen over the question of Dorothy L. Sayers' *The Man Born to be King* which she was writing at that time and which was being broadcast with great acceptance, and indeed with enthusiasm, on the radio. Some of the Church people, including some of the Bishops, objected to the series as being a kind of travesty of the Gospels, and they objected too to our Lord's voice being spoken in "fictional" words over the air. However, thanks to James Welch's determination that the plays should go on, even the severest critics began to see that they were doing a tremendous amount of good, and indeed for a time their impact was almost sensational.

Dorothy Sayers was a strange mixture. She wrote so much really great Christian commonsense, as well as ordinary entertainment, and her death in 1957 was indeed tragic. I found meeting her a great pleasure and indeed I have a letter from her which says in its own way quite a lot. I had asked her to contribute to one of the volumes of *Asking Them Questions* that I was editing, and this was her reply:

Witham,
Essex.
28.3.44

Dear Mr Selby Wright,

I have had a shot at the Powers of Evil, and send it along in the hope that it may catch you before you depart to the Marshall Islands, the Second Front, or the Azores! It is a bit longer, I'm afraid, than you asked for, and I daresay I could cut it a bit if necessary—but anything to do with sin or evil seems to take a lot of explaining these days when nobody believes in sin. I hope it is reasonably understandable.

I thought it well to rule out at once, and firmly, the detestable notion that there is something evil about the body. Misunderstanding on this point does a lot to set people against the Christian faith and Church. Also, to put in a small footnote about hell and damnation, for the "better prevention of scandals".

I hope the thing will do. By the way—you will let me see the proof before you go to press, won't you? and see to it that my name is given in contents—lists and so on, as "Dorothy L. Sayers" and not as "Dorothy Sayers".

Yours sincerely,

Dorothy L. Sayers.

At this time I began to keep a Journal for a few months, since I was no longer technically "on active service" and it is at that point that I should like this Journal to speak for itself for the next few months.

PART II

During the War it was forbidden to keep a Diary, though certain people, notably Lord Alanbrooke, ignored the order. All one could safely keep was an appointment book (which, of course, was very necessary—not least to a padre).

So I didn't keep a Diary, in the sense of a Journal, until I was seconded to the B.B.C. and then only for a short, but for me, an important time. It was a short time because I found that I just couldn't keep it up from day-to-day at the pace I was going, with the added security that could in any way help "the enemy"! And that Diary written at the time will, I hope, speak for itself as far as the early days of the Radio Padre are concerned; and beginning on the day when I left the two Battalions of the Division of which I was padre. These are some extracts from it which, because they were written at the time, are sometimes now rather embarrassing!

2nd March 1942

The 7/9th (Royal Scots) are turning night into day all this week, so coming back late from Edinburgh I was in time to go to my office and lunch at 0100 hours! Very tired, I went to bed after going round the cooks, etc., at "tea time"—0500 hours—and so missed dinner at 0800 hours. I got up at 1015 and John McVie and I had some tea then I left for Alva where I had tea with the 155 Field Ambulance after I had visited the Hospital. On the whole I don't think the average R.A.M.C. new doctor is a patch on those we had at the beginning of the War—no one like Colonel Middleton or Douglas Ross. I like Major Cormack but he belongs to the Old School; Innes, the

E   53

rugger international, is another good chap . . . but they were all very nice however, and wished me luck as did all the chaps I met. I'm sorry to leave the 155 Field Ambulance; I've had some grand times with them, though so many are now away it isn't *quite* the same. From there I called, on the way to the 4th (K.O.S.B.) at Inglewood, Alloa: the Forrester-Patons are always very kind and asked me to stay over tomorrow night with them. I met their daughter Doreen, a grand girl and quite a surprise. So on to the 4th who gave me a really good dinner. Colonel Kelly toasted me and the pipers played—P/M Burgess, Kinghorn and Ford. A really fine evening, and they came out and cheered me off at 11.45 (2345 hours). Such good chaps the 4th—both officers and men—"Chokra" Kelly and "the Duchess", Horace Davidson, Willie Swan, Jim Bennett—a really great Adjutant—Frank Coutts, one of the best subalterns surely in the Army, Charles Marrow, Donald Hogg, Viney Scott, Jock Home-Robertson, and so on—a really good crowd. With them lives the R.C. padre whom I showed round when he first joined the Brigade in September 1941—we both stayed with the 4th on his first week at Pathhead—one of the best types of padres and R.C's—Fr. Lennen, S.J.; the 4th doctor too is a grand fellow, Alan Hill.

Got back to the 7/9th (Royal Scots) in time for my office at midnight! [On this night, though I didn't know it until later, dear Dad passed at last to peace: he died, alas, I heard, fighting so hard to live that he cried out loudly. Poor Maime and Ray as ever were with him. Dear Dad, he was so grand to the end; how we shall miss his lively enthusiasm and pride in all his family; he was only sixty-three and has always been the fittest of us all. "The Lord gave and the Lord has taken away, blessed be the name of the Lord."]

3rd March

Dined at 0830 hours at Bridge of Allan though I didn't wait for dinner, having dined with the 4th at 2000 hours last night! But I got around the fellows at lunch before that (at 0100 hours) and to those I saw I was able to say "au revoir"—it was very hard! When I got up at 1030 all were asleep, but I met Joe Cameron and Hugh Johnston back from their tough course up North, which included Montrose's four-day march. Took Joe as far as Falkirk on his forty-eight hours to Edinburgh. First called on Mrs Johnston, the C.O's wife . . . told her how sorry I was to leave the Battalion and her husband, "one of the grandest men I have ever met". She said how sorry he was that I was going and he had told her that I had been such a help to him. I hope that is even half-true, for I have tried, and because of him and the fellows it hasn't been very hard, but one of the greatest joys a man could have. Had tea with Nevile Davidson at his new Mess, for the 5th K.O.S.B. have left Callander now and gone to Falkirk. Then a very interesting talk in his billet, finishing in the real good Nevile fashion with a very lovely prayer for my new work. Motored from there, as promised, to Alloa, to stay with the Forrester-Patons, Frank Coutts and Viney Scott with us, and Doreen in great form.

Rang up to hear how Dad was and to tell them that I would be along tomorrow. Pip, who had just come up from Southport where he is at present working, answered and told me the sad news—he had died last night. When I saw him on Sunday I was told by the nurse that there was no danger! I had sent Cruickshanks (my driver) away with the car and there was nothing for it but to go back to the cheery crowd as if nothing had happened. It was one of the hardest things that I have had to do. There was no use stopping their evening, so I said nothing but tried to carry on. I think Dad would have preferred that. Poor Maime and Ray and Bob who have had to bear the brunt and are very exhausted and naturally sad—it's a terrible break for us. Thank God Pip is at hand; he should keep them cheery and I'll be along first thing—it will be the first time we've all been together for a while, and I'm sure Dad will be with us for he loved nothing better than being all together with us.

Very tired. I went to bed to find—bless them—that they had made an "apple-pie" bed. A strange strained day after such strains of "goodbyes"—yet none are really "goodbyes" but just "au revoir".

15th March (Sunday)

The first Sunday for nearly four years when I haven't preached (usually not less than five times) at all. I must say I have missed it and I thought down here in Bedford of the various boys that I usually preached to as the clock went round to the various times.

I went first to Dr Welch's rooms in the house of the Vicar of St Paul's, Bedford (the Parish Church), the Rev. Alan Colthurst. We listened in to many services including Nevile's broadcast from Dunblane of the fifteen minutes of the 78 Field Regiment R.A. Service. It was grand to hear the good Scots voices singing the psalms and hymns and it was good too to hear Nevile—so sincere and genuinely simple.

Lunch at the Vicarage is a "big" affair. The Vicar is a grand chap and a "super" Anglo-Catholic; his wife is the last Chapter of Proverbs. They have a large family, all daughters except for one son who is at school away from Bedford. There must have been about fourteen of us for lunch, and considering the war conditions (rationing, etc.) what we received was no mean achievement. I had tea and supper there too. I went a walk with Cyril Taylor in the afternoon through Bedford Park. Staying with the Vicar and taking his services for the day was the Chaplain at Magdalene, Cambridge. I suppose he is a clever chap but he strikes me as being the kind of fellow that is the justification for the break-up of the Establishment—no humour, except at his own jokes (which made me feel I've no humour). In conversation he greatly feared that bombs over London might reach the huge supplies of wine in the deep vaults below (I think) Charing Cross! He is also the assistant cellar-man at Magdalene—a lamentable job for a Chaplain I think. . . .

A letter from the Colonel (F. L. Johnston)—just his usual grand self—from Hugh Rose, the Adjutant, a very nice letter from a really good chap—from Colonel Mackenzie, Colonel of the Royal Scots, a most friendly letter saying how sorry he is that I am off for a bit and that he'll listen-in, how proud he is to be Colonel of the Regiment, and finishing "Yours aye"; he also mentioned that he has still got beside him the N.T. I gave him at Houghton in the Summer of 1940. The new Brigadier, Moreshead, sent a letter too, saying he hoped he'd be worthy of such a grand crowd of fellows as the 155 Brigade, and adding that he hopes I come back when "my six months are over".

16th March

First thing this a.m. I went round to the Regimental H.Q. of the 51 Med. Regiment, R.A. to see if they would be able to put me up. Met their padre—a good chap—who said he was sure it would be O.K. Then on to meet Dr Welch at the Daily Service which he was taking. I sat beside him to learn the technique of it. There is first a Service at 1000-1005 for European listeners, and then the Home and Overseas from 1015-1030. This goes on every day. The singers are first-class. From there I went back to the "Staff Conference" at 52 De Pary Avenue—the Religious H.Q. of the B.B.C. since the re-evacuation from Bristol. A very full session with much discussion. The B.B.C. certainly does take trouble over things: everything is gone into and the programmes are planned months ahead. All last week's religious broadcasts had been put under a very careful scrutiny. At the afternoon session my job was discussed. As I thought, it is going to be very much what I make of it, and I've got a pretty free hand. I've also got to broadcast some of the Daily and Empire Services, do next week's "Lift up your Hearts" and take the Tuesday evening Service next week—my Radio Padre series beginning on 1st April—a very appropriate date!

Cuttings are coming in from the Provincial papers. A Manchester paper says I may well become "the Tubby Clayton or Studdert Kennedy of this War"—some hope! I feel today rather mentally intoxicated. I haven't had to use my "brains" (sic) for quite a time and the machinery is not very mobile. The rooms are too stuffy and the place (Bedford) is very relaxing—neither factor helping me. I miss the Scottish breeze and I miss the Mess in the Battalion and the men. But I've just got to "bury myself in work" and get on with it.

I had a very interesting evening with A. C. F. Beales, the R.C. member of the Staff, who is here only on Mondays and in London the rest of the week. We talked about the Sword of the Spirit Movement of which he is Secretary; it's a grand thing and I hope that all the Churches will get together on it. He tells me that Hutchison Cockburn, the Moderator, is going to ask the Assembly this year to come in on it. I hope they do.

57

17th March (St Patrick's Day)

Went with Eric Fenn to the morning broadcast sermon from St Paul's Chapel, Bedford. Later this morning I met Sir Cecil Graves, the joint Director (of the B.B.C.). I saw to my joy that he was wearing a Royal Scots tie, and mentioning this to him he completely unbent and became most friendly. He had been at Sandhurst before the last War and gone from there into the Royal Scots 2nd Battalion. Having something in common not only has broken the ice, but I feel more at home with the B.B.C. H.Q. already!

I worked most of the day preparing the "Lift Up Your Hearts" (0755) Series for next week; I want to get away from the usual run of prayers and *let* us "lift up our hearts" for the beauty of the world, for friends, for a sense of humour (almost above all for that!), for faith, for the true meaning of peace and so on.

Tonight the post brought letters from many others including Joe Chisholm, the best of the last lot of recruits who came to the 7/9th before I left, saying how much the Battalion was missing me, and sending the best wishes of "all the boys in the billet"; he calls me a "very kind padre who was good to them when they were recruits". Poor chap—if only he knew how grateful I am to them!

Also came a note from the "new" padre—a fellow called Morrison. I don't know him and have never heard of him, but I see that he was a Probationer at the beginning of this year, so he can't have had much experience. He may do very well with the men so long as he doesn't confuse this with not being "in with" the officers, who can so often help the men much better than any padre, *if* the padre can show how and where, and they can trust his "how" and "where". I 'phoned him later tonight. It was grand to hear the boys at the other end. I recognised at once the voice of Cook and we exchanged a few words. Later I wrote to Cook and told him how nice it was to hear a familiar voice and asked him to give all my blessings to all the other Signallers in the Battalion. Wrote more letters and then sat talking to Eric Fenn and Cyril Taylor until after ten, then off to my digs. Eric Fenn tells me that the Musical Department were asked the other day to "please estimate the total cost of 'The Passion'!" Not a bad question for the World to answer today!

18th March

Dr J. W. Welch and Eric Fenn say they like my "Lift Up" series very much indeed, which is a great comfort. I was a bit nervous about them. Everyone here (J. C. W., Eric Fenn, Cyril Taylor, John Williams, Beales, etc.) is so friendly that they don't really care how hard they criticise each other, and no one takes offence at all about it. Actually they are all grand people here, but I do miss the boys.

I got really home-sick tonight. The sudden realisation of what Dad's death means to me. No more now can I write "My dear Dad", no more get these dear Micawberish letters back; no more that loving interest and pride in the smallest things we do. He had fought so hard to live too. He was so lively that it seemed a shame to die. And here I was now in the very street where he had been billeted (in the last War) "when I was in the Argyll and Sutherland Highlanders" as he so often liked to tell people. And I wished that I could go home even for a night to comfort Mum and Ray who have been so very brave and, like Dad, have had a hard time and borne it all so cheerfully. Our family at least had been given two of the greatest blessings of all—love and humour, and we've got to be very thankful for that. Then there's Bob too. He's so much younger and has always had a more independent life. Unlike me, he hasn't a brother his own age like Pip to go about with. He's a grand wee chap and he has got "guts"; I know too how much Dad loved him and how he always takes my advice; it makes me feel very small sometimes.

I wrote to Nunky Brown tonight. He is one of the world's best—always the same. No man is more understanding, more sensible or more wise in his judgments. He has done more for the boys in Edinburgh than anyone else I know, and I personally owe a lot to him. I told him I couldn't understand why I am being made such a fuss of just now and how it all rather terrifies me. "The Ronnie Wright I know is just a chap who likes chaps, that's all." And that *is* all! And always if you like chaps, they'll like you—I'm sure of that. More letters from the Battalion, and about dear Dad. I had a restless night of dreams but later slept well.

19th March

Broadcast the daily service this morning from St Paul's and

after it a Press publicity man got me to sit at the microphone etc., and took about a dozen photographs. I hadn't time to tidy up and was wearing old battle-dress—but what does that matter. In two of the photos Harry, the page boy who looks after the books, was taken with me—handing me a book. He's a good chap and like all the page boys here, has good manners, that blessed thing which surely is one of the virtues of the world.

20th March

Broadcast the Daily Service at 1015 today; previous to that the short morning service to the Empire at 1000 hours. This is recorded and sent out four more times today! The B.B.C. Singers are just grand. Eric Fenn came with me in case I over-ran for the first of my Daily Service broadcasts.

Some grand letters today including a long one from John McVie. He's been very depressed since I left. . . . He's going to carry on Toc H with Joe (Cameron) and Arthur (Brown) and Co., and so on with news so keenly read of the Battalion's doings, and then says, "The last nine months has been one of the finest experiences of my life and I owe the happiness I've had to the remarkable way in which you have been my friend. I hope I may one day be worthy of that friendship and pray for the day when you will be with us in the Battalion again". . . . I remember when we first met at a Schoolboy Club Camp Concert, and then him coming to Camp at Skateraw when Captain of the Royal High School, and having him to help (as a schoolboy) at the (pre-war Territorial) Camp at Strathpeffer the summer before the War, and his keenness to get into the "Dandy Ninth"—his father's old Regiment, and the day— that bright summer typical Gullane day—when he came to join us—an officer now in the "Dandy Ninth" and his sharing my room where the rising sun came streaming in each morning, and in the evening the room was filled with the scent of lavender from the garden; our talks together . . . I know of no better influence on boys than he.

21st March

There is something—in fact a great deal in this "Public

60

School spirit"! It was seen at its finest today when I went to see a Public School boxing competition at Bedford School—the Hall packed with boys, dark suits, dark ties and white collars. The sportsmanship displayed and the courtesy—the young Eton boxers were good, clean and scientific; Bedford on the whole were heavier and coarser; Dulwich were sporting and game and Haileybury just couldn't quite pull it off this year (and there were others too). The greatest ovation went to a young Dulwich boy (aged about 15½). He fought long after he should have given up, hardly able to stand, yet his punches were as strong as ever, until at last he turned to the Referee and said "so sorry sir, I just can't go on" and collapsed—the applause was as loud as it was well-deserved.

What is wrong is not the Public School, its just that there are not more Public Schools, and that there is not an opportunity for everyone to attend or have a similar experience. In a sense Boys' Clubs try to do that; but only in a sense. . . . The only thing wrong with the "old School tie" is its exclusiveness—let's give everyone an old School tie (not do away with it).

To show the Church at its worst. . . . Eric Fenn, with whom I went to the School Hall to see the boxing, told me that he heard the Dean of Norwich (Cranage) preach a sermon quite recently in the Chapel of Bedford School on "The strength of the things that remain". They were not, as one might expect, faith, hope, love, kindness, etc., but (1) The Monarchy, (2) The Three Services, (3) The Church of England, and (4) The Public Schools. (All admirable things—but really!—how amused the Bedford boys must have been.)

22nd March (Sunday)

Began the day by going from my digs to the Vicarage and sitting with Cyril Taylor listening to wireless programmes. Heard Nevile (Davidson) again—good stuff to the 78th at Dunblane; I pictured it all and then "saw" the new padre with the 7/9th and the 4th at Church—the chaps singing and listening as no ordinary congregation ever listens!

My old sciatica came back and crippled me for several hours today; but after lunch at the B.B.C. restaurant at the Cavendish, Bedford, went to hear Bach's St Matthew's Passion at St Paul's, Bedford. A packed Church—wonderful singing with the B.B.C. Singers and the B.B.C. Club Choir—about 100 of them—and orchestra. Thorbald Ball at the organ and Trevor Harvey conducting—a great feast of music and praise. 'Phoned Mum later—all seems to be going well, and I spoke to Ray too.

I spent a peaceful night at the Vicarage. Allan Colthurst, the Vicar, and I talked until quite late about Padres and Toc H and the Scout Jamboree at Birkenhead, and George MacLeod whom he knows well. I slept in Welch's room at the Vicarage—the best sleep I've had for ages. All were so kind and my sciatica got better. Welch is away for a week's retreat, so I'll be able to use his room and bed until he comes back and I'm looking forward to a good week.

Allan told me that the Chaplain of Magdalene is a good fellow and does a lot of good to the undergraduates at Cambridge; he was here for a while tonight again. Perhaps I was wrong about him: I hope so!

23rd March

Allan called me at 0700 hours and later Cyril Taylor came in. He had been firewatching. . . . We had a cup of tea and then went down to the Hall of Bunyan Meeting—taken over by the B.B.C. during the war for studios. There at 0755 I gave my first of my "Lift Up Your Hearts" for the week— "Lift up your hearts for the world as God made it is very lovely"; read from the Hymn of St Francis and finished with the tune that goes with it, "All creatures of our God and King". Then breakfast at the Vicarage—tidy children all talking to a most patient mother; a grand breakfast—truly this Vicarage is the ideal Christian household.

I worked on my talk for tomorrow evening on "The loneliness of power and the loneliness of weakness" all morning.

A large number of letters. Most exciting one from John McVie telling me that Colonel Johnston had been appointed Brigadier of the 157th (H.L.I.) Brigade. We all knew that he would get a Brigade soon, and it's great news—but oh how the Battalion will miss him. I wrote straight off to him. Also a letter from the Dandy Ninth Branch of Toc H signed by all; they had put the wireless in my place and pretended I was there! They have asked me to be their Hon. President and I have replied in "verse" saying I'm just overjoyed and honoured. Melville (Dinwiddie) wrote too agreeing with me that I should make Scotland my first Command and offering a meeting of all Padres and Officiating Chaplains to discuss broadcasting with me. This, coming with an invitation from Glasgow University to meet the S.C.M. men going soon into the Forces, makes me hope all the more that Welch will agree to my going to Scotland first where I know nearly all of the padres. . . . Spent the evening fire-watching at 52 De Pary Avenue, talking to Beales, writing *Canongate Chronicle* etc. Wrote to Nunky and told him to listen in tomorrow as we are having "The Cameronians' Midnight Hymn" ("He wants not love") which he loves. Telephone message from Melville Dinwiddie to meet him at Broadcasting House, London, on Wednesday after I have seen McLurg.

24th March

The Commissionaire at Religious H.Q. called me and gave me a cup of "Army" tea and I went to the studio and took "Lift Up Your Hearts"—"For God has given us friends". As I spoke I had so many friends in mind. . . . Went straight from studio to have breakfast at Lyons with Beales, who had been to Mass. He's a most interesting fellow and has written (among others) a good Penguin book. He was Lecturer on Education at London University. His religion for a time was vague and agnostic; he then began to study for himself, getting, he told me, the greatest possible help from Butler's *Analogy* and was received into the R.C. Church in 1935—since when he has become one of its leading laymen.

I finished the first draft of my Radio Padre talk for 1st April: Eric Fenn is pleased with it. I don't know—it's going to be very difficult to keep it up! Also finished draft for tonight's evening service.

I just loved taking the service in St Paul's Chapel this evening! The singers were grand, the dim lighting, the feeling that millions were joining with us—I chose some hymns I loved. . . . I spoke of the loneliness of power "when evening came He was there *alone*" and the loneliness of weakness—the disciples on the sea in the storm and how Jesus in the power of His loneliness enters into the weakness of our loneliness and there is peace.

When I went back to the Vicarage Mrs Colthurst had a cup of Ovaltine waiting for me—this happens every night, and tea every morning. Welch comes back on Friday—but these days at the Vicarage are just grand!

25th March

I took the theme today that we should "lift up our hearts" for God has given us a sense of humour; read from Harvey's *Ducks*—"and He's probably laughing still/At the sound that comes out of its bill!" And we thanked God for all who bring happiness into the world. . . . I'm sure that the gift of humour is one of God's greatest gifts. It always got us through at home.

The usual good breakfast at the Vicarage and then took the 1015 Service preceding it the 1000 Empire Service. . . . Then the 1108 to London where I travelled with Eric Fenn and Cyril Taylor. . . . Went in the afternoon to see Bill McLurg, the producer of "Ack Ack Beer Beer" at Hereford House, Park Street. He wants me to come into their Variety programmes a bit, at least fortnightly, and talk even for a couple of minutes with the Ack Ack listeners. It seems a good chance and I said I'd do it—but what can one say in two minutes! Then went on—after a tour through the streets, nearly all showing signs of bombing—to Broadcasting House to meet Melville Dinwiddie. It was just grand to see him and we talked for a long time, ate a good supper at an excellent cafe nearby (beside the Queen's Hall, now totally destroyed). Then walked and talked to St Pancras, where I got the train back to Bedford. He agrees that I should get up to Scottish Command as soon as possible to make a real start there. I met a lot of interesting soldiers in London and talked to many of them. They are all always so friendly to padres and so really, in some hidden way perhaps, to religion! Hear that Jimmie Dalgleish's Division is near. When I got back to Bedford I went to the office and found sixteen letters waiting for me. A grand letter from

Mum; she agrees that we should have a small stone for Dad at Cockburnspath where we intend to bury his dear remains, and would like "Here he lies where he longs to be" on it. She is feeling, poor soul, so sad that more wasn't done, for the doctor had said there was nothing wrong, and there *had* been all the time. She and Ray certainly did all they could and no one knows that better than dear Dad. . . . A nice letter from Joe Cameron: "Come back, dear padre, soon to those who really need you!"

26th March

This morning we "lifted up our hearts" because God needs and loves ordinary people, finishing with, I think, Donald Hankey's saying "God must be very fond of ordinary people, He has made so many of us!"

I spent most of today revising my script for J. W. Welch to see when he comes back tomorrow night and drawing up a pretty full memo to him why I should go to Scottish Command and not Eastern, though first seeing Sir Frederick Pile, the C.-in-C. "Ack Ack" Command. There were about twelve good reasons and I'll see what comes of it. It's really most important that I should start with people who will help me because I know them: precedent is most important in the Army and "if it has been done before" then "there's nae bother at a'!"

Went for a short break to see Bedford School sports. More and more I saw the great importance and power and privilege of a good Head Master. I don't think Bedford has got one at present—Rugby has in Hugh Lyon and Edinburgh Academy in Lionel Smith who refused Eton. To turn out good Christian citizens into all parts of life—there can be nothing more important than that. A good Head Master should stamp his pupils like Arnold did.

27th March

The Lift up your Hearts Service this morning was "For God has shown us the true meaning of peace"—a fine passage read from Micklem's *The Galilean* ending with Walford Davies' "Solemn Melody". Then after breakfast at the Rectory and a letter to Maime where I suggested that we might put on Dad's stone at Cockburnspath "Here near these shores he loved lie his earthly remains in peace—as his soul is in peace"—or words to that effect, took the broadcast Daily Service to the Empire at 1000 and to Home at 1015.

A letter from Colonel Johnston today—now Brigadier, 157th Brigade—a grand and typical letter. He is back where the 155th were all last winter and summer—a place we both know so well. "Today," he writes, "is a day of clear pale blue sky, fleeting cloud driven by a brisk breeze, and all the farms and fields a perfect riot of colour—one of those days we both admired in the countryside—God, how I love it all!" He tells how sorry he was to leave the Battalion. "I think I miss the chat over the Orderly Room counter with old friends at 5 p.m. most," but he's with a good crowd—any crowd becomes a good crowd when he is there! Letters too from Willie Tindall and Mrs Thomson of Gullane House saying how much they all loved Tuesday night's service. A grand P.C. from Major F. M. Crum of Gogar with a drawing of ducks—a reference to my broadcast on Wednesday, done by himself, one duck saying "cheerio"! "I have been with you by wireless." What a grand chap he is—typical too of the best type of Regular soldier, and I've never known a better type anywhere than the best type of Regular soldier.

28th March

0755 "Lift Up Your Hearts" for God has shown us the meaning of Faith. Back to the office and sent some more stuff for the May and June numbers of *The Scottish Forces Magazine*. I am keeping on the Editorship of this since I feel it is well worthwhile; we are limited to 12,000 copies a month but as this goes to a very wide circulation, I feel it is well worth it.[1] I wrote and asked C. S. Lewis for his excellent Talks on the Christian Faith which ought to make a good series.

In the afternoon I took the bus to St Neots of happy memories. It was there we spent our first week on our return from France (in June 1940). No clothes except those we went about in! My heart was full of memories and I visited the Churches where we had the Services after our escape. I remember my text "There was no more sea": the sea was what had cut us off from home and from the people and things we

---

[1] I edited the Magazine from 1941 until 1976 when it became again *The Scottish Forces Supplement*.

loved when we were in France, and St John's idea of the City of God was a place where we would be "back home again": and "the sea was as clear as crystal" the sea with all its mysteries was like the world, but in the City of God all things we couldn't understand, or see the unfathomable mysteries would be clear to us: "Now we see in part". Nor shall I ever forget the singing of the 2nd version of the 124th Psalm:

"Even as a bird out of the fowler's snare escapes away
So is our soul set free . . .
When cruel men against us furiously
Rose up in wrath to make of us their prey
Broke are their nets and thus escaped we . . .
Therefore our help is in the Lord's great name . . ."

Just grand it was. (From St Neots we moved to March and then to Beechenwell before we had those glorious months at Houghton Hall, Norfolk, prior to going to "old Scotland again" (Gullane).)

Had tea at the Cosy Café on the Great North Road which we used for the week we were at St Neots as the H.Q. Mess. The folk there had been so good to us and it was good to see Mrs Wise and her two daughters again. We talked of these good days and the grand chaps that were with us—the Colonel and "Quarty" Thomson, the Doc (Dorman), and Walter Scott and Charles Findlay, of Vickers the Mess Corporal; of how tired we all were, of the strawberries and cream we had every day for tea—and so on. I sent Mac (L./Cpl. Walter MacLean) who batted and drove me, a post-card "to remind him". I was recognised by some of the St Neots boys as "the Padre of the Scotties". Wherever the Dandy Ninth went they left a good name and even for a week they remembered us. When I got back to the office I wrote many letters.

29th March

I slept in B.B.C. Religious Department, 52 De Pary Avenue and Warren woke me with a cup of tea. Stayed in and wrote a lot of letters—fourteen—and also listened to a series of programmes for Palm Sunday from St George's, Edinburgh (C. W. G. Taylor and General Thorne), and J. S. Whale, the latter from the Vicarage where I called on my way to the 51st Med. Regiment, R.A. Mess, to which during my stay here I am now attached for accommodation and rations. As my bed has not come from the station yet, I start today to eat in the Mess and expect to sleep there from Tuesday night—lunch in the Mess had the advantage of being "good old Army" (as F. L. Johnston always calls it so rightly) again. Only the Doc—an odd man but pleasant—the Padre, good, young, keen and just a little too self-important, and the Messing Officer—very young and shy—present. I went an eight mile walk in the afternoon alone: an absolutely perfect day, only spoilt because I had to wear uniform, and the respirator always spoils a good country walk. I hadn't meant to go so far today but was refreshed by tea in a wayside house—very kindly given to me. Back too late and too tired for Church, but after a good supper alone at the Mess returned to office to hear the broadcast from William Temple, Archbishop of York, and soon to be Archbishop of Canterbury. Again wrote some more letters and so to bed—"fire-watching" tonight.

Today was a National Day of Prayer throughout the Empire.

30th March

A Staff Meeting which began at 1130 (with Eric Loveday of St Martin's-in-the-Fields present—nice, but what a difference from Pat McCormack!) finished at 1630!

Break for lunch at the Mess where I met a really first-rate Signals Captain (Dunkirk M.C.) from the 3rd Division (Jimmie's Division). We had a grand talk and I found that he was a keen Toc H man. You could tell that there was something about him from the start which marked him out as really friendly and human, the best type of Army Officer. At the Staff meeting we had the usual lot of service jobs, etc., allocated and I came in for a good share! My suggestion that after I see Sir Frederick Pile and A.C.G. Eastern Command I should go to Scottish Command for a month, was "carried".

Received and wrote many letters including one from Nunky Brown about him wanting me to apply for the Headmastership of Heriot's—some of the School Governors seem to think I could do this well (though I know I've not got a chance). So much can be done and should be done for our fellows going out into the world in these days of reconstruction, that is bound to come after the War. Other letters included one from Robin Legget saying that rumour has it that the Battalion is going North to Fraserburgh. Had supper with A. C. F. Beales. Talked to him about the desirability of the Radio Padre having a good signature tune: he jumped at the idea and after discussion his suggestion of the March from "1066 and All That"—"We're going home"— was greeted by me with whoops of delight; it would be just grand and I hope we'll get off with it. He has promised to look into it. I think he is a first-class fellow.

1st April (my first Radio Padre broadcast!)

After a lot of writing, knocking out a script for tomorrow's "Ack Ack Beer Beer" etc., I set off for London to see Beales, etc., at Broadcasting House and get the suggested records from him. Then back to Bedford, more writing, more letters, and a wire from Robbie Fulton wishing me luck tonight. Welch didn't like the record idea very much and I think on the whole he is right; but they all seemed very pleased (much more than I'd hoped even) with the Radio Padre talk which was chiefly addressed to the Battalions I had left behind—much by name and memories of days from Strathpeffer, mobilisation, France, until today.[1] I loved doing it and felt nearer the chaps than I had ever been since I left them. It's going to be hard to keep it up though.

(Later on the 2nd I got a very nice message from Sir Cecil Graves the Director-General, who is very pleased. He says I've to come up and see him any time and never feel lonely when in London, but to come to his room at Broadcasting House—very good of him and very encouraging—Welch is overjoyed! I wish I'd more confidence in the future of this!)

I always try to talk to as many folk as possible when travelling, especially fellows in the Services. They are all always so friendly. One young chap had just been to an R.A.F. Depot to be examined so as to be ready to be called up when he is older; he is only seventeen and he told me he was in the Home Guard, the A.T.C. and in addition fire-watched two nights a week. That's grand service and cheerfully given. Oh why not all this in peace time—well, why not?

Letters from Jimmie Dalgleish, Tony Beilby, etc.

[1] See *The Average Man* (Longmans, 1942).

2nd April

Dictated my script, or at least a part of it, at fever heat! I'm going to tackle the question of "Why we are here on Earth": Wink (Renwick) asked if I'd do it, so I rather rashly said "Yes". Last night's broadcast seems to have gone well and even confounded the critics!

Off to London to the large B.B.C. Studio at Delaware Road to "make my bow" in the variety show "Ack Ack Beer Beer". They were all very "stagey" but very nice, and seemed quite glad to welcome a dog-collar in their midst. Carol Raye, the principal girl in the show (who is acting as co-star with Bobby Howes in a West End London show), was really very nice and such a lady—no "side"; they listened as I spoke of tomorrow being Good Friday and how the trouble with most of us is the same as with the Q.M's braces—we won't give. But God so loved the world that He gave his Son. This has He done for us; what have we done for Him? To have this sort of thing in a variety show for troops is something quite new; but after it was over they asked if I'd come and give a short talk often—at least fortnightly—and if I couldn't come would I send a record? So at least that's something. It shows what we think are non-Churchy folk, do want, and welcome the Church: we just must go out into the "highways and byways" more.

Back to Bedford in time for dinner at the Mess, then the office again. Read over typed copy of script for Wednesday: it won't do as it stands; will need to go hard at it tomorrow. Some grand letters again, including one from Charlie Herriot and one from Walter Scott. . . . A telegram awaited me from Peter Bunn asking me to meet him at Euston Station on Monday. I would like to make it but should go to see the A.C.G. Eastern Command. Peter is a grand fellow. I spoke of him last night—how we slept in the heather last Midsummer's night at Lauderdale and he made sardine sandwiches at midnight and laughed as only Peter can laugh. He is on embarkation leave and I really must try to meet him.

3rd April

Wrote a lot today and got a great many letters; a very nice one from Cruickshanks, my old driver, including a piece of wedding cake. I wrote and told him I felt "I deserved a bit" as I had gone to see the girl's mother in Kings Lynn in the Summer of 1940 when we were at Houghton, and told her that C. was a good fellow! He wants me to remind "them" that they haven't issued the glengarries yet—to get glengarries back into the Battalion was one of my last schemes, and they promised that the boys would get them for walking out; so I've written! Some very kind letters from other padres, etc., about the Radio Padre talk have come in too. But the "highlight" was a letter from John McVie (1/4/42). "Tonight in your first performance you nearly brought the house down. The 'Radio Padre' actually lives now, and as the first example of the results you are about to achieve I must tell you unknowingly you made history tonight. As 9.25 approached imagine the members of the Mess seated at dinner . . . and why? Captain Walter Scott has just delivered a very able speech introducing our new Commanding Officer, Lt.-Col. J. T. Campbell. At 9.24 J. T. C. rose to reply, spoke a few words and was drowned by the voice of an announcer from the wireless in the ante-room. Very fittingly he thought it more fitting to listen to what you had to say. And so each of us listened in silence, smiling knowingly at intervals while you were being introduced over the air. Then came that marvellous voice of yours and it was so real and natural that you might have been speaking to us from that little central table instead of from a studio down south. Walter had spoken of many memories he had of J.T.C. and the Battalion, and it was so fitting that you should continue in the exact same strain with these well-known reminiscences of yours; we were all waiting expectantly for the one about Peter and his sardine sandwiches that night on the heather, and we all tumbled to your various references and were proud to be able to understand them. It was really *marvellous* the way you finished off and said 'goodnight' to us all by name. I did appreciate the compliment. You will be absolutely snowed under with letters from all corners of the realm. . . ." Then he told me that Peter (who I hoped to see on Monday in London) has gone for India and Donald Maitland has arrived. I remember him as a small Watson's boy—the youngest of a good set of brothers. . . ."Joe", John continues, "will be writing probably tonight and he admitted only an hour ago that you are the only person with any power over him by way of

71

bettering his 'way of living' as he calls it. He was terribly pleased that you mentioned him tonight. . . ." Melville Dinwiddie was another who wrote so nicely and looks forward to helping me when I go to Scotland soon.

On the way back to the Mess I passed a huge crowd at a Service near John Bunyan's statue—a united Good Friday Service—fine singing: "When I survey the wondrous Cross". Then back to the Office to revise script for Wednesday, and so very tired to the Mess again and sleep.

4th April

Everything has begun to close down today because of Easter. I finished off script for Wednesday on "Why are we here on Earth?", a question that Wink (Renwick) wanted me to speak about. I'm not very happy about it but I talked it over with Welch and Eric Fenn and they both seemed quite pleased with it. . . . After lunch I went on my own to see "Gulliver's Travels" and "The Saint meets the Tiger"—both first-class films; then to tea with the Head Master of Bedford School Prep with whom Eric is billeted—a nice fellow.

5th April (Easter)

Easter Day in England. Scotland for all its progress, has a bit to go yet! . . . I went to the Office after breakfast and sat with Eric Fenn listening to the various Services. . . . In the afternoon I went for a walk with Eric and saw some of the places Bunyan—who had never left Bedford district—incorporated into *The Pilgrim's Progress*. How a man with such a small knowledge of places and things could have written the books he did is just another of the miracles! I took part in the Easter broadcast . . . reading the Easter story with Trevor Harvey, Cyril Taylor and John Williams, and both the A and B singers and Thorbald Bald at the organ; just grand. Then I, at the invitation of Alan Colthurst, the Vicar, sat in the stalls, all in black! . . . Welch preached a very vague and tired sermon—the poor man must have been very tired; he had had a number of broadcasts today, and even after this there was the last of William Temple's Holy Week Services (he has been broadcasting each evening this week) which W. took.

After supper in the Mess I went back and fire-watched—Eric Fenn again there and more talk—as usual—with him most interesting.

There were some good broadcasts today, notably J. T. Christie on "The Greeks had no word for it" (agape) and Commander Kimmins postscript on Malta. But I missed Easter with the boys and Easter Communion.

6th April

I received many letters today, chiefly about last week's broadcast and all very kind. One lovely one from Ian Gillan, S.C.F. Ack Ack Command Scotland, giving me a long and most interesting list of units to visit, etc., during my stay in Scottish Command at the end of the week. Geoffrey Gilbey also wrote enclosing a copy of his book *Pass it On* and some most interesting papers, etc., on his Young Soldiers' Training Battalion Camp, which he has asked me to visit. All are under twenty and all have been sentenced to detention, but had their sentences remitted by the Army Commander to go to his Experimental Camp. I've written and offered to go for a day or two at the end of the month. . . .

Later I went to London to see Peter Bunn, now en route for India. We had a grand—though short—time together, dinner in a place off Regent Street (we arrived too early at "Joseph's" in Soho). Much talk about the Battalion and all its grand chaps. Peter was so glad I mentioned him in my talk on Wednesday; it had cheered his mother a lot he said, and him too. Of course Peter is quite unique—a grand fellow, full of good fun and one of the best laughs I know. . . . Back to Bedford and bed.

7th April

I went to the Eastern Command today at Luton Hoo—a huge house—to see the A.C.G. and Command H.Q. McKew, the A.C.G. is a grand man—rather like "Tubby" Clayton in Tubby's early days. He gave me a grand welcome and spoke most frankly about broadcasting to the troops. I had lunch at Command and met some first-class Staff officers, all of whom were genuinely keen on the "Radio Padre" idea, and out to help in any way they could. Kemp-Welch, the C.-

in-C's A.D.C. was particularly helpful and wants notices to go up in all Commands about it each week. "This side of our work is as important as any, and more important than most." He Captained the Cambridge Cricket XI some years ago and is now in the Grenadier Guards. I was made most welcome by them all and felt there is no fear from Eastern Command. . . . Some grand letters on return, from, e.g. "Wink" Renwick: "I miss you very much padre, maybe I'm wrong in saying this but there is an emptiness in my life somewhere—especially at the Church Services. We had a Communion Service today—remember my first one at Aberlady? . . . I would like to thank you very much for all you have done for me, I only hope I live up to your standards, remember . . . (and so on). I've had a quarrel with my wife and we are still rather in the dumps, but neither of us wants to give in, but as I go on leave everything will be O.K. I wouldn't like to have kept that from you. . . . It's our anniversary today . . . every best wish, Wink." Good old Wink, he's quite one of the best. I wish the original plan of his coming with me, which had been agreed on, until the W.O. went back and said "no batman", could have been carried out; it would have helped and cheered me so much. Then a very sweet letter from Ray—who is quite one of the bravest people I know. She is to have another operation, is keeping Mum cheery, and Oh how she misses Dad! She writes about the things they did together, and talks they had, and "these things will never be again". She understood dear Dad better than anyone and he'd do anything for "Day Day".

8th April

This has been a busy day and no mistake! Left by the 0815 train to London and met Welch at Oxford Circus at 1000 going straight from there to Stanhope to see General Sir Frederick Pile, C.-in-C. A.A. Command Home Forces. He was most friendly—a small cheery man—very keen on the Radio Padre idea and out to do all to help—to write to the Chaplain-General; to get me made up to Major (3rd Cl. C.F.); to get a car or promise of conveyance, a secretary, etc. He talked a lot and most enthusiastically about the men under his command and is so keen on them. Before we left he said "You must meet General —, he's a bit mad you know, but he ought to be of some help to you!" General—was interested and before we left in the C.in-C's car the C.-in-C. called out, "Remember now, come back any time you like—you're really our padre you know!"—a good and encouraging interview.

The rest of the day in London was spent in visiting B.B.C. officials—Adam and Adams and Nichols, programme directors and publicity—too keen on publicity I fear, but I suppose it's necessary to get the job done.

I got the train back to Bedford and got to the office in time to revise and partly re-write my script for tonight. I spoke at 9.25 p.m. on a question that "Wink" had asked me: "Why are we here on earth?"—so I talked on man's "Chief end—to glorify God and enjoy Him for ever". It seemed to go off all right. Then back to the office and wrote letters till 11.30 p.m.

9th April

After the business that concerned my job had been dealt with at the Staff Meeting . . . I went to my office and dictated next Wednesday's script on "some of your homes I have visited"—not particular homes but the whole question of homes and their breakup in war time. Fr Vann O.P. was here today too. Beales is keen that *The Picture Post* should have a Radio Padre article: this may mean a break with my colleagues in the R.A.Ch.D. and Church in general "advertising and all that"! The snag is that this job by its very nature IS a public job—and about as public as you could make it! Unless you are known you cannot get round posts freely, and make the contacts that are needed. I still feel that a job like this should be for a more able and preferably slightly older man of 3rd Cl. rank and possibly C. of E., as far the larger number are C. of E. in England certainly.

A nice letter from Jimmie and Mary Dalgleish asking me to come down and stay with them for a bit and "padre" Jimmie's Regiment. Of course it can't be done, but I've written and asked Jimmie if he'd meet me sometime and we could broadcast together, comparing the old days with today. Nunky Brown also wrote urging me to put in for Heriot's Headmastership as quite a number of folk seem keen on it. Oh dear no!

75

Began packing my things to get ready to move into Scottish Command tomorrow.

10th April

Left Bedford by the 1115, having first been to the office. It's a long journey but whether it's because I'm going to my homeland or whether it's because of the new light nights with double summer-time, I don't know, but it seemed shorter than the journey down!

It's always strange what interesting people you meet in the train! Almost every railway carriage contains at least one sermon. Among the fellows I met was a young R.A.F. doctor from Aberdeen called Inglis—a very nice fellow. Some good Yorkshire folk who got out at Leeds gave me some of their sandwiches—you can't get food on the train now.

When I came to the Borders my heart beat faster! There was a lovely night sun—evening sun—on the Borderland. I thought of the boys of the 4th (K.O.S.B.) Hawick: "Wink" and Spence, Scottie Gordon, Scott, Myles and so many more, and David Haddon from the 7/9th; then Galashiels with Murray and Amos; nearby Selkirk with Ford and so many of the band. "Braw, braw lads"—how Dad used to love these words, and how true they are; and dear Maime came from Hassendean, Hawick—so there's a bit of the Borders in me too, Oh hope! . . . How "the Colonel"—Freddie Johnston—loves it: "Hills green to the top, padre, a line and the trout, bees in the heather and the wind blowing through the telephone wires. . . ."

I got back to Edinburgh after 10.00 p.m.—dark and rather strange; but the first words I heard were, "Hullo Mr Wright" and there was Harry Smail, one of the old Club boys driving a taxi. It was a good home-coming and he and I shook hands and talked a bit, much to the embarrassment of a L./Cpl. in the taxi, who wondered what a Captain was doing holding him up like this! Then to Acheson House where Robbie Fulton and Jim Stephen were ready with a cup of tea. And so through the grand old place again—each room with its own "smell". Were I to be struck blind I would know when I'd come to Canongate and I think I could tell every room in Acheson House by its smell!

76

11th April

A letter this morning from the Duke of Montrose, this year's High Commissioner to the General Assembly, enclosing a very good short article by him for the May number of *H.M. Scottish Forces* (the Forces' Magazine) called "Where Adolf goes wrong". . . . I went down home (12 Saxe-Coburg Place) as soon as possible and had lunch with Maime and Ray in that lovely homely place. It's so quiet down there without Dad and "Paddy" (the dog)—how quickly things change! (Even Dad's beloved Budgie was found dead in its cage just after Dad died.) Both Maime and Ray are bearing up well—though both look tired—and Maime very white. After lunch I went round to see "Nunky" Brown—in his usual good form and then back via Inverleith Park where I stopped to watch the different teams playing football; I used to know nearly them all but I know none now. I remember how Shaw and I never missed a Saturday in the Park with our Club teams—what a team our First was, with only two losses in two years! Stanley McLean, John Davies, Robert Roadnight, Jimmie, George Flannigan, Lackie (Macmillan), John Banks, and so on. Again how quickly things change! Tea at home with Maime and Ray—again that homely atmosphere and we talked of Bob's future and how glad we were that Pip and Clare were so happy, and we laughed rather sadly—for you can laugh sadly—at some of the escapades of Dad and "Paddy" and "Jock" and "Donald", and all the other dogs he had and loved. I had supper out and met a sailor at the same table who had just been in a Destroyer escorting back these grand Norwegian folk who had broken through the mine-infested and carefully watched seas, to the freedom of Britain. About twelve set out but only two or possibly three got to this country. He told me how there were hundreds of civilians on board, women and children, and how they cheered as the British rescued them from the Nazi slavery.

Heard that the 7/9th are in Cruden Bay and Peterhead. Oh how I wish I were with them! If they go into action without me it will break my heart!

12th April

I spent the morning finishing off my script for Wednesday

and it took all morning to do this. . . . I preached in the Canongate at the evening Service—a good crowd was there. . . . After the Evening Service I went home and had a cup of tea with Maime and Ray then back to the Boys' Club. Jim Macfarlane up on leave from the West Indies. He had seen the Duke of Windsor—looking very fit and well when he had come to inspect them. The whole Club seemed in good form. . . . I'm sure that the Club has done more to teach boys to worship and lead them into the Church than anything else.

13th April

Worked a bit on the June number of *H.M. Scottish Forces* (the Forces' Magazine). The final proof of the Daily Prayer card sent by the Oxford University Press. I'm quite pleased with it, though I wish now that I'd put a more simple "home" prayer. They also sent a notice that it is going to be put in all the papers—I suppose I'll be blamed for that! . . .

Met Maime and Ray and went to a really first-class film version of "Rebecca". . . . Tea with Maime and Ray at Fullers. Supper with George MacLeod and Dr A. Vidler and Uist MacDonald at the St Giles' Grill. I went off by myself to the New Club and had coffee and read a detective book for an hour (what peace!) and then went round to John McVie's folk to see them all.

Acheson House pretty full tonight with the meeting of the Iona "Chapter" so I slept most comfortably in the "powdering" cupboard off the Tapestry Room, which I always use now as my study. The Headmastership of Heriot's was filled today. I'm glad in a way I didn't apply, though I'm told that I stood a very good chance. . . .

14th April

Alec Vidler, Editor of *Theology* stayed with us at Acheson House overnight and this evening George MacLeod had him to dinner at the University Club (in Princes Street). He is one of the most striking characters I have yet met. This afternoon he spoke to a large gathering at Acheson House most ably, though rather closely cross-questioned later by Principal D. S. Cairns—the grand old warrior! I had tea with Melville Dinwiddie and we discussed future arrangements in Scottish

Command. (Alec Vidler asked George MacLeod what sort of a pacifist he was and after a short pause George answered "51%!")

16th April

. . . In the evening I went to Toc H Meeting at Dalry House to discuss the future of Toc H Scotland—Melville Dinwiddie, G. E. Troup and Newman of Fettes there. A most interesting meeting. I personally can never forget all I owe to Toc H, for it was through it I first learnt the meaning of service and met so many good friends—these early days in Edinburgh were great days indeed: George MacLeod, Canon A. E. Laurie (whom I succeeded as Padre), Hugh Lyon, now Head Master of Rugby, General Dudgeon, Nunky Brown, Evan McAndlish, Tom Curr, Roy Sanderson, Tom Ritchie and so many others. Toc H in Scotland may have had some hard knocks since then, but surely it must not be allowed to die.

19th April

Breakfast in bed this morning! A lovely Gullane day . . . before I went to the back row of the Episcopal Church (where H. T. Coles was preaching in the absence of J. M. Ballard who was so good to our boys when they were here) I took a walk and saw a grand Polish service (R.C.) outside where the Mess is (Waverley of hallowed memory) hundreds of Poles singing (how they *could* "sing the Lord's song in a strange land!") and in the distance I heard the Scottish psalms come from St Andrew's—our own folk and strangers in our midst each worshipping God. The Poles had candles and an altar, though in the open air, and a priest in full vestments. Had tea at the Roses after a visit to Whiteholm on the way up . . . where we talked, Mr and Mrs Rose and I, much about Walter who was killed at Hong Kong with the 2nd Battalion Royal Scots, and Hugh, who I told them—and meant it—is one of the straightest and best Adjutants any Regiment could have, and the 7/9th are fortunate to have him. Then supper at the Thomsons and the bus back with Coles, home to see dear Maime at present alone as Ray is in Perth and Bob at the Boys' Camp. Home is always the same: "Home"—there's no word that can describe it. She gave me such a lovely salad and tea. The only word better than "home" is surely "Mother"!

79

When I got back to Acheson House a great surprise—
Jimmie Dalgleish up on leave, and there he was the same grand
old Jimmie (Sergeant and M.M.) sitting with Mary his wife
and George MacLeod and Robbie Fulton. Was I glad to see
him! . . . arranged to see him on Wednesday, my only free
afternoon so far for ages. A really grand day.

20th April

A long but very interesting day. A F.A.N.Y. L./Cpl. called
for me at Acheson House with a fine Ford V8 and we went and
picked up Ian Gillan at Fairmilehead and then, past so many
"well-kent" landmarks, to the sites on the Coldingham
Moors of the Light A.A. Gunners—lonely posts manned by
small bodies of men—about twelve—all waiting, so far in
vain, to have a crack at the Hun. I talked to many of them and
found them very bright and cheery and smart. They "put on"
various things for me, spoke about the wireless which is a
great boon to them, etc. I met two of the old Battalion who left
us at Houghton—good to see them again. We had a grand
simple lunch and then set off to another old haunt—
Archerfield—now too full of Poles. Passed *en route* again
Cockburnspath and the way to the Hut (at Skateraw) and the
bridge when Stan decided to join the Guards, and so many
good days came back. Yet here was I living some good days
still with the old friends as true as ever, though now far
apart—what a lot there is to thank God for . . . found too that
they listened to the Radio Padre. From there we drove to
Dalkeith Palace, an excellent O.C. Battery of Searchlights
(formerly Lincolnshire Regiment) Major Smith. The whole
H.Q. here is really a first-class show, spotlessly clean, Smith
all out for the men, the chaps a good type. We had tea there
after looking round; and after tea went to see the A.T.S. H.Q.
at the Palace (which belongs to the Buccleuchs, though the
family haven't lived there since 1913). Then Smith came with
Ian Gillan and myself to one of the loneliest Searchlight
posts—twelve men—good fellows (they were playing cricket), very lonely but their loneliness was covered over by their
friendship. They had a pet lamb given to them by the farmer
and they were very good to it. So, dropping Smith at Dalkeith, we motored back in the evening. A good show and a

grand day. . . . I had dinner later at the New Club with General Dudgeon . . . during this the Duke of Buccleuch came and spoke to me, as usually, so nicely. Then I wrote letters till late, trying to keep up with the ones I've got. Such nice letters too today from John McVie, Jimmy Wighton, Stan (from Eretria), Hilary Dorman, etc. A wire from "All ranks of the 7/9th" signed by the Adjutant asking me to come and stay with them, and a charming letter from Nevile (Davidson) who feels he *ought* to go back to the Cathedral if the Army authorities will let him, though he has never been so happy as in the Army. He says to me "Your friendship at meetings and talks and all kinds of odd moments and varied places has contributed more than almost anything to the happiness of my almost two years in the Army; and I miss you constantly nowadays". . . . I greatly value his loving friendship and counsel—so many places indeed—Newbury, France, Norfolk, Tyningham, Dirleton, Dunblane, and so many more.

21st April

Had dear Dad lived he would have been 63 today.

26th April

What a day! Left Acheson House at 0830 hours prompt followed by a W.O. photographer and went to lonely Searchlight sites on the Pentland Hills where after some photos with the chaps I took a Service in a Hut there.

27th April

In the most glorious sunshine I left with Ian Gillan—that "good companion"—for Inverness and the West. Oh what lovely scenery it all is! We were met at Inverness by an A.T.S. who drove us to the A.T.S. Training Centre—the Camerons' Depot taken over, I hope temporarily. The C.O. of the A.T.S., a cousin of Ian Gillan's,[1] took me round and I was more than ever impressed with the first-class way the A.T.S. live. We had tea at the Mess, and then went to the Camerons' Mess which they have still managed to keep to themselves. There I met Major (soon to be Lt.-Col.) Pringle-Patterson (a son of the philosopher)—a really first-class Regular soldier,

[1] Helen Nimmo, who later has done so much for the Canongate and me.

and I know of no higher praise than that! From there we went to the Castle Mess where the A.A. R.A.S.C. has its H.Q. and was taken round. It's a lovely and happy place and I met some good young soldiers, from England chiefly, who had just finished their training. The 52nd Division were finishing a scheme in these parts and "my heart stood still" as I saw a 55 (the 7/9th number) vehicle in the distance with what looked like Arthur Brown in it. We dined with J. F. Marshall, now D.A.C.G. in this Area. At dinner to my great joy I met Colonel H. A. Kelly of the 4th K.O.S.B. and he arranged to meet me on Friday and take me across to dinner with the 4th Marshall, Ian and I talked until midnight in the hotel about many things—chiefly about the Church after the War—a very serious subject. All men like and help padres, nearly all are most religious and Christians, but so few see the answer in the Church as we have it today. . . .

28th April

Just one of the most wonderful days I have ever seen. We motored to Poolewe from Inverness through some of the finest scenery in the world, and the sun shone brightly the whole time, not a cloud in the sky, the rivers and lochs deep blue and the trees feathery green with new leaves; even the grass was fresh and the crops were beginning to come up. Here and there blossom could be seen and thousands of daffodils. I never remember a day like it for beauty of sea and weather. We stopped at Garve where we are to stay on Wednesday night and at a transit camp at — where I had a talk with four fellows all from England in the IV Hussars, R.A.C., Tank Corps and Derbyshire Yeomanry. They have rather a lonely and miserable time at this post—nothing but guards, no good recreation room, very lonely indeed—not even the wireless. As I expected, their officer-in-charge is not a Regular (a Regular officer would never have allowed this) but turned out to be, alas, a combatant Minister of the Church of Scotland! Then lunch at the beautiful Gareloch with Padre Ross—a really grand little man who "does" the Area. His wife Jane gave us a really good meal and Ian Gillan and I were sorry to leave such grand folk. Ross who was at Dunkirk, etc., puts in a power of good work—a real good Highland Scot. Then on to the 58th H.A.A. at Poolewe—men chiefly from Kent and Manchester and a really good crowd. I liked their Colonel (aged thirty-two) and visited some of their sites—miles and miles apart. The men like this place. They haven't been here long and have just come up from Manchester and so far they have had nothing but sunny days. I'm afraid when it rains it won't be such fun! I liked these men from Kent—really good cheery fellows—and I liked their officers, one especially who had brought down a German plane in Kent and got an M.C. for it. . . . We dined at Poolewe Hotel where we are staying the night and later went to Mrs Sawyers' wonderful house and garden of rhododendrons, daffodils, and various sorts of trees. Yet ninety-five years ago nothing grew on this promontory except one willow (I should imagine a weeping one!) Mrs Sawyers' father, Osgood Mackenzie, planted all we saw—hundreds of trees and one of the most lovely of all gardens. Across the Loch we saw the other promontory—bleak and bare, the same as this had been ninety-five years ago. Two pictures and a very telling sermon. On the way back on this perfect evening of a perfect day and passing the R.A.O.C. which too we had visited in the afternoon and various town boys from Kent and Manchester walking in dream-like amazement by these lovely Scottish shores, we called in on the Y.M.C.A. for a cup of tea with Mr Forbes (whom I had last met in Thetford in Norfolk in the summer of 1940). We got back to the Hotel late and found the door locked, but I got through the window and after a bath slept a glorious sleep, the fresh Highland air coming through the window and knowing that all around were men from all over Britain, taken from their homes and loved ones, ready to defend us; and H.M. ships lying out at sea watching for the enemy's coming; and all that disturbed the waters of the sea loch were seals—it was peace!

29th April

I thought it would be impossible to equal the glory of yesterday, but today has been another day like it—"Every prospect pleases" and man is just grand! Again not a cloud, glorious sun, unsurpassed scenery. We motored up to a very lonely Coastal Battery R.A. where we saw Major Crockett, cousin of S.R., a most interesting and quite unique fellow, a regular soldier and a philosopher, very like an Oxford Don. He told me many things, one of the most interesting being that he invented and brought back the word "browned-off". I wish I'd known about this before I'd recorded the talk I'm broadcasting tonight. Like some of the officers we have already met on this tour, he is worried about Russian relations with Great Britain and our loose use of the word "democracy". The Church, he maintains, must take a very strong part in reconstruction—beginning now. . . . I was sorry to leave him and his fellows; it was a lovely place but the men are a bit tired of it since there is so little to do, but this weather has cheered them up, and they really are extraordinarily well looked after. Then we went to a Light A.A. site for lunch—Major Harper and five other officers . . . all seemed good fellows. The men there were a bit older and definitely not so intelligent as the Heavy A.A. whom we visited after lunch. They were a Troop of the lot we saw yesterday under a grand Subaltern called Davies, a most friendly fellow who seemed most sorry that we couldn't stay longer but at least cheered up when we went to see where they lived—a little cottage. More sites after this and then a first-class R.A.M.C. Camp at Gareloch—a real happy family. Once again we saw the difference a good officer makes and there are hundreds of them. Tea in the hospital and a good crack with the patients . . . most of whom are getting sunburnt outside—very friendly and very cheery, full of praise for the surgeon from Bart's and the doctor and nurses. They, like so many others, I find are interested in the wireless and seem to like (probably from politeness) the Radio Padre. We joked about tonight's (forthcoming) talk and unwillingly I left them all and Ross, who was there too, and Crockett who had come down from the Coast Battery. Ross and I agreed that it was impossible to believe in the depravity of man if you were a padre. I wonder at, and thank God every day for, the goodness of man. The same lovely journey by road took us back to Garve where we spent the night at the Hotel. I remember how in July 1939 when the 7/9th were camping at Strathpeffer, I came here with Ronnie Alexander, Bobbie Gunn, Harry Evans and Ernest Lawson (all privates then, but now all officers) and still the food is pre-war. Ian Gillan and I along with Miss Mackenzie, the talented proprietrix of this grand hotel, listened after dinner to the recorded broadcast of my talk on being "browned off". . . . A fellow wrote the other day to ask if I believed in miracles: what greater miracle than sitting in a Highland Hotel and listening to myself and words that I'd spoken some days before, and realising that throughout all the land people were (or could) listen too at that very same moment! After this we spent a most interesting evening talking to General Sir Robert Carrington the recent retired C.-in-C. Scottish Command (General Thorne succeeded him). He was most friendly and interesting and had many things to talk about connected with the Army, e.g., the Adjutant-General is keen to have one Infantry Regiment (like the R.A.) and scrap all separate Regiments . . . that de Gaulle was only a greater hater of the Germans than of us, that Sir Alan Brooke who was with us in France in 1940 (the 52nd Division) had to make one of the most difficult decisions ever taken by an Army Commander, when he brought us back, and of an interesting interview Brooke had with the King of the Belgians—a good fellow really—a few days before Belgium gave in, thanks to traitors who were there when Brooke saw the King. The Canadian soldiers who are stationed round here were called out during the night to put out some of the huge fires that the drought has caused.

30th April

The sun, if anything, is stronger than ever today, and though it's lovely for us I hear the Forestry Commission are very worried about it, and the strong winds have made the lands drier than ever known in memory and fires on the moors threaten the woods—a very serious matter. Rested at Garve all morning and I appreciate the rest. Then we went on to Invergordon via Strathpeffer of peace-time Camp memory (summer of 1939—white spats, white belts, blue patrols, etc.!) . . . Then to the transit camp at Invergordon with a most enjoyable haversack lunch by the Moray Firth on the way . . . met Padre Dalgleish and motored across to a lonely Light A.A. site on the Black Isle, one of the happiest sites I've seen. A young Sergeant with older chaps under him, very isolated, but all so contented in their community life that they didn't want "to go ashore"! Went then to Dingwall, calling on sites on the way to have tea with Jack Macphail who is now the Minister there. It was grand to see Jack again. . . . Then on to Muir of Ord where I stopped for a bit and spoke to some grand young soldiers of the 2nd Highland Regiment (formerly 70th A. and S.H.). At Beaufort Castle we just missed Lord Lovat, back from a most successful commando raid, who had gone out for a walk with his wife; there is a fine sundial there which tells the time to a minute. It has been a good day and when I got to the Station Hotel at Inverness I greatly valued a good hot bath. Marshall gave us a grand dinner there and we talked till late. The sites I have visited were lonely, but with good officers and good N.C.O's they can be, and usually are, very happy.

1st May

. . . said "au revoir" to Ian Gillan who returns to Edinburgh plus some eggs for Mum. Ian has been just grand, most helpful, and a good companion on the way. He is a first-class S.C.F., a perfect gentleman, and a great Christian, and I was very sorry to leave him on this wonderful tour.—Is very stiff and not very impressive; we visited some of his sites and saw the men who guard the aerodrome at Lossiemouth—a sad lot, but pleasant. . . . At Elgin I found Joey Ogle, the best of all Mess waiters, from the 4th K.O.S.B., who had come from Buckie to meet me, and we had tea in the Hotel and a walk around Elgin, and Joey gave me all the news. I was picked up by Colonel Kelly and "the Duchess" (Major McLaine), and the ever-faithful Middlemas the driver, and taken to the 4th H.Q. where I got a grand welcome from everyone there— Alastair Thorburn, Donald Hogg, Horace Davidson, John Elliot, etc. After dinner I motored to Cullen to the dance there (B and D Companies are there) and greatly rejoiced to meet the ever-faithful "Wink" who seemed as glad to see me as I was to see him . . . later in the evening I walked round with Doc Allan Hill and talked and went to bed—tired but happy, back in the old Brigade again with all its good fellows around me. It's hard to beat the good Borderer. . . .

2nd May

Had breakfast with the K.O.S.B. at Buckie, lunch with the 52nd Reconnaissance Regiment at Keith, tea with the 155th Brigade at Turriff and supper with the 7/9th Royal Scots at Cruden Bay. In addition I passed through the 5th K.O.S.B. at Banff and the rest of the 7/9th at Peterhead. I was sorry to leave the 4th after such a short stay. Williamson, the padre's batman motored me to Keith where I saw Jack Hankey, one of the best of friends and one of the greatest soldiers I've ever met. Jamie Stormonth-Darling was, alas, on leave. Neil Murray was acting Adjutant with a good fellow Telfer as Assistant. Jack Hankey is the first Colonel of this Battalion and has made a wonderful job of it, as he would.[1] He got Dr Anderson to motor me across to Brigade H.Q. where I was due for tea. . . . The first man I met at Brigade H.Q. was David St Clair-Erskine and it was good to see him again . . . quite a family tea-party for Ian Crawford is still Staff Captain. They were all so nice . . . Morrison and the faithful Cruickshanks picked me up and motored me back to the old Battalion—tired but happy to be "home" again even for a short time. . . . After supper I went for a walk with John over the dunes of Cruden and not even the air-raid warning could stop the joy of the evening, its peace and its contentment. We stopped to hear the last post played most beautifully—the sun setting behind the Hotel where H.Q. and "D" Company live. I remembered so well the night before we left for France (11th June 1940) hearing Reid play it—and how many changes since then! I got back to the Mess and found John Campbell, now C.O., waiting for me. He was in grand form and most welcoming. . . . There were hundreds of letters waiting for me and it's going to be a job to get through them all. Also the new volume (No. 4) of *Lift Up Your Hearts* with three articles by myself. I have no sermon for tomorrow (Sunday) but mentally I am very tired so I had a bath and slept like a log, happy to

[1] When at the end of the year I was S.C.F. of the Division, General Ritchie told me that he regarded it as the best Battalion in the Division.

be with my own Battalion again among friends, and happy too to think of the friends I have yet to meet tomorrow.

3rd May

I preached to the 7/9th A, B and C Companies, at Peterhead and H.Q. and D Companies at Cruden Bay. It was so good to be with them all again. I spoke about "Tom, Dick and Harry" (S.M. and A. in Daniel 3) "Our God will save us . . . but IF NOT . . .".

At Peterhead the pipes and drums turned out and played the Battalion to Church to my favourite March, "The Muckin' o' Geordie's Byre"—a very nice gesture, for which I thanked them at the beginning of the Service. They had their first march-past for a bit afterwards, and John Campbell, now C.O., took the salute. He had read the Lesson. The Church was ugly but the fellows fit, sunburnt; cheerful faces made you forget the rather dull surroundings! At Cruden Bay the Service was in the Hotel—now a billet, and was taken from a rather shaky platform composed of two trestle tables. The music was led by the ever-faithful Eunson, Smith & Co. on brass instruments. In all this padre Morrison was most helpful.

I had a good chance to talk to the fellows after the Cruden Bay Service, and they came round and talked too. Ted Cook and Jimmie Wighton, the Walkers from Aberdeen, Willie Urquhart, and so many more.

In the afternoon I went for a walk with John McVie round by the old Castle, the fishing village . . . stopping to talk to fellows on the way, and then back to the usually good 7/9th family tea. The feeding is always so good in "our" mess (better than when I was P.M.C. at Yeovil!) and the mess waiters led by Docherty, now a Corporal, excellent. After tea I wrote a bit and then went up and talked for a while to the chaps again. They were all so friendly and welcoming: "How do you like the new job sir?"; "When are you coming back to us?"; "Can you get us this . . . or arrange about that?" and so on.

After dinner John McVie, Bob Rutherford and I set off for Peterhead where I had promised to meet Melville Dinwiddie

at a Toc H meeting. . . . After tea there and it was about 10
p.m. we went on to B and C Company Mess at Peterhead
where we got a grand reception. Joe Cameron in great form
and all the others too. All day today I felt I had never been
away, but that I'd just woken up from a happy dream to an
even happier life that I so much love.

4th May

I set off with Morrison and driven by Cruickshanks,
immediately after breakfast, visited Division H.Q. at Aberlour (about eighty miles off). We drove through some very
lovely country and eventually got there and found John Fraser
most friendly and happy. He took me to see "Johno" (Lt.-Col.
Johnston, Royal Scots) the G.1 a real good chap. . . . J.F. says
my return to the 52nd will be pretty safe. From there after
lunch at a wayside house at Craigellachie, we went in search of
Ray's babies, Nita and Thelma, whom after some time we
found—looking brown and fit but very thin. I promised Ray
that I would try to do this and I am so glad I managed it. I wish
we could get them home as I don't think they have got a very
nice place for evacuation. Then, rather sadly, leaving them we
went to Rothes where the 155th Field Ambulance are—a very
changed lot compared with the good old days of David
Middleton! Few left here though I was glad to see Lance-
Corporal Oliver—a good type of the fit young soldier of the
best Territorial kind. Then to Keith to tea with the Reconnaissance Regiment—sorry to find Jack Hankey out, but had a
good talk with Crawford the second-in-command. . . .
When eventually we got back in time for dinner to Cruden
Bay we had the sad news that Bob Rutherford was due to go
tomorrow morning on embarkation leave (told this afternoon). Thus he joins Arthur Brown and Frank Paxton, etc.
Only six Second-Lieutenants left in the Battalion; how
changed from last summer when we had about twenty-five!
John Campbell told me how worried he is about losing so
many officers he wants to keep. . . .
A good, rather exhausting day, covered much ground and
met many people and none more glad to meet than Robin
Legget on the way home through Turriff, who rushed out for
a few cheery words. He is on leave next week and John McVie

is due on leave then; Arthur Brown is already on embarkation leave, so we all hope to meet. That, in the well-known words of Robin "will be the cat's whiskers"!

It's funny, but when I saw Ray's babies today I nearly cried and could hardly speak. They are not happy and think the woman on whom they are billeted is a witch. She told them that she knows all they do and say wherever they are (and they are afraid to speak).

5th May

Bob Rutherford came rushing into my room this morning to say goodbye. "Would I sign the prayer card I'd given all the Battalion?" I do hope I'll see Bob again; he's a grand little enthusiast and a first-class sportsman—one of the best. . . .

I sat in the Mess and tried to tackle some of the letters this a.m.—over 300 of them! Docherty brought me tea at 1100. It was "my other home again" and no mistake.

A long gap in my 1942 Journal due no doubt because of letters, travel, etc.

11th June

I travelled down to London from Bedford this a.m. with John Williams and lunch with Beales at Broadcasting House. After lunch I listened to the Service of Enthronement of the new Archbishop of York—what wonderful singing . . . I thought how Dad would have loved this; somehow I felt he was listening to it and he felt very near. Then I went to Maida Vale to Ack Ack Beer Beer where I spoke on the wireless about Arnold of Rugby and then about comedians and my favourite gramophone records. Met Albert Sadler and his trio on the same programme and, most interesting of all, Gerald Kersh, the author of *They Died with their Boots Clean*—the best story of the Army I have read. As I had taken the Overseas and the Daily Service I had broadcast four times today.

I didn't feel fit today and fainted just before I shaved this morning; no one saw me or was there and I skinned my knee a bit. It was soon over but it shook me up a bit for the rest of the day.

Lots of letters when I got back from London . . . I should

90

have gone to Hounslow tonight to stay with the Rev. G. H. Woolley, V.C., M.C., and been Guest at the dinner of the Middlesex Regiment, but didn't feel fit enough to take it.

12th June

My birthday and Jimmie Dalgleish's birthday. A wire awaited me from dear Mum and all at home, also one from Jimmie . . . and later Pip and Clare and Keesh wired. I remember two years ago today receiving a wire from Maime and Dad just as I left for France (though they didn't know!). . . Two years ago! We thought then that we were to be in France for some time—years possibly. And yet within a week we were back—all our kit, except the Carriers, lost. I remember the march beside the Colonel from Burleigh House to Newbury Station, the embarking from Southampton and Laing singing "I'll walk beside you" on the deck in the dark, and the cheer I got just suddenly from "D" Company as I passed them in the twilight; I remember the destroyer going with us and the ships with the 4th K.O.S.B. and 5th K.O.S.B. on board. It was a great adventure—so soon to finish—and it was my birthday. I remembered too it was Jimmie's birthday . . . I wondered what had happened to him until just a few days before we left I got a note saying he was back safe from the rearguard action at Dunkirk and later, when I came back from France a note to say he had got the M.M. . . . . And here *today* the same telegrams first thing from Mum but not Dad, from Jimmie . . . and I thought of all this today and many other things.

I didn't feel too well today—tummy and exhaustion. I should have gone to the Bishop's Palace at Peterborough to speak at a Padres' Conference—but I wired it off, just couldn't make it. I was in the Office nearly all day working until I felt even more exhausted; so back to the Vicarage trying to finish my script for next Wednesday on "Going Absent"—"Absence makes the War grow longer"—and so to bed.

13th June

Travelled up to London from Bedford today with a grand old Captain now in the Intelligence Corps—a Regular all his

91

life, joined when he was fourteen, his father an R.S.M. and he later the same. Said he would not have had a better life anywhere and he'd go through it all again. Went straight from there to St James's Club to meet the Marquis of Queensberry: he had left a message to meet me at the London Casino (soon to be called the Queensberry Club) which he is going to turn into a Club for all ranks and all War workers, and he wants me to take on the religious side and preach to 2,000 on Sunday mornings in the Big Hall. He is very keen on this and so is his manager—they want religion in the Club they say. They want me to do it as they say I can get across better than anyone, and that the men all want me to do it (*THEY* say!!). . . I said it was a great chance and I'd let them know. I met Naughton of the Crazy Gang and Teddy Brown; nearly all the actors have joined the Club. Went to lunch with Lord Queensberry and his secretary: a not too large lunch cost him £2.19/- for the three of us plus 6/- for the tip. My impressions of him are reservable! Then I went to Westminster Abbey and heard 400 choirboys sing most gloriously with Sir Sydney Nicholson conducting—really wonderful. Tea at the Authors' Club and then a taxi to the H.Q. just outside Wormwood Scrubs, with a Mixed Heavy A.A. Battery, for London stay. I visited Wellington Barracks in the afternoon. The Guards are there and there is no one to touch them. I saw the S.C.F.—a rather stiff chap. I feel that the Guards of all people need a padre who is not stiff, to play off against the other side of their life. . . . Went with the padre here—Anderson—to some of his sites. Still feeling none too fit and sleeping badly.

My post today brought among other letters one from Hilary Dorman from India . . . one from John Newton asking me down to Dorset and telling me that Jimmie Mason-Brown is now a Lt.-Col. at Oxford.

28th June

Peterborough: a good day. Preached at Gun sites—excellent services and first-class officers. Visited many other sites with Guy Teale in the afternoon and had tea at Brigade H.Q. with Brigadier Anderson—a good fellow. At night had dinner with the Divisional Commander, General Crossman, and his wife, a most enjoyable family evening—one of the best.

Spoke to H. F. Ellis (of *Punch*) about the publication of the A. J. Wentworth stories in *Punch*—very funny. I think he will have them published.

29th June
Peterborough.

30th June
Aldershot.

1st July
Bedford.

2nd July
Bedford, London and Bracknell.

3rd July
Bracknell, London and Bedford.

4th July
Bedford, Tidworth via Salisbury.

5th July
Tidworth. Preached in the Garrison Church in the morning to a large number of Scottish Troops—mostly R.A.C. Afterwards there was a Service of Holy Communion to which quite a number came. Later I went round the Y.M.C.A. and parts of the Camp—a really first-class show. Lunch at the 61 Training Regiment Mess was followed by D. A. C. G. James taking me to his house where I wrote broadcast for Wednesday on "Padre, do you believe in Heaven and Hell?" Found it very hard to concentrate on this—this kind of life not suitable for writing good wireless talks! Tea with Mr and Mrs James and then to the Methodist Garrison Church to take the evening service—a great experience. Church full of fellows, most enthusiastic singing and very "receptive" congregation. I'll never forget the singing of "From sinking sands He lifted me" and I thought, as I told them later, of the hundreds of R.A.C.

men who must have sung that in this Church and were now fighting, or prisoners, or dead in Egypt or Libya, where the great battle is raging. After the service the padre, Roy Smith, had an At Home—more hymns, tea, solos, talks—a really good night. . . . Altogether nearly 2,000 men attend voluntarily services at Tidworth just now—an amazing tribute to the fact that religion isn't dead in the Army, at least among the more intellectual type of fellows—for these R.A.C. chaps are on the whole all very intelligent. Supper later in the evening with Smith, James, etc. . . .

Got back to the 61 Mess (Assaye) and had another go until late into the morning at my broadcast.

I watched the 61 Regiment R.A.C. at drill this morning. It was worth coming miles to see—quite magnificent, the band playing, first-class "guards" drill, one hundred per cent turnout. The secret, is, as usual, first-class officers under a really excellent C.O. from IV Hussars. . . .

6th July

Padre James took me to Bulford where we went to H.Q. Salisbury Plain Area and through the Bulford Garrison Church—a very nice place. Then met S.C.F. Airborne Division, who took me first to meet the Divisional G.O.C. Major-General "Boy" Browning—a really first-class man, a Grenadier Guard and incidentally the husband of Daphne du Maurier. Later in the morning I heard him lecture to his officers—worth going a long way to hear—first-class stuff. Lunch at Divisional H.Q. where I met another Grenadier, Lt.-Col. Goshen, also an excellent chap, and Cowan of the R.S.F. who used to be in the 52nd Division. In the afternoon went to Nethley to see gliders and paratroops—very interesting—General Browning has fixed a period a week in each Company for "Padre's Hour" in the training programme—not as an extra. I went to one of these and because I was to be there they were all Jocks (who had, incidentally, been in a tough raid recently). They listened, asked questions and were most friendly. . . . The "Padre's Hour" is a grand opportunity . . . and should do real good. . . . Many of the men are "devil-may-care" chaps but with this good G.O.C. and a tighter and more sensible

"Guards" discipline, they should do better. Only four miles away at Tidworth 2,000 attend voluntarily services on Sunday nights, whereas here not fifty do. What is Truth? The feeling among many of them here, the padre told me, is that they are "Hired Assassins" and so "why bother? Make the best of the life we've got while we have it". Good padres are needed here for the men are good fellows. I feel that the padres here are not strong enough for them.

Went back to Tidworth at night to stay with Mr and Mrs James at the Senior Padre's house—Zooch Manor. Went to the Church of England Institute, packed with troops. The A.C.G. Todd rang me up and was very kind; he said my talks and tours were doing great good and were a fine example and advertisement for the Chaplains' Department. Very encouraging, but I still want to get back to the 7/9th Royal Scots and 4th K.O.S.B.

After supper James took me to the far part of Tidworth. . . . Told me about the last padre there whose services were so popular that he had to take over the theatre.

7th July

Tidworth, Plymouth. J. A. James, the D.A.C.G. and his wife have been most kind to me . . . James motored me to Salisbury where I had time to visit the Cathedral where I heard part of the Service—glorious singing. . . . Got the train for Plymouth and talked to a young Marine officer—a good chap and very friendly. He was a good Churchman too . . . he told me how they had to spend a winter in the South of England under canvas, nine in a tent, even under snow. Later talked to two young sailors on their way to Devonport—full of enthusiasm about their job. The S.C.F. and padre Murray met me and took me through the most awful ruins to the Royal Citadel Barracks where I am to stay. The bombing of Plymouth and Devonport is dreadful—whole streets in ruins. I walked round it a bit later and then went to see Martin Fairgrieve now a sergeant in the Royal Artillery and an old Club boy. He is at Dover now, but I met his wife—a nice girl—who told me that "Martin was worth his weight in gold". In the late evening I walked round the ramparts of the Citadel, a glorious series of views on a lovely night.

I told Murray that I had come to the conclusion that the best way for religion in the Army is to have compulsory Padres' Hours . . . in the training programme and voluntary services on Sundays, and he agreed.[1] He took me to the Royal Chapel—a very interesting place. His C.O. is "all for" religion—a good regular and so the padre's battle here is half-won already.

8th July

I left the Royal Citadel Barracks with padre Murray and picked up the S.C.F. Jackson. Then from the *Mayflower* steps I went with them to Drake's Island, saw over it and met the chaps there who even put on a show for me of manning guns, etc. We boated back to the Citadel for lunch and then set off for a tour of the Coast Artillery round Plymouth—a long and rather tiring tour of inspection. . . . The places varied according to the officers. The usual complaint was "not enough padres". One officer—a good chap who had been a master at Lancing, asked if padres couldn't come to take a service on a week-day since their Sundays were so full—an offer which I am glad to say Murray accepted willingly.

After tea I went to the B.B.C. Plymouth where I was to spend the night. I had a good supper there, wrote some letters and broadcast on "Heaven and Hell on Earth"! After this I talked to some Home Guard fellows, good young chaps; then wrote my broadcast for next Wednesday and sent it to Bedford. I got to bed—a most comfortable room—after 1 a.m. One good thing about this job is that you sleep like a top on it!

9th July

Parsons, the famous cricketer of Warwickshire, now S.C.F. of the 77th Division, called for me at the B.B.C. Plymouth Studio at 0900 hours and took me to B— Cornwall, through lovely scenery, to meet the 11th Battalion of The Devons. I spoke to them and they asked questions. He told me they were a tough lot—and by jove they were—but one of the best lots I have yet met. I talked for a long time to groups of them who

[1] Later in the year 1942 when I was S.C.F. of the 52nd Division I arranged with the G.O.C., the great Neil M. Ritchie, to have no parades on Sunday but all were expected to go to the Church of their denomination.

clustered round full of ideas and questions—criticism of Church parades, of the Church, of the Army system, etc., yet not of the Christian Faith, or of the teaching of our Lord. Some of them were fiery but very friendly. "I like you," said the first, "you're a decent bloke. I wish you'd come and stay with us for a bit." I liked them too and wished I could. Their padre is a hopeless creature who can't see beyond "Mass"—a bad type of Anglo-Catholic. The 77th Division is not good from a religious point of view, but with Parsons as their S.C.F. they should be better. He is a first-class fellow and a real Christian and quite fearless. I motored all day with him and talked and answered questions—of which there were many. I went to several camps . . . and saw the 70th Royal Ulster Rifles—a Company of young soldiers with a hopeless Company Commander. One of them told me "We'd have done anything for our old Company Commander—nothing for this chap". . . . Others I talked to were Anti-Tank Royal Artillery, R.A.S.C., Divisional Signals, and a Battalion of the East Surreys, a Brigade H.Q. and a platoon of the Duke of Wellington's. Many questions were asked—about conscientious objectors, the teaching of Jesus and the war, hypocrites in the Church, compulsory religion, etc. There is no lack of interest in religion, no lack of criticism of the Church, and no lack of keenness for the real Gospel. . . . But with a good dose of Parsons, who hasn't been with them long enough to make his presence felt, things should be better. . . . I got to Tavistock very tired, saw "Wavell's 30,000" at the local cinema after dinner and went to the Canteen and talked with some of the chaps. I find that many listen-in wherever I have been and are keen and interested. Spent the night at the Queen's Hotel, Tavistock.

10th July

After writing some letters Parsons called to pick me up and take me to my next "halt"—Exeter. There I was met by the S.C.F. Exeter Garrison—a Regular padre called Price who took me round to visit units in the district—an all-round run of 100 miles. Price quite a good chap and very kind, but too keen on the "position" of the padre as officer. Much of what I saw

97

was a repetition of what I had seen in other places. The most interesting visit today was probably to B— where I saw the Mercantile A.A. A young Bombardier there had just got a high award for bravery and bringing down an enemy plane, from the Queen of the Netherlands. He seemed a good chap and it was fine to see him with an unusual ribbon. I talked about my work today, but, unlike yesterday, no questions were asked—strange how days vary so much. Went back to — Barracks, Exeter, where the other padre, a local one for the Barracks, a good fellow, met me and took me to my billet. After dinner in the Mess where I met an old Fettes boy called Hepburn—a Lieutenant aged about twenty, who told me he remembered my sermon at Fettes in 1938!

I walked to see the bomb damage in Exeter at night. I called at the Deanery and S. C. Carpenter, the Dean, kindly took me round and showed me the damage to the Cathedral, which is pretty considerable. He takes it well; "It is bearing its part like other folk, and has proud wounds too". . .

The countryside all this week has been lovely:

"When I consider the works of Thy hands
What is Man that Thou art mindful of him?"

11th July

Price the S.C.F. called for me after breakfast in the Mess and after I had watched young gunners training he took me to the Station where I set off for Bristol through lovely Devon and Somerset country. Saw some of the damage at Weston-super-Mare. Thorpe, the padre of the 133rd H.A.A. (mixed) Regiment where I am staying for the weekend, met me and took me to the Mess. Later visited Clifton College and Chapel (Newbolt's: "This is the Chapel . . ."). It is now an O.C.T.U. for R.A.S.C. I felt very exhausted and rested in the afternoon—the first rest for ages!

12th July

Bristol and District.

13th July

Yeovil, Sherborne and District.

14th July

Lyme Regis, Portland, Weymouth, Dorchester and Sherborne.

15th July

Bristol.

16th July

Left Bristol by the 0750 train with Welch to London. Went to Broadcasting House and saw Sir Cecil Graves the Director-General of the B.B.C. who was most enthusiastic and was so keen that I should continue at the B.B.C. and not go back. He said that these Talks were "one of the best things I'd ever put over"! High praise indeed. He is so very nice—and also a Regular Royal Scot. I explained why I'd like to go back to the chaps again and he understood that, and didn't see why I shouldn't do *both* in winter. I agreed; but will the War Office and Welch welcome this? Had a talk with Beales, an early lunch at Broadcasting House and then got the train to Bedford where I found another huge pile of letters to try to get through—it's really quite impossible! I wrote and read and then at the Office fire-watching all night. I really should have spoken on Ack Ack Beer Beer programme tonight but I was far too done to stay on later in London.

19th July

Pirbright. Attended the 0800 hours Church of England Communion Service at the Church of England Chapel—a lovely and most effective Service. Young Guardsmen (about seventy of them) from Grenadiers, Coldstream, Scots, Irish and Welsh, also Life Guards, etc., there, most devout and reverent. No rank here. . . . David Cairns and I made our Communion too—no denomination either. Oh if only it was always like this! I preached to the Coldstream Guards in the large Camp Theatre at 1000. Their new C.O. let them walk to the Service on their own and not parade—how very much better. The Armoured Training Wing representing all branches of the Guards and Household Cavalry, were there too. . . . The Coldstream's Band played the hymns and the responses and it was a good Service. At 1100 hours in the same Theatre I preached to the Scots Guards—a good Presbyterian Service. The C.O., Lt.-Col. Alan Swinton,[1] read the Lessons. Both Services were most impressive. After the Service I went with the C.O. and his wife and David Cairns round a bit of the Camp and saw the very lovely garden round the Church of Scotland Hut. Played croquet (a favourite game in the Mess) after lunch. Father Andrews, the Guards R.C. padre, a Jesuit friend of his, David and myself, talked together in the afternoon. There is much more affinity between R.C. and Presbyterian than between R.C. and Church of England! We went to the Camp Theatre and saw an excellent film of "Dr Jekyll and Mr Hyde" (Spencer Tracy). Large numbers of Guardsmen present. I've never seen men stand so motionless when "The King" was played at the end.

Later, after the most magnificent dinner, I went to the C.O.'s; he and his wife were with the Senior Commandant of the A.T.S. at Pirbright (the "Top 'at"!) We spent a most pleasant and friendly evening talking.

I was greatly impressed with everything for there is no bluff about the Guardsmen—everything is just first-class, and say what you like there is nothing to touch them in smartness, efficiency, manners, and all-round good soldiering. But as I told them—one lot of them—this morning "a really good soldier keeps even his mind clean". Here too they are very much better than most folk. I'm *sure* of that.

20th July

Pirbright. In the morning I visited various parts of the Camp. I talked to the great R.S.M. Archer whose smartness has to be seen to be believed. I saw a special drill squad on the square and have never seen drill like it. I was allowed to attend the C.O.'s orders—a quite unique sight—one hundred per cent discipline and drill and saluting and *justice*. They put a small boxing show on for me in the Gym—the Coldstream Gym (all so far today had been in the Scots). I saw P.T. and firing, the battle course, the canteens, etc. I find that a large number of fellows listen-in to my Talks. In the afternoon I spoke to some squads of the Coldstreams in the Church of England Chapel (a

[1] Father of Major-General Sir John Swinton.

100

really good show, most interesting and very friendly). They shook hands with me at the door and said such nice things: "Good luck sir", "All the best sir", etc. Prior to that I had attended the Church of Scotland Squad in the Church of Scotland Hut when David Cairns spoke of "What happens when I'm shot". . . . None had any other idea than that immortality was "right" and indisputable and all joined in. We talked too of Jekyll and Hyde since we had all seen the film, and all agreed on the lessons to be learnt from it too ("We're all like that sir"). . . . In the evening the Church of Scotland fellows just up from Caterham had a party in the Church of Scotland Hut. Team games and songs (mostly Scottish). I talked at their request of my job and they gave me a great welcome and loved my "action" songs. David Cairns in great form too and Bailey (the Church of England padre) came up later. One of the officers, Tony Phillipson (the son of the late Hylton Phillipson, M.P., and Mabel Russell, the actress) joined with us. A most happy, friendly evening, concluding with the 100th Psalm and family prayers and a quite charming vote of thanks from one of the boys. They too all shook hands: "Goodnight sir, and I hope we'll meet again", "Give my love to Scotland when next time you're up sir", "God bless sir, and don't forget us", "We'll be listening", "Could you send your photo sir?", etc. Tired but happy, Bailey, Cairns, Phillipson and myself sat drinking tea in Bailey's room till midnight. It has been another great day among great fellows. How I wish more folk realised what a lovely person is the ordinary chap!

21st July

Before I left Pirbright I went to the Hospital to see Sergeant Ginger Reynolds of Longniddry, now the M.T. Sergeant. I asked him a lot about Stanley McLean for though Stanley writes about every ten days, he never mentions the war. Reynolds told me how Stanley had been with him a great deal of the time during the (desert) fighting, including some pretty hot bayonet charges where they had done a great number of Nazis in; some, he said, were chained to their guns. Stan very fit and it's a good thing he's in Eritrea now for his Company "F" of the 2nd Scots Guards have all been captured. I was sorry to leave Pirbright again.

Had lunch in the United Services Club (London) with Eric Gillet and Longman the publisher who wants to publish my Broadcast Talks. He's welcome to them. . . . Later went with Eric Gillet and talked to a Meeting in St Martin's-in-the-Fields—very enthusiastic and friendly. From there I went to the War Office to see the Chaplain-General's Chaplain for a preliminary talk about my future plans. I don't know what to do! This job I'm doing seems to be worthwhile and valuable, but I long to get back to the chaps again. The Chaplain-General is more or less willing to do as I want to do, a very difficult position as it puts the onus on me.

When I got back to Bedford I found the usual mass of correspondence; Major Crum's MS. of his book in which he wants me to write the Preface; acceptances and refusals for my new book *Asking Them Questions* (*Soldiers also Asked*), a request from the Archbishop of Canterbury to go and talk over our forthcoming broadcast, a request to talk to the 15th Division padres at Morpeth, and so on. I wrote, and talked to Eric Fenn until midnight.

The loss of my notebook and diary is a great nuisance.

22nd July

After attending to correspondence I went to Bid-denham . . . to rest for a day and read a bit, and wrote a Foreword to Major Crum's new book. I got a bit of peace this afternoon—the first for months! In the evening I was motored into Bedford and gave my Broadcast to "The Unknown Leader". Beales liked it.

23rd July

I worked hard in Biddenham all morning trying to cover some of my post and after lunch went to the office at Bedford to tackle some more—an almost impossible task, but so rewarding and most illuminating. . . . Caught the train at tea-time for London and after leaving my kit at the Authors' Club went to Lambeth Palace to see the Archbishop of Canterbury (William Temple). He was most friendly and I sat for a long time in his study talking to him. (He showed me some of the results of the bombing of the Palace too.)

24th July

I attended Mass and Holy Communion in the private Chapel in Father John Groser's house, and afterwards had breakfast with him and his household, walked round his garden, fed the hens and bade him "au revoir"—a real saint of God. I arrived at Broadcasting House and had coffee with Welch and Beales. We met the Archbishop of Canterbury at 1215 and I asked him some questions at the microphone which he answered about the Palaces, stipends, etc., of Bishops, about the Church's message to the world today, etc. Our interview (to be broadcast on 12th August) was played back to us almost at once. I think it should create some interest; it's grand to have an Archbishop of Canterbury like Dr Temple, who is prepared to do this sort of thing. After the recording Welch, the Archbishop and I went to the Athenaeum for lunch—a most enjoyable affair. I was greatly struck by the way the Archbishop knew nearly all the clergy in the Church of England and a good deal about other clergy too. He is so very human and has an amazing brain. We sat in the Library of the Athenaeum and drank coffee and had a most interesting conversation. Later Welch introduced me to Lambert, the Under Secretary to the War Office, who is very interested in my job. In the afternoon Welch and I were photographed together at the mike. They want a photo of William Temple and myself and also one with Jimmie Dalgleish. I had tea at the Travellers' Club with W. H. Elliott, now the King's Chaplain at the Chapel Royal. We had a most interesting talk—the King, he said, was one of the most spiritual men he had ever met; Sir Stafford Cripps too is most religious and a man of very high principles and "the next Prime Minister"; he regards John Macmurray's book *The Clue to History* as the greatest book so far of this century; he told me too that Joad would soon be one of the greatest Christian apologists in Britain! At the moment he is a Rationalist, but William Temple tells me that he has now become a Theist. Talked a lot with Elliott about belief in immortality, about which he is going to write in my new book. A most interesting day.

103

Returned to Bedford to tackle again masses of letters, including a most interesting one from Tom Arnot about the effect in his Mess of my talk on "The Unknown Leader" which had evidently "won" them. Also a letter from Gerald Kersh including a poem that he had written. (This was "Stay with me God" which everyone thought was anonymous.) Lovely letters too from Maime and Ray.

25th July

I left Bedford for Pontefract, getting there about tea-time. My destination was Geoffrey Gilbey's Young Soldiers' Training Camp. A very thrilling experiment it seems to be. All the fellows here are young soldiers (under twenty) who have been in trouble and are generally regarded as being pretty "hopeless". Yet Major Gilbey gets 85% successes out of them. It isn't hard to see why. His own personality and that of his officers inspires confidence "Arnold-like". He had a good dinner in my honour after a very good discussion with three young airmen who had come to visit him.

26th July

The parade of the young soldiers was as good as anything I'd seen outside the Guards and the 61st R.A.C. Training Regiment. I preached to them—an all-denominational Service—and some A.T.S. at the Barracks. Some of the A.T.S. had been inoculated and during the Service five fainted! After the Service back in the Camp I spoke to the N.C.O's—a really fine crowd of young chaps. This Camp is run on the system of the ideal State I think. Real good discipline, but the absolute right of every individual considered.

27th July

Geoffrey Gilbey invited me to attend his orderly room this morning. This is a happy Camp, but it is no "cissy" Camp; it's just and absolutely fair; that's its secret. Played in a cricket match later with Geoffrey and the boys.

28th July

Bedford. Jimmie came today. It was just grand to see him again. There is no one quite like him. We laughed and talked of

104

so many things, his love of May, his pride "of being a father soon"; rightly he's one of our "family" too. "What's Mr Selby been up to?"—roars of laughter; "How's Bobbie?"; "And Mrs Craig's (Ray's) babies?"; "How is your Mother?" "Do you remember when your father and Paddy (his dog) . . ." and so on. We talked over the script for tomorrow, etc.

29th July

Jimmie here all day. We went through the script in the morning, adding and taking from it like the old Club days of early 1938 (when we broadcast with other Club boys: *Asking Why*, O.U.P.). In the afternoon while I attended a Staff meeting he went for a row on the river and then to the cinema for a bit, coming back in great spirits. We had supper together, joined by Eric Fenn, Father Gerald Vann, O.P., and Beales, at the Cavendish, and then we walked up together to the Park and watched the cricket. We talked so much of old days and of days to come, of Dad's death and the meaning of death, of old Camps; and he especially remembered the prayers around the flag at Reed Point as the sun set. And we sent messages jointly signed to the Club (best wishes to you all—carry on), to Maime and Bob, to Stanley McLean in Eritrea and to George MacLeod at Iona. Then the rehearsal for the broadcast and the broadcast itself; coffee at the Swan and more talking. It was the most perfect summer night, befitting a perfect friendship, and we were both so happy. I went so far to his Billet and he shook hands as only Jimmie can and smiled as only he can, then "Goodnight sir, I'll see you in the morning"! We arranged to meet at the station at 8 p.m. to get the 8.19 p.m. to London to see Mary off to Edinburgh. "Don't be late," he added, and once again, "see you in the morning, sir." We waved until each of us was out of sight. Another raid tonight—some incendiaries and a little high explosive. (The raid went on until early the next morning with fatal result.)

30th July (The death of Jimmie Dalgleish)

James Welch came into my bedroom this morning and told me that Jimmie had been killed while putting out incendiaries. I just couldn't believe it. I thought it must be a nightmare. I dressed in a daze and went up to the Hospital. Yes, he had been killed all right. I am still in a daze. He was my best friend and the finest character I've ever met—truly "Goodnight sir" BUT, as truly, "see you in the morning". In a daze I wired his father and mother, his mother-in-law, to break the news gently to Mary who couldn't know until the evening; I wired home, and Shaw, Brown and George MacLeod, Robbie Fulton, Stanley McLean, T. and H. Smith, his old form in Edinburgh; then I went to my office and cried till I thought I'd never stop. What a wonderful life—fit, healthy, the best type of man this country wants, gone from this earth so suddenly BUT yet so radiantly happy, but yet doing his duty as always, and helping folk; at least we had him over two years longer than Dunkirk, where so many of his friends were killed. I wrote to Mary, to his Father and Mother, to his O.C., to Bill Loos, etc. I cancelled all I had to do (except a necessary recording which I did from Bedford in the afternoon) and packed straight off for Edinburgh, arranging a Memorial Service for him on Sunday at the Canongate which I hope to take myself. All day I was dazed—he was so fresh and cheery last night—so like the Jimmie I knew; and now he's gone:

> He's gone
> I do not understand
> I only know
> That as he turned to go
> From his young eyes a certain glory shone
> And I was dazzled by the sunset glow,
> And he was gone.

He has left a wonderful memory. Praise be to God for him. Welch, Eric Fenn, Cyril (Taylor), John (Williams) were all splendid, so was Seiveking. I left by the 5.15 p.m. from Bedford for London to get the night train to Edinburgh; I'll have the comfort of Maime and Ray, of Pip and Bob, and will be able to feel more settled again, I hope.

2nd August
Memorial Service in the Canongate for Jimmie Dalgleish.

4th August

Jimmie's funeral day in the Dean Cemetery next to Dad. About 2,000 at the funeral.

(Here the Journal[1] of 1942 ends except for a few short notes.)

11th August

Iona.

24th September

Appointed S.C.F. 52nd (L) Division to take up duties on 1st October. The Chaplain-General told me this great news. He was very kind when I saw him today at the War Office. I only hope I'll do the job well. There is nothing I'd like more— Senior Chaplain of the Lowland Division—whoever thought I'd ever become that? Certainly not I!

1st October

Report to 52nd (L) Divisional H.Q. as S.C.F. and leave for a fortnight's leave. A very fine "A" Mess—General Neil Ritchie, fresh from Commanding the 8th Army; Jim Cassels the G1 and Tom Craig the A.Q.

22nd October

Received a most mysterious Top Secret and Most Secret message in two envelopes to go to Aberdeen and meet two people there from M.I. and not to tell anyone—but of course I had to tell Neil Ritchie. Can't write anything about this as SECRET! It will mean carrying on Radio Padre broadcasts from the Division, but with a slight but important difference!

5th December

Goliath—General Ritchie's big scheme; my car very full. . . . Lockie driving. . . . Wallace (Campbell) and myself, with masses of luggage behind.

---

[1] The MS of this Journal is now in the National Library of Scotland.

Jimmie Dalgleish, 1937
with Nobby

Harry Richmond, 1950
with Barney and Dougal

"Mac"

"Wink" Renwick

Wallace Campbell

George Colmer

Ack Ack Site—Protecting London, 1942
The Radio Padre

Mixed Ack Ack Site, 1942
(Second on right Sgt. Mary Churchill (now Lady Soames))

11

The Journey through Europe, 1945
George Colmer, Roy King, Self, Charlie Chislett

With Roy King on Hitler's Balcony
Berchtesgaden 1945

12

"Nunky" Brown

Norman Davidson, Captain Scottish
XV, 1953 with Pringle Fisher, Captain
Scottish XV, 1967

James Shaw

Fr. Coles

The Evening Story—Skateraw

Arthur's Seat, May Day Sunrise Service

Holy Communion at Holyroodhouse, 1960

The General Assembly, 1972

Installation of Governor of the Castle—Sir Michael Gow—1979

PART III

Chapter 1

From my Journal it can begin to be seen that the job I was given as Radio Padre, as well as being a most interesting was also most exhausting; and since with the blackout and other war-time restrictions people had not much to do in the evenings except listen to the wireless broadcasts, my voice soon became very well-known and my listening audience gradually increased from five to seven and then to ten million: indeed Melville Dinwiddie, that great Scottish Director, to whom I owed so much, told me I had the largest radio audience at one time, apart from Tommy Handley's ITMA.

It is obvious from my Journal too that though I greatly enjoyed meeting people and frankly began for a time to enjoy the unexpected publicity—large crowds as well as the huge audiences I met with everywhere I spoke, I longed to get back to my own Division. I found the work not only more and more exhausting, since I not only had to do a weekly fifteen-minute broadcast each Wednesday, but also to do at least weekly some further broadcasts, including Services, or B.B.C. prayers for the Empire and Home broadcasts and travel all over the United Kingdom, often in a different bed each night and travelling in war-time conditions which even at their best were pretty bad; and at the same time trying to tackle a post that brought in anything from 100 to 1,000 letters a day (indeed on two occasions I got over 1,000 letters).

By no means all the letters I received were from H.M. Forces, though many sailors, soldiers and airmen did write very often about their family troubles or their difficulties or their temptations. A large number came from families—mothers, wives, sweethearts, and they too were very much on the same lines, always seeking some kind of faith to give them courage and keep them going, but though the post was so large you could very often foretell just what it would contain. However, sometimes there were certain exceptions, and here is one which I got in 1942 which I thought was quite delightful:

Hednesford,
Staffs.

Dear Radio Padre,

I have just been listening to your talk over the wireless, to the man just joined the Army. I am writing to thank you for all your talks, and for all the help I have got from them.

I am only a schoolgirl, I am just fourteen years old, but I always listen to your talks, and so does my Granny.

I go to Church every Sunday, I have always gone since I was a little girl, and I have been confirmed.

However, before I listened to your talks God never seemed very real to me, but now after some of the things you said, I really enjoy going to Church, and I try to do the things you say.

I now have great belief in prayer, and if ever I can't do anything, particularly at school, I just pray inside myself and I generally can do it.

My brother is sixteen, and he is in the Merchant Navy, and since you said to the men to be worthy of the folks at home, I try to make myself a sister worthwhile.

Please don't imagine I am a good girl. I giggle a lot, I like boys, and go to the pictures about once a week. But I think God didn't mean us to go about dull and gloomy did He?

I have a great love for the country, as I live in it, and I always try to thank God for it.

I have not told anyone about this letter, they might think I'm silly, but I hope you won't mind.

So I will close, and say once again, thank you, I do enjoy

your talks, they have explained such a lot to me, and I think we young people need helping by people like you.

                    Goodnight Sir, God Bless You,
                                        M.M.T.

There was another letter rather like it which I received a year afterwards. It was like it in the sense that it was slightly different from the ordinary letter and showed too that there was a younger audience as well as an older one listening:

                                        Stamford,
                                    West Byfleet.
                                        5.3.43.

Dear Mr Selby Wright,
    I rather hesitate to write because I know you must be inundated with nice letters, on the other hand "appreci-ation" is a thing I feel one can always do with just a little more of. So here goes.
    On his last visit before going back to Wellington a nephew of mine aged sixteen and a half, *not* a saint by any means—was listening in with me to your talk. At the end I said "Oh Ian, I do hope the Tommies do listen in" to which he replied "I don't know about them, we do". I said "Do you—at Wellington?" "Oh yes, always, we turn it on in prep, I think he must be an awfully decent sort of fellow."
    May I just add that the aunt feels the same!
                                        M.H.

But most of the letters were from the Forces themselves, from the Navy, the Army, or the Air Force, and from their homes—fathers, mothers, wives and sweethearts—homes that had been broken up through the death of a loved one or for other reasons just as sad. There were many about unfaithfulness—a wife who had gone off with another man; a soldier who had gone off with another woman. One could almost say that the larger number of letters were concerned either with immortality or immorality.
    There were some very happy letters too, but many of them

                        111

were very sad, and one was often left with the privileged burden of trying to answer them as best one could.

(Of the many letters I have received from listeners, some of which had nothing to do with the War, and indeed some which were written after the War had finished, are most interesting. As an example, among many, I include this, dated 3rd July, 1951:

Having listened to your two Lift Up Your Hearts full of Dr Thomas Arnold, I venture to think you may be interested in the fact that I am the daughter of Theodore Walrond (born at old Calder Park, Glasgow, in 1824) whose whole character and career he would himself have traced back to the teaching and personal example of his great "Head". When Dr Arnold died at Rugby in 1842, my father was his Head Boy, and he afterwards wrote the biography of him in the *Dictionary of National Biographies*. Since then my family has never lost touch with the three generations of Arnolds. The poet Matthew Arnold was my father's dearest friend, who used to stay with us when I was a child in Bucks, and used to have great talks at breakfast with my father and dear old Principal Sharp of St Andrews, about their common idol Wordsworth. My father died in June 1887, and Matthew's elder daughter who had married Fred Whitridge of New York always said her father never really recovered from the shock and loss, before he himself died of angina pectoris in 1888. When my father died, my step-mother obeyed his dying request, and destroyed all the many letters he had received from his many friends; twice this year people working on Matthew Arnold have asked me if my father had kept his presumably large correspondence, and I had to say there was nothing left. But my father applied after several years as a fellow of Balliol and then a master at Rugby, for the headmastership of his old school, but was disqualified in those times by not being in Holy Orders, a number of his friends, such as Matthew Arnold, Tom Hughes (whose *Young Brooke* was admittedly drawn from my father) and others wrote testimonials to make any daughter proud. In Clough's letters to his sister, there are often references to my father, who was also with

112

Matthew Arnold, a member of the famous reading party of *The Bothie*. And he would certainly have said "I trace all I am and can be back to the years at Rugby under Dr Arnold".

I am,
Yours sincerely,
Georgina G. Buckler, D.Phil. Oxon.
(wife of Wm. H. Buckler, D.Litt. Oxon.)

One of the great pleasures of course of the Radio Padre's work was getting around and meeting various people—all sorts of people. James Welch used to arrange, from time to time, conferences of small groups to which he very kindly invited me. There one was able to meet people like Rose Macaulay—so full of wit and wisdom, and incidentally with no small knowledge of theology, as can be seen in her *Towers of Trebazon*; I have a specially vivid memory of meeting and lunching with C. S. Lewis when he was still at Oxford and when he was producing these quite brilliant radio talks, which were later published in three series under the title of *Mere Christianity*, some of which he allowed me to publish in the *Scottish Forces Magazine* which I edited from 1941-76. His talks, so full of commonsense and, written in a language that people could understand, had tremendous impact at the time and still have in many places today. His fellow Dons were not too pleased with him because I think they thought he was entering into a field for which they felt he was not properly qualified; but I could not help feeling that it was just jealousy, because he was getting across to thousands of people what was bringing them comfort and strength, in a way that was denied most other people at that time, and he could write and speak with special emphasis as he himself had at one time been an atheist.

It was not surprising, therefore, that I began to feel very exhausted and suffered from bad attacks of neuritis—which had its repercussions after the war.

Officially, as mentioned, my Radio Padre talks were to finish after six months; but I was told to carry on, with one big important difference—I would be returned to my Army Unit, to my great joy. The Chaplain-General told me I had been

113

appointed Senior Chaplain of my old Division—the 52nd Lowland—and I would start officially on 1st October. I found myself living in "A" Mess with the nicest crowd of people you could meet—the Army Commander was Neil Ritchie,[1] the G.I. Jim Cassels,[2] and there was also the A.Q. Tom Craig and Colonel Berne, the A.D.M.S.

I now once again had an Army car and I had an excellent young clerk in Lance-Corporal Wallace Campbell who did so much to help, and was able to tackle my correspondence most efficiently. The B.B.C. still received my letters. Some they could answer formally, some they sent back for me to answer personally, and some that could be acknowledged personally. In all this and so many other things Wallace Campbell helped me tremendously.

I was told now to limit my broadcasting to one fifteen-minute talk each Wednesday evening and to concentrate on my duties as Senior Chaplain with the most loyal band of padres, all of whom gave me the greatest encouragement and support, despite the fact that I was probably the youngest of the lot.

The padres of the 52nd Division were among the finest you could ever meet. I had succeeded two distinguished senior chaplains in Joseph Gray of Lansdowne and John Fraser of Hamilton, who had left to become D.A.C.G. in the West of Scotland. They had both been in the First World War and were greatly respected and beloved by everybody. Among the padres I had with me in the Division were Nevile Davidson, who was soon to leave to go back to Glasgow Cathedral, and indeed with whom I had been for a short time as an Assistant; Willie Tindall who later became Professor of Practical Theology at Edinburgh University; Jimmie Wood who had taken over my old 7/9th Battalion of The Royal Scots, a great mountaineer and skier, which greatly suited the Division when it became "Mountain", but above all a great pastor and friend—always so much loved and respected by everybody; John Morrison who later became a well-known regular army padre and who had the distinction of having three sons who all got into "Pop" at Eton; James P. Stevenson from the Church

---

[1] Later General Sir Neil Ritchie.
[2] Later Field-Marshal Sir James Cassels.

of England, who, too, later became a regular army padre, but for good reasons fell foul of the more regular senior army chaplains, and later went to Australia where he wrote a most interesting but hardly complimentary book about the Chaplains' Department; the High Church and devout Bernard Haddlesley, and so many others.

Noticing that the officers used to go off for what were known as T.E.W.T.S., which means Tactical Exercises Without Troops, I felt it would be a good idea to have what I called E.E.W.P.S.—Ecclesiastical Exercises Without Parishioners. We tried to tackle some of the questions with which we might be faced as padres. Jim Cassels was greatly amused and he and General Ritchie encouraged and helped our E.E.W.P.S. in all that the padres tried to do. Soon after I arrived I asked General Ritchie if he would meet all the padres for the Division, and he gladly agreed to do so. So we got them all together and he shook hands with them all and talked with them, and they all had a cup of tea together. That evening he was able to discuss the various chaplains he had met that same afternoon, by name, and give me a most accurate summary of what he had thought of each one of them, mostly, but not always, to their credit! This was typical of the kind of personal interest that the General took in everyone. I remember his orderly telling me how once he had been "warned by the General not to get into trouble". He had said to him, "When I was your age I nearly got into trouble in the same way as you, and I don't want you to get into the same mess that I might have got into". The General changed that young man's attitude to life though he was killed not long afterwards.

The Divisional H.Q. was at that time in Aberlour House, and each week I had to motor sixty miles each way to Aberdeen and back to broadcast. The Divisional work was made easier in that I knew so many there already. I had such wonderful backing, not only from the padres mentioned, not only from the General and his Staff, but also the four Brigadiers and the officers and N.C.O's of the Division. I was indeed a most fortunate man to be where I was, and so very happy again. And then something happened that was to ultimately change the whole outlook again.

I had hardly been in the Division a month when on 22nd

October 1942 I received a sealed envelope marked "Most Secret", and inside a further envelope also sealed and marked "Top Secret". Wondering what on earth it was all about I opened both envelopes to find directions for me to go to Aberdeen to a certain hotel there at a certain time, where I would meet two people whom I had not met before and would be expected to know when they greeted me—a Lt.-Col. Winterbottom and a Miss Mabel Howatt of the A.T.S., who would explain the object of this strange request for my appearance there. The Division was just preparing to go on a very big scheme called "Goliath"—one of the schemes that General Ritchie ran so successfully. Here was I, a fairly new Senior Chaplain, suddenly dashing off to Aberdeen without even "by your leave". So I thought I ought to put it before him privately and also before the G.I., though I had been told not to inform anybody of this correspondence. Their confidence of course was absolutely secure and they told me to go ahead and that they would quite understand, and when I came back I was to join the exercise wherever I found it. Since I was Senior Chaplain this was not very difficult since it was a Divisional exercise and took over a very large part of the North of Scotland.

Well, I went to Aberdeen and met Colonel Winterbottom and Miss Howatt and the gist of the conversation was that the War Office wanted me to go on broadcasting as Radio Padre and to combine this broadcasting with certain work for M.I.9. It happened that a great many prisoners–of–war were listening to my Radio Padre talks (there is a short reference to this in the book *Return to Colditz*). It was felt, therefore, by M.I.9 that they could get some messages across to them if part of my talks were coded since they would be listening in any case. It would mean ultimately giving up my Chaplaincy of the Division to which I had gone so happily. It would also mean slightly altering the beginning of each of my Radio Padre talks. When I began "Good evening Forces" it meant that I would give them a coded message. If I left out the words "Good evening Forces" it meant there would be no message for them that week. When I came to the word "but" it meant that the message was over.[1] Of course I felt very sad about the

[1] See reference to this in *M.I.9 Escape and Evasion 1939-1945*, by M. R. D. Foot and J. M. Langley (The Bodley Head, 1979, p. 115).

prospect of resigning from the Division, and it turned out that I was able to stay on until February 1943, and both the General and the G.I. hoped that I would be able to come back again as their Senior Chaplain—a hope that I more than shared, but which, alas, was never fulfilled.

I was posted Senior Chaplain to the Edinburgh Garrison in 1943—a job that I disliked intensely—but I was able to take Lance-Corporal Wallace Campbell with me who was seconded from the Division. For the whole of that year the talks I did as Radio Padre beginning "Good evening Forces" were coded when sending messages to the prisoners-of-war. I still had a good deal of travelling to do, a tremendous amount of correspondence to attend to, and the strain of not only writing weekly broadcasts and sometimes knowing that these talks were going to be adapted and even in places paraphrased, as well as the extra commitments one was expected to do. It came to me as a great relief at the end of September 1943 that the War Office from their point of view no longer needed these coded talks, and therefore they suggested that after the end of October I should be able to get a little rest; they suggested three months' rest but said it was up to me when I wished to continue my Radio Padre talks. There was no chance of my getting back yet to the Lowland Division and I was anxious to see something of the War from a different angle and also to make a break from broadcasting, and all that pertained to it, though, as will be seen, it was several years later before my Radio Padre broadcasts were to finish.

Chapter 2

I found myself luckily posted to the Middle East at the beginning of November and joined the troopship *Stratheden* to Cairo with a Battalion of the Cameron Highlanders on board and with a strange assortment of other passengers, including Harry Roy and his band. We went in a large convoy—one of

I

the first to go through the Mediterranean again—and we took a longer route than usual into the Atlantic before we made for the Straits of Gibraltar and the first non-blackout nights I had seen for over four years as we passed Tangier and Gibraltar—it was appropriately enough on Christmas Eve. I shall never forget that troopship Christmas Service, the shout from a passing corvette in the Mediterranean of "A Merry Christmas . . . how are they all at home?" and our reply from the deck, "All is well with the folk at home!" Nor shall I forget the proud thrill of seeing Malta, G.C.

On board the *Stratheden* I was able to realise that not everyone enjoyed the Radio Padre or his talks. I was one of those detailed to censor the letters of the 5,000 troops on board, an exacting if sometimes quite an amusing job. In one of them I found a fellow writing home to his grandmother informing her that the Radio Padre was on board the troopship that he was on, and that she could listen to the wireless without the risk of hearing him! That letter I handed to one of the medical officers who was acting as a censor, since I thought his signature at the end would look rather better than mine under the circumstances!

However, as a compensation for this there was one lady who used to write to me very frequently, always signing her letters simply "Radio Friend". They always included at least one £5 note to help me to get some more tobacco and frequently some Devonshire cream (the postmark was always from Devonshire). I never knew who she was until after she died when she left me not only some beautiful and very valuable prints, and £500, but also a magnificent silver tea-set and quite a lot of silver. The letters and the gifts had continued quite some time after the war had finished, and indeed until she died in 1967. She was truly a "Radio Friend".

I shared a cabin with Adam Macpherson, a fine Regular padre who became my lifelong friend. When we reported to the Assistant Chaplain-General in Cairo we found he had really no work for us to do. Indeed his first words to me were "What are you doing coming out here and doing a decent man out of promotion?" I said to him that as he was a Regular soldier he ought to know that we went where we were sent; and he accepted that.

In Cairo I had the joy of meeting Tom Torrance, whom I was to meet again later in Italy and who was doing so much good work for the Troops. Once in Alexandria at this time I experienced a feeling of almost bewildered loneliness. I was billeted for a few days in an hotel with strange people, none of whom I knew, and most of them wearing the kind of hats associated with Tommy Cooper, and my bedroom had no view, either of the sea or of any living thing. I had been visiting some Army units but I was alone in the evening. I wrote and told George MacLeod just how lonely I felt, and I was glad I wrote for this was his reply: "I am glad, my dear Ronnie," he said, "you are mouldy and lonely, so was Abraham when he went out from Ur of the Chaldees and Moses from Egypt and our Lord from Nazareth. The road to the Kingdom is paved with broken hearts. . . . Christians are pioneers, not map-makers and we are fool enough to expect that electric lights and drawing-boards and central heating will accompany our journey. So, in your mouldiness, realise it is the true element for worms who alone really fertilise the earth; and in your loneliness realise that only the lonely find it necessary to knock at doors and only those who knock will ever find or enter. Loneliness is the permanent home of those who belong not to this world. It is frustration only to those who are fool enough to live in suspension; it becomes fruitful for those who, not of this world, seek the one eternal in the heavens." That did not quite cure, but it comforted my loneliness.

On the return journey to Cairo, driven by an African driver who could not speak English, we got completely lost in the dark and after a rather alarming hour or two in the desert I was never so relieved as when I saw a Union Jack illuminated in the distance.

In Cairo had one rather strange experience. I obviously wanted to see as much of Cairo as I could and I went to see the Pyramids on a camel and the man who owned the camel insisted on reading my fortune from my hand. I told him I didn't want my fortune read but could not persuade him not to do it, and since I was on the camel and he was on the ground he began to do it. Among other things he told me was that I was accustomed to speak to millions of people, which at that time was true and which he simply could not have known, and he

119

went on to say that I had not been very long in Cairo, which probably from the colour of my skin was pretty obvious, and that I was going back very soon, which seemed to me absolute nonsense at the time since I had only just arrived there. However it turned out not to be such nonsense after all, because not knowing what to do with me they decided that I should go up to Jerusalem, and so I went up by car, accompanied by Duncan Macgillivray, from Egypt to Jerusalem, across the desert.

In my monthly *Pastoral Letter* to the congregation of Canongate I wrote:

My dear People,

I am writing this letter to you in Jerusalem where for the time being I have temporary headquarters at Saint Andrew's Hospice. From my bedroom window I see Zion, and below the valley of Gehenna. On these last four Sundays I have preached at a desert camp by the Suez Canal, at St Andrew's, Alexandria; at St Andrew's, Cairo; and twice today at St Andrew's, Jerusalem. In addition I have been speaking at many camps and centres in Egypt, and now in Palestine.

I had a most wonderful run from Cairo to Jerusalem across the Sinai Desert. I passed very near the traditional place where the children of Israel crossed the Red Sea, arrived at Beersheba as the sun was going down, and very lovely it looked (you remember Abraham lived at Beersheba). When I came to Bethlehem it was now dark, and I entered the Church of the Nativity, and went with the Rev. Duncan Macgillivray, with whom I am staying here, to see the spot where Jesus was born "in the days of Herod the King", and where the manger lay. We went together led by the light of a candle which a bearded Franciscan monk gave us, and that night I was able to say my prayers at the very spot where Jesus was born.

Yesterday I saw some more places, having spent a day going around Jerusalem and seeing something more of the wonderful work done by the Church of Scotland Huts out in this part of the world under the inspiring leadership and foresight of Mr Macgillivray. Well then, yesterday I set off with him again, this time to Tel Aviv and Jaffa. I saw where John the Baptist was born, where Samuel is buried, the village in which Joseph of Aramathea lived; I passed through orange, lemon, and grapefruit groves, all just laden with fruit. This coming week I hope to visit the rest of Palestine and then some of Syria, before I return to my H.Q. at Cairo.

I have already mentioned the work done by our Huts out here—no praise could be too high. In a broadcast recording I did from Cairo which by this time some of you may have heard on the B.B.C., I mentioned some of the things that have struck me most out here—the spirit of the men most of all, so I won't repeat it here, though I may publish it in next month's *Chronicle*.

Everything is of the very greatest interest, but, I repeat, it is a lonely job. It is just grand being with Mr Macgillivray, who is one of my best friends, just now, and I have met quite a number of people I know. Tom Arnott, now a Captain and Technical Adjutant at the Royal Armoured Schools, M.E.F., took me for a grand run in a Sherman tank in the desert; then too I have met Drum-Major Rooney of the Camerons; contacted Mr then Major, now I believe Lt.-Col. Alastair Blair, whom I hope to meet when I go back to Cairo, and who used to do so much for the Boys' Club; and any number of Scots, and there are quite a number of Edinburgh fellows. I have had a fine opportunity of meeting the Padres out here too, and have spoken at quite a number of their conferences. I shall have much to tell you when I get back—which, because the B.B.C. want me to start my Radio Padre broadcasts again, may be sooner than I expected.

This, I fear, is rather a hurried note, written as I journey along, and at the end of a long and rewarding Sunday in Jerusalem during which, in addition to the Services I have mentioned, I have also talked at a detention barracks, met a Chaplains' Conference and done a fifteen-minute broadcast for the Palestine State Broadcast (I am expected to broadcast from Beirut this week too).

I hope that you are all keeping fit and well (I'm very fit and sunburnt!) and that the old Church is going along as well as ever. I often think of you all, and never a day passes without a mention of the Canongate.

My blessings to you all. The Lord be with you.

Jerusalem, 30th January 1944.
As from: G.H.Q., M.E.F.

After spending a day or two in Jerusalem I suddenly got a cable ordering me to return immediately to Cairo and to prepare to leave that night for the United Kingdom. I immediately flew from Lydda to Cairo that very afternoon and was on the troopship that same evening. The reason, I discovered, for this very sudden move was that I was wanted again to do more work as the Radio Padre; at this time especially for M.I.9 in time for the "D" Day landings: and so I had to start all over again after this very much shorter break than I had intended (indeed I had expected to be out in the Middle East possibly for the rest of the war) and once again I had to start to do these radio talks. This time they were rather shorter, not fifteen minutes but possibly seven or eight minutes: they were to be directed to Forces overseas, though other people could and did listen in, for most of them were of course coded.

In order to give me some kind of posting I was appointed Senior Chaplain, North East London. This gave me Headquarters in London though I was billeted in Jordans, after, for a few days, in Chelsea Barracks.

I had greatly enjoyed my short visit to the Holy Land—a welcome change from Cairo and Alexandria. And Jerusalem, the view of Mount Zion from my window at the Scottish Hospice; coffee at the King David Hotel, and many talks with Eddie Galloway who was soon later to be killed; the walks in and around the Holy City with Jock Elder who had been Senior Chaplain in the Highland Division when I was Senior Chaplain of the Lowland. What a thrilling experience it was to see the Holy Land—trees laden with oranges, lemons, grapefruit and "there is the road to Emmaus . . . to Bethany . . . to Jericho". And the journey by plane from Lydda where St George, they say, killed the dragon, back over the desert to Cairo. And the voyage back to Britain—Etna pink with snow in the early morning, the massive grandeur of the Atlas Mountains, the monkeys at Tangiers—and so "home", for certainly all Britain became home to me—yes even England to a Scot!—tired, almost exhausted and, let me confess it, though, always counting myself as one of the luckiest fellows alive "remembering my good friends"—strangely lonely.

And so from Chelsea Barracks to stay each night at "The Sheiling" in Jordans in lovely Buckinghamshire with its sustaining memory of the dewy, heavy-scented, birdsong laden mornings, and the lovely peace and cool of its evenings, and the kindly people who lived around as befitted the village of "the Friends". Dear Jean Brants, the beloved "Miss Matty" of the village, was my very kindly hostess and the friend and helper of everyone; and with her, her sister Mary and her brother-in-law Janek Vojacek, dear Alison too and all the Coopers, and Professor John and Betty Macmurray. John was growing a beard and was soon to succeed A. E. Taylor in Edinburgh as Professor of Moral Philosophy—two wonderful people.

There was something very wonderful about Jordans with its Recorder evenings, the nightingales at Hodge Moor, and the walks through the bluebell woods. The evenings when one still believed in the good things of life, for even in war it was a peaceful and happy place with lovely people, and I was glad to be there.

There was more reason than one why I went to Jordans. In addition to my daily visits to London where, as I have mentioned, I was Senior Chaplain in North East London, I visited from time to time Room 527 in the Hotel Victoria, Northumberland Avenue, a rather mysterious John Buchan-like visit where I entered by one door and left by another; and used to go, when at Jordans, with Alison Cooper (to whom I dedicated *Small Talks*) and her dog Gay across the golf course at Seer Green—not in uniform—with a new script, and hand it over to someone there, by arrangement, which was taken to "Camp No. 20" which was nearby, and, which people will know from books which have come out since, connected with Military Intelligence. I didn't know at the time that M.I.9 was run by Brigadier Norman Crockatt; and though I got to know him well when he was Colonel of the Royal Scots and indeed took his Memorial Service when he died in October 1956, he never once mentioned the fact to me and I didn't think many people knew about it until the book on M.I.9 was published in 1979. Those who knew then and who know now the great work that he did were surprised that he didn't receive higher honours, though he himself was not the kind of man who bothered about that; and he held the highest honour he knew he could receive—to be Colonel of the Royal Scots, his own Regiment, who were so proud of him.

London was to me at that time indeed a very frightening place, with the bombs dropping, first the V1's and then the V2's, which even ventured above the sky beyond Jordans, and the outskirts of London. How greatly I admired the courage and good humour of the Londoners.

The "second front" had now begun and I shall never forget the sight of the fleet of gliders passing across the sky as I watched them from Jordans going to Arnhem. My immediate need for the Radio Padre talks was now over, and I felt even more exhausted than ever—indeed so exhausted that I went before a full Medical Board of rather stiff-looking Brigadiers who asked me if I would "like to be invalided out". I told them I had no desire to leave the Army whatever and what I needed badly was a complete and utter change from radio work, away from this country (though I was sad indeed to leave Jordans) and back again with an active Division. I was then sent to Italy to become Senior Chaplain to a Division there; but once again it didn't turn out quite, in the first instance, as I had expected.

Chapter 3

The voyage to Italy was marked especially by two events—first the breakdown of the engine in the ship of our convoy in the middle of the Bay of Biscay which took a day or two to mend. We had to be left behind in dangerous U-boat waters and the ship rolled pretty badly, so that we were all very seasick—not a pleasant experience in a ship over-full of passengers unaccustomed to sailing; and the death of one of the naval gunners whose funeral I took as we were approaching

Naples—my first sea burial. We had a large number of padres on board and since I was the only Senior Chaplain and the only Church of Scotland Chaplain there, I was put in rather an unenviable position.

We disembarked and stayed a short time at Naples and were then moved—at least the padres were—to a small place called Nola near Mount Vesuvius. That Christmas Eve we spent sleeping on a very hard marble floor. On Christmas Day I took Services for small groups of troops scattered around the area.

In my Pastoral Letter of Christmas Day 1944 I wrote:

My dear People,

I'm writing this to you from an Italian villa—used now as an Officers' Mess—surrounded with wooded hills with in the distance snow-topped mountains, and looking very much like our own Scottish Highlands; except that I can walk around the garden and pluck and eat as many tangerine oranges as I like—and, believe me, I do like!

I had a good voyage out, and on the Sunday too a service at sea for the Royal Navy—an unusual privilege for an Army Padre, and one I very much appreciated. I also had the sad privilege of taking a naval burial at sea—a service with full naval honours—the sailors, soldiers, and airmen standing round, now at attention, now at the salute, now with heads bowed in prayer—the body "committed to the deep", the three volleys of guns, the bugler blowing last post and reveille, and the ensign at half-mast while the ship sped onwards towards the Mediterranean.

On Christmas Eve I went to the midnight service in the big camp here—a lovely moonlit night. The camp chapel was packed to the door and we sang the old carols. I thought of all at home and in the Canongate and felt "very near" you all. It is at worship, surely, more than at any other time that one feels "bound together across the world by the unseen chain of God's love". We slept that night—the other padres and I—on the tiles (quite literally!) for our beds had not arrived, and our temporary beds were on the marble floor of the villa, wrapped round in our blankets—and, though we kept all our clothes on, it was a cold and rather hard bed! And that was how we woke in the morning to wish each other "A Happy Christmas"!

And now, it's Christmas Day—my sixth war-time Christmas, and all away from home. But it has been a remarkably good day really. We, rather stiff, got up and shaved in cold hard water, went into the garden and ate tangerines, had breakfast and walked to the Camp with some excellent R.A.M.C. doctors who are here with us, to sing more carols with a great crowd of men. Then I motored six-and-a-half miles through lovely country where I spoke at a Church service of more troops—a fine experience—and visited the local Y.M.C.A., an excellent bit of home tucked away in the little township. I motored back to that place at night as they asked me to take a carol service for them—and what a fine evening we had. A good log fire, crowds of British soldiers, really grand singing, much laughter, real reverence and as fine a congregation as one could wish for. So I drove back—another lovely moon-lit night, along the white Italian roads. I had missed the marvellous Christmas dinner at the mess—for it was now late—but they kept me some turkey, plum pudding, fruit salad and coffee—which I'm sure you agree, wasn't bad.

I hear my camp bed has now arrived and, believe me, I'm ready for it! So, my love and blessings to you all, and a very good and victorious New Year.

The Lord be with you and all you love.

I had been promised a Division but when I got to Italy I found I had been posted to an Area—No. 54 Area—about the size of the South of England. I found myself O.C. train that took us across the Appenines in freezing cold weather, from Naples to Bari, which was to be my H.Q. It was a terrible journey—a story in itself—where we brewed tea from the hot water from the engine, and had a very difficult time keeping unauthorised passengers from jumping on to the train as it chugged up some of the high mountains, before we got into the olive-laden country around Bari.

My stay at Bari was quite the worst part of the war for me, but fortunately I didn't need to stay there too long.

126

In my Pastoral Letter of January 1945 I wrote:

My dear People,

New Year passed out here very much as Christmas did—the same enthusiastic Services and the same friendliness everywhere. It was cold too, yet we still ate tangerine oranges from the trees in the garden! The twenty-five doctors and nine padres were still together—a wonderful crowd to be with, and quite a number of Scots too. . . . Now we have all split up to our various postings, but you can't split a fellowship!

I've seen quite a lot of places recently—Naples and Vesuvius, Pompeii and Herculaneum, Salerno and Taranto, Brindiṣi·and Bari among them. I have had an all-night journey over the Appenines, thick with snow, lovely in a bright moon, and colder than any day in Scotland, or room in Acheson House—sunny Italy! Then I commanded a troop train—although I explained that a Padre does not do that sort of thing—and for twenty-three-and-a-half hours we travelled in it—endless stops, piercingly cold, broken windows, some adventures about which I cannot write now. We had dry rations—bully beef, raw bacon, tinned milk, bread, etc.—but nowhere to cook, no fire, no water! And then one of those things happened so characteristic of the army; some young sappers suddenly arrived at my carriage and took us in hand. When the engine halted they cooked the bacon and brewed the tea from the boiler water (grand tea too), and brought us boiling water to shave and wash, and did all they could to help. And so it turned out a grand journey in the end with that typical kindness of the British "Tommy" and "Jock". . . . And when next the soap box orator gets up to run down the old country tell him just to find a better if he can (they can't) and go to it!

And now I'm the Senior Chaplain at present of an area about the size of Scotland. I have to get round all this and administer the work of the Chaplains there. As I write this I look on the Adriatic Sea, and from my window I see the Union Jack flying and the White Ensign, and the Stars and Stripes. The Canteens are excellent, and the Church of Scotland Canteen has the best cakes I've tasted! I've seen the

127

grand work of the hospitals, and met my good friend the M.O. of the Dandy Ninth—we marched out side-by-side when the war started—Lt.-Col. J. J. Mason-Brown. And Toc H is doing a fine job too. The Service on Sunday night was packed to the door, and a more worshipful crowd it would be hard to find. Most folk here seem to know the Radio Padre, even those from New Zealand and South Africa, and all are so kind.

The day will not be too far off, I hope, when I'll be able to *tell* you more than I can write. But will you remember when you feel the war not going fast enough the amazing bravery of the men on all fronts fighting in really miserable conditions, and pray each day that the time will soon be here when we all get what we long for most—not at first a new world—but just at first the old world of our fireside and slippers and a "comfy" bed, and most of all those we love; to "hear our names called by the voices we love"; that is the peace which comes so near the peace of God which passes all our dreams. God bless you and be with you all.

The H.Q. Mess was not a happy place, composed chiefly of fairly senior officers with chips on their shoulders, very discontented, and not too well looked-after troops. There was much drunkenness among some of the troops through an inferior cheap vino. Indeed the only redeeming feature for me was the olive-laden countryside and the sea, and there at least "every prospect pleased"—and a very fine sermon I heard preached by one whom I soon got to know as a good friend, Dr Leslie Church, in the Waldensian Church at Bari. He later wrote a charming Foreword to *Whatever the Years*.

I immediately claimed "through the usual channels" that the promise of a Division had not materialised, and that I was still hoping to get one and leave the terrible place I had been landed in. The Division that I was meant to have had gone to Greece; and it turned out that my posting to an Area was a temporary one, and I soon received a reply apologising for the mistake and an order to report to the 8th Army H.Q. There I met the Deputy Chaplain-General who was one of the finest men one could ever hope to meet. Padre J. M. Layng had been

128

Chaplain at Balliol College, Oxford, after having been a Regular soldier, and from the moment we first met I knew I had a friend, a man I could really admire and feel it a pleasure and an honour to serve. After the war he became Archdeacon and Canon of York. He gave me my various instructions and I continued up the Appian Way to Rome, where I stayed for a night or two, and then on to Florence, until I joined my new Division in the line north of Florence.

In my Pastoral Letter in the *Canongate Chronicle*, February 1945, I wrote:

My dear People,

I am writing this to you from Rome on my way back to Assisi, the home of my beloved St Francis. Two most wonderful motor runs have brought me here: the first from Bari, over the Appenine Hills, through Benevento to Naples, where once again I stayed, this time for only two nights—and preached; and then from Naples by the famous Appian Way to Rome. Everywhere I went I saw again, with all the glorious scenery, the ravages and destruction of war, and it was made all the more interesting as my driver had fought his way along the way we now so safely motored. There is so much I'd like to write about these journeys and others I have done before them—but there is neither time nor space to do it now. It was a great joy to me to meet the Rev. Duncan Macgillivray in Bari (I have met so many friends out there!) and an even greater joy to meet him again in Rome. In one year we met in four different capitals— Cairo, Jerusalem, Edinburgh and Rome—and as we parted we hoped it would be Paris or Berlin, or, really best of all—Edinburgh again! . . . I haven't had very much time, but I saw the excellent Church of Scotland Canteen (and, of course, sampled their tea and cakes), and with Mr Macgillivray and Mr Ross visited St Peter's, the Sistine Chapel and one or two other famous places. What a tremendous place Rome is, and what glorious treasures it contains! No, we did not have an interview with the Pope—though, by chance, we *nearly* did; for we happened to go into the Audience Room just before he was due to appear, and we had a look round it and saw the quite magnificent Young Swiss Guards with new battle axes and bright uniforms, all in "glorious technicolor" as the Hollywood Directors would put it. Once again time and space is the difficulty, but I will have a lot to tell you when I get back. And now I'm off to Perugia to stay the night with the Rev. J. F. Marshall who is the only Scottish D.A.C.G. out here (incidentally, I find I'm the only S.C.F. from the Church of Scotland out here!) and then we go together to Assisi—he to conduct, and I to "direct" the course for Chaplains for eight days. Oh, and I really forgot to tell you the best bit of news of all for me. I've got my ambition again (I'm really a very lucky fellow) and have been made Senior Chaplain of an 8th Army Division in the line, and none other than the famous 10th Indian Infantry Division. More later! Remember me in your prayers. The Lord be with you.

The Division I had been sent to was the 10th Indian Division, and I soon found I could not have been more fortunate. The General was Denys Reid "the famous fighting leader of a dozen desert battles" who had recently escaped to Italy, and it was under his inspiring leadership that the Division was to see the war out. He was a remarkable man and I took to him at once, partly because of our mutual admiration for Neil Ritchie, under whom he had served when in the Desert war, partly because he was a first-class fighting soldier whose men came first and whose leadership was quite outstanding. He had been in the first war, a young Subaltern in the Seaforth Highlanders, where he had won a D.S.O., M.C. and bar, and later had gone into the Indian Army. He was a son of the Manse—rather a wild son at that—and a great supporter of the padres.
From my Pastoral Letter of February 1945 I wrote:

10th Indian Infantry Division,
C.M.F.,
28th February 1945.

My dear People,
   I last wrote to you, I think, from Assisi. Since then I have

been to Florence—that lovely "City of Flowers" where I preached to large congregations at the Scots Church there and in the Chapel of the Church of Scotland Canteen—a quite excellent place run by Mr Stewart—and incidentally met Norrie Dye, who, as you know, is a Sergeant in the Lothian and Border Horse. Later I joined my Division up the line, and what a fine crowd they are! The General is Major-General Denys Reid, C.B.E., who has a bar to his D.S.O. and a bar to his M.C.; he is a real good Scottish Presbyterian (a nephew of Dr Drummond of Lothian Road), and so very like my old Colonel, Brigadier F. L. Johnston, that to describe him as such I can find no higher praise! I have now pitched my tent at his advanced H.Q., and though its a bit "lively" at times, I feel quite "safe" for on one side of me is George Flannigan, and on the other Harry Holt, and though they are quite far apart I hope to see them both very soon. I have a fine car and an Indian driver, and instead of my Indian batman (who brings my tea in the morning with a "Goo' morn Sahib"), I am arranging to get a Scot from the Lovat Scouts. Though this is an Indian Division (and what a grand crowd these Indians are!) it is no secret to say that like all the Indian Divisions there are a great many British troops, and in these are a very good proportion of Scots.

I have been visiting as many units as I can, and everywhere have had the most friendly reception possible. The weather, too, has been quite wonderful, and the countryside and scenery really so fine that no words of mine can describe it; all this more than compensates for the dusty, bumpy roads which make me feel very sleepy (as now) when evening comes!

I had lunch with the Rev. Duncan Macgillivray and the Rev. Tom Torrance at our rear H.Q. last week. Mr Macgillivray has now gone home for a short time, but I'm glad that Mr Torrance is still here and quite near where I am. He is an old friend of mine, and one of the ablest of our younger Scottish Ministers, and is at present Minister of Alyth. He is one of the great personalities out here, and the work he has done in this Division in particular has become quite proverbial. He says nothing about that himself, but everywhere I go I hear his name and hear of his deeds—how under fire and on hands and knees he carries buns and comforts to the front line; how nothing is ever too much trouble to him; and how he helps everyone. I feel so proud to know him, and that he has borne so high the name of the Church of Scotland. With men like him, like the Rev. Allan McArthur, C.F., of the Scots Guards, and others like them, there is, I feel, a grand future for our Church leadership in the days that lie ahead.

When you read this probably it will be Easter. I shall especially remember you all then on this greatest day of the year. I shall be with you at Communion—for we, too, I hope, will be able to have our Communion that day. At no time are folk more united than at Communion, united with all the Church on earth and the Church in Heaven; yes, "with angels and archangels and all the company of the heavenly host"—and many of our friends have joined that company since the war began. They will be with us too round the table, "for all are one with Thee for all are Thine". Yes, we shall be very near them and each other. Let us all go out, resolved to love God more and serve Him better in the days to come; let us realise anew our "oneness" in Christ Jesus and as one body, let us go forward "conquering and to conquer" indeed in this greatest of all wars, the war to "finally beat down Satan under our feet", we must be "more than conquerers" for we go out to win for Jesus Christ the hearts of men, and it takes "more than a conqueror" to do that. So God bless you all, and a happy Easter to you. The Lord be with you.

I was given a good Indian servant, and in George Colmer of the Kent Yeomanry I had one of the most loyal, most helpful and most cheerful of driver-batmen, who remained with me until the war was over. My joy was increased when I found that Tom Torrance had attached himself some time before my arrival to this Division. He was working with the Church of Scotland Huts and already had become almost a legendary figure for his unselfish and courageous service to the troops, British and Indian alike. It was a great comfort to have him near and around me, for though I was Senior Chaplain I was the only Church of Scotland Chaplain in the Division. He had his own jeep with "Church of Scotland Padre" painted across it, and ran gift-shops, barber-shops, canteens, and almost anything you wanted, right in the front line, and would often visit some of the outposts well within reach of the enemy. I had last seen him in Cairo in January 1944 and I greatly welcomed the re-union.

As mentioned, the Division was very much in the firing line when I joined it near Monte Grande and had already done some very hard fighting in the desert and in Italy itself. Monte Grande is a hilltop north of the Sallaro river, fifteen miles from the outskirts of Bologna. It was a place of ill-omen which had seen much heavy fighting and the Germans had set great store by it. Much of it was deerstalker's landscapes with high look-outs and deep scours, and I shall never forget how when the Lovat Scouts came to join the Division under Cameron of Lochiel, the well-trained Scouts could pick out the enemy posts with such ease and speed compared with the ordinary infantryman. They were fairly exposed posts in many ways and a smoke screen had to be set up to cut off the enemy from ourselves. Sometimes I walked in the hills at night with Walter Goodman, then the C.R.A.,[1] and to the end a very great friend, and we used to almost bump into German patrols and even at times exchange a passing wave.

An Indian Division was, of course, larger than a British Division, since each Brigade contained at least three Indian Battalions and one British Battalion (some had more) and most of the Indian Battalions at that time were officered by British officers and there were as usual a great many supporting Forces like the Artillery. We had for a time the Scottish Horse beside us, for example, of which Robin Barbour was Adjutant and George Flannigan, one of our old Club boys, was, among other things, a drummer.

I stayed with the Division until the end of the war and while

---

[1] Later Major-General.

it fought its way up to Italy, sometimes going down to Florence, and on two memorable occasions to Padres' Conferences which I ran at Assisi, and where a fine brotherhood of chaplains met to re-charge their batteries before going back into their units again.

From my Pastoral Letter of February 1945 I wrote:

Assisi, February 1945.

My dear People,

I am writing this to you from Assisi. The conference for Church of Scotland Chaplains which I started over a week ago is now nearly over, and it has been a fine experience. Assisi is, I think, one of the most lovely places in all the world, and never surely has the spirit of one man more dominated and permeated a place than that of St Francis and Assisi. From the days when I was a boy I have always loved St Francis, and now I have been privileged and thrilled to see the places I seemed already to "know" so well. The Church he built still stands, and when I visited it the friars were still using the same "office". Here too, the lovely Carceri where he used to go for prayer and rest and meditation, and where you can still see the actual places he used (it is now a small convent, and the Franciscans call them monasteries where only two or three friends live at a time), and the "actual tree" where he preached to "his little brothers the birds". Then there is the fine Basilica Church—or rather three Churches. Far below is his own very simple and lovely tomb above one of the Churches with its famous frescoes, and above that the Church with its famous set of frescoes of St Francis' life by Giotto. There is so much to see, so much to write about.

And with me are such good companions from our Mother Kirk of Scotland as well as some Presbyterian Chaplains from New Zealand, Canada, and for a time U.S.A. Among those with me here are the Rev. James Marshall, of Renfrew, our Senior Scottish Chaplain in Italy, and a great power among us all here and the Rev. Dr W. Neil from Bridge of Allan; and the Rev. A. Allan McArthur, Glasgow.

The Chaplains' Centre at Assisi is a fine idea of the Royal

134

Army Chaplains' Department out here. It is run by the Rev. F. B. R. Browne, S.C.F., the Sussex cricketer, and the Rev. Robin W. Woods, C.F.,[1] a son of the Bishop of Lichfield (another son of the Bishop runs the British Chaplains' Centre at Tidworth).

We began the day with morning prayers taken by the D.A.C.G. After breakfast there is an hour's Bible study, and then after a short break, I have been giving a series of lectures on the World that faces the Church and the Church that faces the World, with special reference to the Iona Community, the "Returning Soldier" and the "Church at Home", and our work as Padres. This is followed by discussion. In the afternoon we visit Assisi—a week is not enough—and the country around. After tea we have group discussions, and then there is in the evening a Service followed by an address by Mr Marshall. I wonder if ever before the old Scottish Psalms have been sung in Assisi! And certainly not as we sing them! Certainly it must be the first time that a Scottish Communion has been celebrated in the town of St Francis, and "St George's Edinburgh" rung through the Cumbrian Plains.

It has been a great experience and refreshment to us all, and has given us new strength and vision to go out to our work again.

Tomorrow I go to Florence, and then to join my Division "somewhere up the line".

And so from Assisi I send you the blessing of St Francis:

"The Lord bless you and guard you, show His face to you, and have mercy upon you, turn His face towards you, and give you peace. Brother, the Lord bless you!"

At Florence I would visit the Officers' Clubs, and there sometimes sadly wonder as one saw fit, young, already battle-scarred officers singing round the piano, how many would still be alive before the week was out.

In Florence I attended one of the most outstanding Services I have ever been to, where the Archbishop of York, Dr Garbett, confirmed what must have been hundreds of young soldiers, most of whom had come straight down from the battle line

[1] Later Bishop of Worcester.

and who were going straight back again afterwards. I shall never forget them, with their open-necked shirts and their shorts, looking so clean and fresh, kneeling in Confirmation; nor shall I forget the Sermon preached then by the Archbishop "Be ye faithful unto death and I will give you the crown of Life".

From my Pastoral Letter of April 1945 I wrote:

10th Indian Infantry Division,
C.M.F.,
8th April 1945.

My dear People,

I am writing this to you in the garden of a South African Hospital (which also takes in our own men). The place is a mass of blossom, and the old walls of the house that faces me are just covered with wistaria in full flower—and even some roses are out, and the sun is beating down from a cloudless sky—as it has been doing for nearly three months now with hardly a break. There are a lot of butterflies about too, and the birds are singing, and every now and then a lizard dashes across the path in front of me. I have been visiting the wounded here, and taking a Service, and this is the first quiet bit of afternoon rest and peace I've had for quite a time.

As you all know now, as I write the 8th Army is in the midst of another fierce battle, fighting over what Reuter's correspondent has called "the worst battlefield in the world". But the *holding* of the line, the patrol activity and the artillery duels experienced during these last months of so-called "waiting" were, I can assure you, no rest or "picnic". There is a constant tension, fellows get wounded and killed and sometimes the noise is terrific—that of course, is one of the horrors of war. With all the grand comradeship, the humour, the loyalty, even the glory, there's that other side. What we must discover after the war, not now, is the moral equivalent of war, and the spiritual equivalent of war, and—in the grand words of the old liturgy—"finally beat down Satan under our feet".

The day after this new battle started I attended a Service at

136

15th Army Group; it was held in a garden like the one I am in now—rather smaller. An open-air altar was surrounded with blossoms and flowers, and once again all around were birds and butterflies—and the glorious sun shone brightly on the Union Jack and the Stars and Stripes beneath which stood picked men from Great Britain and the U.S.A. The singing was just grand—led by the full band of the Royal Ulster Rifles, General Mark Clark read the lesson: "Therefore take unto you the whole armour of God . . . having your feet shod with the preparation of the Gospel of peace . . . above all taking the shield of faith". . . . Then the Archbishop of York preached a great sermon on "Christ the King". Later in the day I saw the Archbishop confirm 200-300 young soldiers just down from the line and soon to return, and preach on "Be ye faithful unto death and I will give you the crown of Life".

When we had tea with the Archbishop he spoke to me about the grand work Dr George Macleod is doing.

There is so much I'd like to write about—about the night that George Colmer, my driver from the Kent Yeomanry, and I met Field-Marshal Alexander with his staff on a lonely mountain road—the greatest of all our Generals; of giving George Flannigan a lift one day in my car when we talked of the "old days and the days to come", of the visits we had from the Army Commander, Sir Richard McCreery, of the time when Harry Holt suddenly walked to my tent—or the night when General Reid with his C.R.A. and his A.D.C. and myself set out for a Service in his jeep, but without lights and with the windscreen down, for we were under enemy observation—so much and so much.

But let me finish with this: the Sikhs have carved for me a lovely Iona Cross to use at my Services and to take home with me when the war is over. As you know, they have their own religion and their Service Book is guarded in the little "temples" they set up wherever they go. For them it is no dead book, it *lives*. And so it was that one night recently a big black bearded Sikh came to my tent with electric cable in his hand and spoke. I asked one who understood his language what he said. "He would like to give the Padre Sahib light for his tent because he has a sacred book and works for

God." Here indeed was light from one not of our faith—and what better, more challenging or more humiliating to one who but feebly tried to be a Minister of Him who is the Living Word.

I'm going to sleep now in this sun for a bit, or in the bit of shadow there by that tree. And after that a bath, what a wonderful thing a hot bath can be!

So God bless and be with you all.

There in that last stage of the war in Italy as we moved up towards the river Po, one saw again the horror of war, the constant burial of dead bodies—young men, German and British and Indian; and with it the sacrifice and comradeship and cheerfulness born of sharing common hardship and anxiety, yes and even fear, but most of all common service and sacrifice in face of a common purpose.

Chapter 4

One of the great pleasures at this time was meeting the various visitors to our Divisional Headquarters who would look in for a talk or a meal (since we were an Indian Division our curries were very popular!) held in our Mess Tent or sometimes in the open-air beside our caravans; and two especially stand out in my memory at this time because in the absence of Denys Reid I had to entertain them myself. First the Commanding Officer of the Scottish Horse, Lt.-Col. George Murray. One could not meet a more delightful man and we soon found that we had several friends in common, not least Geoffrey Gilbey for whom we both had so great an admiration. When he left to return to his own Headquarters he gave as usual his cheerful goodbye. He was killed the next day—the only casualty the Scottish Horse had that day, and too on the day before the war in Italy finished, to the great sorrow of his Regiment, for he was a greatly beloved Commanding Officer. Had he lived he would have been the next Duke of Atholl, his son eventually succeeding to the title.

The other was Lt.-General Sir Bernard Freyberg, V.C., the Commander of the New Zealand Army, who told me of his gratitude and surprise when Sir James Barrie was giving his famous address on "Courage" at St Andrews University, and how he suddenly turned and pointing towards him and said, "He is a V.C. now, and you would not think to look at him that he could ever have presented such a disreputable appearance, would you?" Freyberg was not only G.O.C. New Zealand Expeditionary Force, he represented the New Zealand Government and was directly responsible not to Churchill but to the Prime Minister and Government of New Zealand, and as a result exercised unique independence. With his sense of independence he had also the same dry humour that could be seen in the men he commanded; and the story went that once when a senior British General remarked to him that his New Zealanders didn't salute very much, he replied "You should try waving to them—they always wave back!" By this time, though greatly admired and respected by his men, he wasn't so much liked by them as Brigadier (later Major-General) Kippenberger, whom the New Zealanders regarded as their finest soldier; but I found Freyberg most kind and friendly and easy to talk to.

Lochiel, too, who was commanding the Lovat Scouts, would visit our Headquarters when his Battalion joined our Division near Monte Grande, who with their great knowledge of the moors and hills, were more quickly than others able to pick out the German outposts. Donald Cameron of Lochiel later commanded a Battalion of Cameron Highlanders and became their Honorary Colonel—a fine soldier and a fine man, later to become a Knight of the Thistle.

I had for a short time a driver who had worked on Lord Baldwin's estate in Worcestershire, and he was never tired of telling me how kind Lord Baldwin was to them all; and previously I had met a young officer whose father had been a Labour Cabinet Minister and he too told me how friendly Stanley Baldwin had been to the Opposition as well as to his own Party, and how his speech at the time of the General Strike "Give peace in our time, O Lord" had had such an effect for good. I was sad therefore to see what a bad press he was getting, and when his wife died on 17th June I felt I ought to

139

write and tell him how sorry we all were and that he was on no account to acknowledge my letter. I was surprised and delighted therefore to receive a Forces Air Mail letter, written in his own hand, and sent to me at the 10th Indian Division in Italy:

2nd July 1945.

My dear Mr Selby Wright,
   It was the kindest of kind thoughts that you should write to me, and that one like yourself, bearing the brunt of war in a far land, should think of me with such sympathy and find the time to say so touches me very dearly. Such a letter could not fail to bring help and comfort, and it has.

I am most gratefully and sincerely yours,

Baldwin of Bewdley.

And I can assure you that such a gracious letter was a great comfort too to me.
   Surely the historian Dr G. M. Trevelyan, then Master of Trinity College, Cambridge, was right when he said "He remains the most human and most lovable of all the Prime Ministers".
   When victory had come to Italy on 2nd May 1945 the whole world seemed to change. At night I was able to sleep in my tent beside my caravan in peace and in the sky Very lights were let off in all directions in sheer joy that the war was now over.
   In my Pastoral Letter for that month I wrote:

10th Indian Infantry Division,
C.M.F.,
31st May 1945.

My dear People,
   Since I last wrote you so much has happened that I would require not a letter but a book to get it all in!
   When I last wrote we were in the mountains round Bologna, and now the war out here has been over for a month! Actually we had two "V" days here—VI day and

VE day. And what days they were! Everywhere crowds of fellows gathering for short informal Services of Thanksgiving, and then the great Day of Thanksgiving. Field-Marshal Alexander has told us to observe these days with "sober satisfaction and gratitude" and we certainly did. It is significant—or I hope it is—that when we were "down" and "at our finest hour" we turned as a nation to God, and when we faced our hour of triumph, for it was nothing less than that, we again turned to God in thanksgiving.

Of course it has not been without its cost as we in the Canongate know, and certainly as we in the 8th Army know. Personally, I have heard some terrible things and seen some ghastly sights that I shall never be able to forget; but out of the horror and terror of it I have seen some glorious things appear, and I shall not forget that either. . . .

We still had some anxious moments as we moved up towards Ferrara and Padua and Venice towards Trieste, as we were not quite sure what was going to happen there with Tito's Forces, since we really did not know whose side they were on. Indeed we slept with our steel helmets within reach in case of sudden attack! It was a tense situation.

From Gorizia where we were now stationed, driven by George, I used frequently to go down to Grado or Sistiano to bathe, always taking some of the British troops with me. And what wonderful days these were in the warm waters with such wonderful comrades around. Occasionally I would go into Yugoslavia just across the border to take Services for small groups stationed there; and it was in Udine, where I had to go to hospital for a short time, that on 6th August we first heard of the A bomb dropping on Hiroshima, and we knew then the war with Japan too was over; although in our excitement and great relief we did not realise just what the dropping of that bomb meant.

One night while having dinner in a mess-tent on the Yugoslav border, I heard this story from the Colonel of a famous Indian Regiment. Our conversation had ranged rather trivially all over the place, and then I mentioned a famous regiment (I don't think that's giving anything away, for what regiment

141

now *isn't* a famous one?) One of this regiment's regular battalions had been nearly wiped out in the Far East in the early days of the war. "Did you ever hear", said the Colonel, "the story as to how some of them got away?" I told him I hadn't. "Well," he said, "it's a most interesting story and I have it from one of the men himself." Then he told me how this great and gallant battalion had fought its way most brilliantly, contesting every mile of ground till now there were only about 200 left, and the position was really quite hopeless. But there were still some aircraft—enough to take about seventy men—and the Colonel was determined to get as many as possible out—to save as many good lives as possible—to let the battalion's fate be known and to show others how best to profit from the lessons they had learned. Two hundred left and seventy to be chosen. How was he going to do it? How would you have done it? Well, this is what he did, and I think you will agree it was a very good way—in fact, the best way possible.

He got the men round him and told them quite simply and bluntly that the position was desperate, that they had all fought as he'd known from the beginning they would, brilliantly and bravely, and now he called on them to do one thing more. He wanted about seventy men to volunteer for a suicide job—a job that might mean certain death. It was a lot to ask, he confessed, but he had no doubt that he would get them. Well, he got them all right, and chose the first seventy volunteers and so, they who were willing to lose their lives for the sake of their comrades and their country found they had gone to almost certain life. Risking all, their very lives in the service of their fellow men (and may it be said, in the service of God), willing to lose life itself, they found it.

Chapter 5

These days, stationed in the hill country north of Trieste, were among the happiest I can ever remember. The war had now finished, the countryside was beautiful, and my caravan was pitched beside the Isonzo river, and one could jump in for a bathe before breakfast and in the evening, until the river had to be put out of bounds for bathing, since for some reason someone had died by being poisoned by it. But, above all, I was surrounded by the nicest set of fellows you could meet, and these trips we made, driven by George or Roy, to Grado and Sistiana where we bathed in the warm waters and dried ourselves in the warm sun, are never-to-be-forgotten.

In addition to visiting the various units in the Division and their supporting troops, I had, of course, to take quite a large number of Services. Sometimes these took me into quite lonely positions on the border, and often with quite a small number of soldiers. I remember well on one occasion when I was taking a Service of young soldiers whom I had never met before, and before the Service one of them came to me and said he had become an atheist and didn't wish to attend any parades in future—as was his right. I explained to him that when people changed their denomination in the Army the usual procedure was to have instruction in their new denomination, but since I didn't know any atheist padres I found that rather difficult! But however I understood his point and perhaps next time I called I said we could have another talk about it. I then asked him, just as a matter of interest, whom he admired most in the 8th Army and he said without a single moment's hesitation "Field-Marshal Alexander, sir". So I explained that Field-Marshal Alexander was one of the best Christian people you could ever meet and I wondered whether perhaps he would feel like pitting his own mind against that of the Field-Marshal's whom he so much admired. Perhaps, I suggested, he might be wrong and the Field-Marshal might be right. Well, a fortnight later (because in these distant, isolated, posts, I could only visit fortnightly and not usually on Sundays, in order to cover ground) I saw him again; this time he appeared at the little service we were having. At the close of the service I said to him "You know, it is very unusual to see an atheist in Church and joining in so well". He smiled and said to me, "Well you know what you said about Field-Marshal Alex, sir; I thought it over and it is rather conceited on my part, isn't it, to think I should know better than he, and in any case I think I was wrong. It was just that I was feeling completely fed-up at the time and could not see the use of anything, but I feel much happier now thank you—thank you sir". I used to meet him each time I took the service in that lonely spot—always so friendly and so cheerful; I wonder what he is doing now, and so many others like him.

It was while I was stationed on the Yugoslav border that I received a signal from 13 Corps H.Q. telling me that I was to get leave from the Division for an unspecified time in order to visit all the 8th Army Land Leave Route Camps that had recently been set up from Italy to Calais. Many of the men had not been home for a long time—some indeed for years—and this was the journey home for them. I was told to visit each Camp on the way up and on the way back I would be allowed a certain freedom of route before I returned to H.Q. to report.

Of course I took my ever-faithful driver, young George Colmer of the Kent Yeomanry who had been with me ever since I had joined the 10th Indian Division, and used to make remarks like "beggin' your pardon, sir, but it's an 'ell of a way". I also asked Roy King from the Main Divisional Signals if he would agree to join us. He was not only an excellent fellow in himself but he was a good driver, and I thought it might be as well to have a spare driver with me as well as another good companion (and it is very important when one is on a journey to have the right sort of people with you). I had got to know him well when I visited, as I constantly did, the Signal Section in their caravans when I used to go in the late evenings to have tea with them, and it was to him that later I dedicated one of my books, *Whatever the Years*. George was twenty years old and Roy was twenty-one, and almost as an after-thought I took with me an older man called Charlie Chislett who was in civilian life a Bank Manager and had volunteered for the Army. He was an expert photographer. Once I got to know him as well as the others I was very glad I had taken him as he was a most cheerful fellow who had travelled a lot before the war, so full of good stories, and he made an excellent addition to our little party. So you see, I could not have had three better travelling companions: the people we travel with make all the difference, whether it is a journey across Europe or through life itself, and sometimes we tend to forget that until it is too late. Well Roy and Charlie and George will never let me forget it.

144

It turned out to be a truly wonderful journey through much of battle-scarred Europe, from Trieste through most of the North of Italy, Austria, Germany, Luxembourg, Belgium and France. The whole story of the journey would in itself make a book—Villach to Spittal, Salzburg, the birthplace of Mozart, Munich where the Nazi party was founded, from Munich to the concentration camp at Dachau; though not on our route we felt it was so near Munich that we should go and see it, and we were glad that we did. Then on to Ulm on the Danube where we stayed with the 16/5th Lancers. It was practically in ruins except for its glorious Cathedral with its spires that Rudolph Otto said described what he meant by "the numinous", and where I preached in the Lutheran Church which was shared by the Roman Catholics as well as by the Lutherans because so much else had been destroyed. Then on to Darmstadt, Mainz, Trier, and so through Luxembourg, Sedan, Le Cateau, Arras, St Omer, on to Calais, every moment had been interesting and a few perhaps outstanding. One had to remember that the war had not been over for more than a month and there were still many living memories of it, including some of the German troops straggling back to their homes, the bombed roads where one could travel for some distance and then discover that one could go no further since the road had been blown apart, the bombed bridges on which one was very careful not to go too far in case one found that half-way along it continued no longer.

What I remember so vividly too was the destruction of some of the cities, not least Ulm, parts of Munich, the horror of Dachau where we visited the gas chambers and still met some of those who had been interned there, the young Jewish boys with their numbers ever imprinted on their arms, a visit to General Paton's H.Q. at Munich where the padre told me once he had heard the General addressing some of his men and telling them they were like a bunch of bananas—some were green, some were yellow, and the rest were just rotten!

I think the most moving part of the journey was to see some of the young children coming out of the woods, almost starving. We had been told on a huge notice on entering enemy territory that there was to be no fraternising with any Germans. It was an impossible command and made even more

145

impossible when one saw these young children living literally in the woods, and they ate the bars of chocolate we gave them like ravenous wolves. Some of the younger ones could speak quite good English and told us of the horrors that they had gone through, their homes bombed, their parents killed, and I wondered what had happened to them during that winter that was soon to follow.

And then one of these strange coincidences happened when we got to Calais. Some months before George had got very homesick and began to feel that he would like to get back again and see his own folk and the places he knew best at East Ham in London. I said to him jokingly "Well George, never mind, I will show you the White Cliffs of Dover by your twenty-first birthday". When we got to Calais we went to see the White Cliffs of Dover and the young sailor who showed them to us said, "Look at them, sir, you could not have seen them more clearly than you can this morning"; and George turned to me and said, "Do you remember your promise to me sir? That I would see the White Cliffs of Dover by my twenty-first birthday? Well, sir, I happen to be twenty-one today."

On the way back George developed a high temperature of 103° and we had to leave him at Sedan, but he turned up again and joined me in Italy. Fortunately Roy King was able to take over and drove the 2,000 miles back; and what an interesting journey we had back. We didn't visit the Leave Camps this time as we had already seen them, but we went to many other places instead, and the most interesting of all was Berchtesgaden. I think we were the first British troops to go there, since that very afternoon we went they were expecting Lord Tedder, and we were able to have a prior inspection ourselves!

We visited Hitler's house and Goering's house and the S.S. Barracks, which had all been blasted with incredible accuracy by the R.A.F., and then 8,000 feet up we went to Hitler's Eagle Nest where you can look down on the world.

Berchtesgaden is one of the loveliest places surely in the world, and yet it was there that Hitler dreamed his dreams and hatched his plots. As mentioned, most of his H.Q. had been blasted—his house, Goering's house; and we were able to walk round them, though neither of them of course had been at home for some time! It was a glorious sunny day and how

146

lovely was the countryside, and high though Hitler's house stood—Roy had had doubts as to whether the car would make it, and even greater doubts as to how the brakes would hold on the way down—high though it stood we got into a jeep and climbed still higher, very high indeed, in fact twice the height of the highest mountain in Britain, to Hitler's mountain hideout which I have mentioned—the Eagle's Nest. And from that high mountain you could look down upon the world and imagine yourself master—an "exceeding high mountain" where he dreamt of world power. One of the young American soldiers who was occupying the Eagle's Nest turned to me and said "gee, this *is* an exceeding high mountain isn't it sir?" And suddenly the words came back to me "The Devil took Him unto an exceeding high mountain and showeth Him all the Kingdoms of the world and the glory of them, and he said to Him, 'All these things I will give you if you will fall down and worship me'". And Hitler from the "exceeding high mountain" fell down and worshipped the Devil; and because the Devil is always a liar, Hitler at the expense of great suffering to countless innocent people, was beaten off the face of the earth. And then I thought of that other hill, not a mountain this time—"a green hill far away, outside a city wall" where the only real Man who ever lived did not fall down and worship, but from there went out conquering and to conquer—not lands or the kingdoms of the world, but the hearts of men.

The rest of the journey back we took more easily and these were more restful days, for frankly we were a bit tired by this time. One night at a little Inn in the Tyrol there again a strange story emerged. I had prepared a speech in rather a diffident French and German and Italian, to ask for three beds since George was no longer with us; but when I went into the hall of the Inn I was met by a delightful old gentleman and his wife who greeted us straightaway in English and asked us what it was we would like, and I told him that I would like three beds and he said we could have as many as we wished. He turned out to be an anti-Nazi Professor who had taken refuge in the Tyrol from Hitler and his gang. He and his wife had two sons, one happened to be in the American Army and the other in the British Air Force, and they used sometimes to see the British planes going over and wondered whether their son was among them. And then one day as the Americans came nearer they suddenly came up the valley and burst into their Inn, and the first person they met was the Captain of the American troops—and he was their son! They had not seen him for ages, they didn't know where he was, he didn't know where they were, and there they met in this amazing way. We stayed a day or two with them in that beautiful country round the Tyrol.

We had one adventure which might have been fatal. The Professor told us that down in the cellars there was quite a lot of loot taken by the German, and possibly by some of the Italian, troops and if we liked to go down there and see if there was anything there we would like, we could have it, as he didn't know what to do with it. Well, Roy and I went down a narrow staircase into a cellar, switched on the light and at that moment up jumped some German troops who had been hiding there. Neither of us were armed and I had a sudden feeling that this might be the end, and I whispered quickly to Roy to run upstairs and tell any troops that he could see what had happened. It all finished very peacefully because the Germans came very quietly with us. They probably didn't know how many people were behind us (as a matter of fact there were none until Roy went up and brought some down). Had we been armed or had Roy been armed, because I as a padre would not be carrying arms, things might have been very different; but Roy at the beginning of the journey had been carrying a revolver which he decided to give up halfway through—and had he been armed he might have brought out his revolver and we might have felt the opposition too strong for our comfort. The loot in the end turned out to be pretty tawdry and tatty stuff. I brought one or two forks and spoons back with me which very rapidly were used up at the Boys' Camps at Skateraw.

We went from the Tyrol, which we were sorry to leave, down the Brenner Pass back again the way we had started, back from an unforgettable journey and unforgettable friends, the brew-up times, the talks we had together, the various places we had visited, the people we had met, and we gave ourselves a toast at the end, "may our journey through life be ever as pleasant as this journey, and may we travel and meet with such good companions on the way". "And to think", said Charlie, as he helped himself to more jam, "that we are being paid for this!"

Chapter 6

We got back to Divisional H.Q. on 13th July 1945, having spent the last evening at Villach, each with a room to ourselves and each with a German batman! In just over a fortnight we had covered about 5,000 miles, and with only a day's break I found myself on the Sunday broadcasting to the 8th Army and the Desert Air Force. We were still not quite sure what the Yugoslavs were going to do under Tito, and had to keep a fairly watching brief on the border, but centred as we were, around Gorizia and Udine, we were able to get in a lot of marvellous bathing at Sistiana and Grado, and I still had all the British units of the Division to visit, along with the attendant supporting units there, chiefly the Divisional Signals who were the most delightful people.

We still had with us the 1st King's Own, the 1st Durham Light Infantry, the 2nd Loyals, the 1st Northumberland Fusiliers, the Kent Yeomanry, among others. For a time too I found myself acting as D.A.C.G., since my old friend, Adam Macpherson, D.A.C.G., had gone on leave, and so had to visit the 13th Corps H.Q. and some of the other units of the 8th Army. Although officially the 8th Army had broken up on the 29th of July, I took Roy and Pat Garrett with me to visit Victor Pike,[1] their splendid A.C.G. It was also the day when the Desert Air Force ceased to exist. George was still away and so I was motored by Roy King and we were able to combine the duties of visiting with the joys of bathing in a new-found world of peace.

On the 8th of August I had to go into hospital at Trieste, and after a few days' stay there was moved to hospital at Udine, where I was joined by George Colmer who had now returned from his sick leave. It was in the hospital at Udine we heard that the Japanese had given up and that the war had at last

[1] Later Bishop of Sherborne.

finished. Ill as some of us were, we leapt from our beds with excitement; the atomic age was upon us but we didn't realise or think about that at the time—all we thought about was . . . it is all over now.

After a week in hospital at Udine I left for the convalescent home at Velden where I spent about a fortnight in glorious surroundings. George Colmer who had, as mentioned, by this time joined me there again as my driver and batman sometimes used to row me on the lake, or make visits with me to Klagenfurt and places round about.

In my Pastoral Letter of September 1945 I wrote:

10th Indian Infantry Division,
C.M.F.,
September 1945.

My dear People,

Perhaps by the time this letter appears in the *Chronicle* I shall be back in the U.K., so this may be the last letter I write you from the C.M.F.

Since I last wrote I have spent twelve days in Austria—at first convalescing at Velden by the lovely lake—the warmest in Europe, called the Worther See.

Much has been happening round about where we are now, still near Trieste (though soon I expect to be near Milan and Genoa), swimming, riding, athletics, football, cricket, etc., to add a certain interest to the men's lives and to stave off a feeling of boredom and frustration, both very natural consequences of the ending of the fighting. But we sometimes still have moments to let us see that there are some things not quite settled yet, and to show how difficult the peace is going to be.

The outstanding features of the last week I will never forget—a full scale beating of retreat by the Royal Navy and the Royal Marines with the massed bands of the none too small number of H.M. ships at present near us—the sailors in their spotless white uniforms, the arrival with trumpets blowing, swords and bayonets flashing, of the C.-in-C. Admiral Sir John Cunningham, the playing of "Abide with Me" as the White Ensign was lowered, and the marching to the crashing of the Band! And then a day later the great Searchlight Tattoo, the massed bands, the combined pipes and drums, the marching of the Scots and Coldstream Guards, the drill of the Gurkhas, the trick cycling of the Royal Corps of Signals, the horse riding of the Bays and Lancers and Hussars, and the march past of British, Indian, Gurkha, American, Italian, and Jugo-Slav troops, and crowning all Field-Marshal "Alex" himself, cheered by all the nations as our much-loved, honoured, and respected Supreme Commander.

But, too, there have been other possibly more lasting, and certainly more important things. Personal talks with individual soldiers about their future and their homes; large and eager congregations at Church, and discussions about the past, the present, and the future.

And in one discussion recently some very wise and telling things were said by some young soldiers here. The subject was "The Church we want to see" and one point about that "Church" was quite clearly this—the Church must be worthy of the faith we have, worthy of the God we worship: it must be bright and clean and cheerful, and lead to reverence; it must be friendly and speak the language of the people—"the common people" must again "hear gladly" the voice of their Lord. Applied to the Canongate, as I actually applied it all through the discussion, in my own mind, it means that we've got to make our Church bright and cheerful and clean—even a fit "Home" of the God we call our Father. "Some people", said the young soldier who was speaking, "think that these 'outward' things don't matter; but I believe they matter far more than these people think." The other soldiers all agreed and so do I—and so, I hope, do you too.

We must not lose the "ordinary" sailor, soldier, and airman when they come home—for they are the greatest fellows in the world.

May they all be home as soon as possible to homes worthy of their love, and a Church worthy of our God.

I got back to the Divisional H.Q. at the end of that month and continued taking Services and visiting there, watching various other parades and Tattoos and the like, and occasionally doing the odd broadcast. Later that month I left Goritzia with George Colmer for Asolo and stayed at a beautiful house called "Casa Dusé", then owned by Lord Iveagh, but formerly used by the great Elenora Dusé, whom D'Annunzio called "the symbol of all the beauty and the loving in the world". It was in perfect condition although it had been used by the Germans as an officers' mess, and even the photographs in their frames remained untouched and unharmed on the mantelpiece. We were able to go round the beautiful countryside at Asolo with ripe grapes hanging from the vines and the sun-capped mountains in the distance—a view most memorable in itself. Asolo is associated too with Robert Browning and Freda Stark, and, for that matter, with Napoleon.

From Asolo we went via Verona and then on to Lake Garda and through Milan to Piacenza which was then the Division's new H.Q. I still each Sunday took Services for the various units, sometimes three or four on one Sunday.

I officially gave up the Division on the 24th September when my successor, Padre Brown, arrived. A decision had to be made as to whether or not I would stay on with the Division when it went back to India, but on the good advice of Padre Layng, the D.C.G., and the 8th Army A.C.G. Victor Pike, and also the fact that I was pulled very much to get back to my beloved Parish of Canongate, I decided it would be better if I returned there, when my service was over.

Immediately after I had given up the Division I went to Lake Como and took George Colmer with me. I stayed with the South African School of Religion and there I met the South African troops who were really one of the finest crowd of men I have ever met. I had to address the School on various occasions while living with them, and they gave me a great send-off when I left, first for Milan and then for Genoa, returning to Lake Como shortly afterwards. After three days at Turin where I had the great pleasure of seeing George Flannigan, whom I had not met since I saw him in the Scottish Horse in Italy, I went on to Rapallo and Portofino. At Rapallo the South Africans had a School of Religion there too, and once again I met the most delightful people you could ever hope to meet. We bathed and boated in the beautiful warm waters, diving off the side of the boat. I had to address the Conference several times, but again it was chiefly the friendships I made there and the really happy atmosphere of the whole place I remember best. I spent over a week there and the time went very fast.

These Schools of Religion for the South African troops were really based on the Moral Leadership courses which were first begun at Assisi under the expert leadership of men like William Neil of Nottingham University and Robin Woods, later Dean of Windsor and now Bishop of Worcester, and which were continued later under James P. Stevenson in Austria, which set out to prepare men for life after the war; and splendid places they were too. Of all the many men I met during the war and after, there were none finer than these South African troops whom I met at Como and Rapallo, and Portofino. They were the most cheerful, friendly and loyal men one could ever meet and it was a great joy to be with them. As I got to know them I felt great affection for the South Africans and I was greatly impressed by, but not converted to, their Christian justification of apartheid, and their sincerity in their belief. They certainly bore no hatred for anyone and truly felt that their way of life was the right way, both for themselves and for the coloured peoples of Africa. They were, of course, volunteers, and it was a strange mixture of Professors in the ranks and their students sometimes officers, but off parade you would find them all playing tennis together in the most friendly way possible, and I could not have had a better or happier ending to my stay in the Central Mediterranean Forces and was indeed sorry to leave them and sorry too to leave Rapallo and Portofino, which I did on the 19th of October, calling to lunch with the Kent Yeomanry at Genoa on the way, before going on to Lodi where the General, Denys Reid, gave me a farewell lunch. I left for the Excelsior Hotel, Milan, where I had my release papers. Roy King had arrived back from leave that night and came to say goodbye to me the following day.

I stayed at Milan for three days before leaving by train for Dieppe, passing through Switzerland—a wonderful journey. But by the time I had arrived at Dieppe I was very sick and tired. We were held up at Dieppe for a few days because of the storms, and I was able to take some Services there on the Sunday and visited the local countryside and the Canadian cemetery.

After five days of storm we eventually set off at four in the morning and got to Newhaven at 7.30 a.m.—a still rather stormy trip with a warning that there were some enemy mines about, which didn't help my general state of mind at that time!

We got to London the same day and that same evening I left for Edinburgh, arriving there on the 30th of October and reporting to Redford Barracks. I was able to have tea with my mother.

These six years of war were nearly over now—six years that I would not have missed for anything in the world, six years of a fellowship unknown in civilian life, six years in a world of good fellows where we lived together sharing fun and fear, laughter and tears, when each was out to help his neighbour and the tired man helped the man more tired, the hungry man shared with the man more hungry, where each man carried his own pack but was never too weary to help someone to carry his, or never too proud to allow another to help him on his way. And as I lay down that night I thought too of some of the wonderful sights I had seen. The wonder and amazement when I saw certain parts of the Dolomites and the Tyrol; of the views from my window of Lake Como from Catannabbia, or of Mount Zion from the Scottish Hospice in Jerusalem. But most recently and perhaps most wonderful of all, travelling up from Milan through Italy and through the Simplon Pass, travelling the North West corner of Lake Geneva and seeing the Castle of Chillon and the beautiful town of Lausanne, and then further out the great panorama of the Alps, the great snow-clad vassal mountains stretching for over 100 miles and it seemed into eternity, with Mont Blanc the king of them all and the Dents de Midi and the Matterhorn as very royal princes. All these and so many more were wonderful sights, but the greatest memories of all were memories of comrades and friends I had met on the way. And now it was soon to be over and I was to start again in what had now suddenly become the finest sight of all, "mine own romantic town".

As I lay down to sleep that night the words of P. H. B. Lyon came back to me with new meaning:

Now to be still and rest, while the heart remembers
All that it learned and loved in the days long past,
To stoop and warm our hands at the fallen embers,
Glad to have come to the long way's end at last.

Now to rejoice in children and join their laughter
Tuning our hearts once more to the fairy strain,
To hear our names on voices we love, and after
Turn with a smile to sleep and our dreams again.

Then—with a new-born strength, the sweet rest over,
Gladly to follow the great white road once more,
To work with a song on our lips and the heart of a lover,
Building a city of peace on the wastes of war.

PART IV

Chapter 1

When I eventually got back to the Canongate in December 1945 I must confess I felt at first strangely lonely, rather lost, and very tired. Certainly all was well with the Church and Parish, since during my absence Robbie Fulton and Duncan McNeil, assisted by men like John Summers and George Wilkie, had kept everything going splendidly under the very kindly fatherly eye of George MacLeod, who had himself looked after the Manse at Acheson House, his Edinburgh Headquarters, both for himself and for the Iona Community. What the Canongate owes to George MacLeod is part of its history, as indeed is what the whole Church of Scotland owes to him—part of the history of the Church. Much has been written about him and more has yet to be written, for surely he is the most outstanding Scottish churchman of our generation. As Moderator he dedicated the new Boys' Club Headquarters at Panmure House when H.R.H. The Princess Royal opened it, in 1957. He also dedicated a restored and reoccupied Manse at Reid's Court in 1958, and the restored Russell House in memory of the late Sir David Russell, in Reid's Court. As Lord MacLeod of Fuinary in 1968 he opened the Annexe to the Boys' Club which we called the Harry Younger Hall, of which Lord Home had laid the Foundation Stone in 1967.

I had to try to settle down again after the hectic war years, as indeed hectic they were, and a life that only the Army could give, and a fellowship that no civilian life could ever quite match.

I had to get to know again the young people of the Parish. The fourteen-year olds when I left were now young men of twenty; most had served and even given their lives in the war, and the present fourteen-year olds had been eight when the war started. As an effort to do this I took over an old empty farmhouse from the Bowe family called Aikengall, in the Lammermoor Hills near Oldhamstocks, within fairly good walking distance of Skateraw, and fitted it up with fifty air-raid shelter beds, and there we had some memorable Camps, about which I have written in *Our Club*.[1]

I wrote in August 1946 in my monthly Pastoral Letter:

My dear People,
    This month's number *is* more or less a Pastoral letter! As will be seen, I spent my two months' "exile" at Aikengall—in the kind, friendly Lammermoor Hills I love so much; where from the gate one can look down the valley on to the grass road to Oldhamstocks and up to the sea to that lovely little bay bounded by Fast Castle point. I have had many folk around me here—nearly 200 boys, all over, for a start! And I have carried away with me very happy memories on this the first peace time summer since 1939: that hot summer's day when Mr Coghill and I sat by the burn in peace; the first evening the boys and I saw a fox; the long walks made short by the good fellowship to my Hut at Skateraw and back; that splendid lot of our B.B. fellows with such grand officers; the walks and talks over the moors and the finding of white heather; Billy Brown's care of the French rose and combat with the cow; John Hood jumping off the high dive at Dunbar; Harry Richmond's rabbit; Mr Sellers making scones; chips for supper; Mr Inglis chopping sticks; Pinkey's laugh; Mr Fotheringham's longing look at the distant house when on the skyline above the moors; John and Charlie and Jimmie felling trees; Billy Reid, who like Felix of old "kept on walking"; Jim Kinnaird's putting monkey puzzles into all the beds (except mine and Mr Wilkie's I think); Bill Urquhart's great cross-country win; the sports night with Dalry and St Giles'; reading Kipling and Brooke to Mr Roy Hogg—or later Brigadier Gerard to

[1] *Our Club* (Oliver & Boyd), revised edition 1969.

the "resident members"—(as I came to call Harry, Billy, John, and Charlie) round the log fire at night; General Ritchie's tea party; and "please, sir", "please, sir"— questions, questions, questions . . . and prayers in the quiet barn we have made our Chapel, the cross from the Carpenter's hand at Assisi, the candles and the lamps, the "lights of evening round us shine". He led us by still waters, He restored our souls.

I have come back to Aikengall to "tidy up". I have just walked alone over the well loved places—I saw a hawk and some wood pigeon, some grouse flew out from my feet, a wild duck rose from the duck pond; the many sheep, endless rabbits are left in peace, and around are the everlasting hills looking so lovely in green and purple. But it wasn't *quite* the same.

It is the Feast of the Transfiguration. Somehow I feel we have *had* ours. Was not the Lord of all Good Life transfigured before us? Did not the very prophets and law-givers of old stand out in new clearness and under-standing? "Lord it is good for us to be here." And, as we "came down from the mount"— were we not transfigured ourselves, sunburnt and fit, and very happy. We who have been so privileged have a job to do. "Lord it was good for us to be there"—but there is a crowd at the foot of the mount that needs us all—and, strangely too, we need them now: and we know that though the vision has passed, though not to be forgotten, "Jesus is with us" still. Yes it is the Feast of the Transfiguration—let us lift up our hearts.

6th August 1946,
The Feast of the Transfiguration.

The Appeal had brought in by this time almost all the money that was required to achieve its three-fold purpose— the restoration of the Church, both inwardly and outwardly, the acquiring of Panmure House as a Headquarters for the Boys' Club, and the obtaining of Reid's Court as a Manse once more. Some of this had to wait for several years, but we were quickly able to make a start on the outside of the Church. And as soon as possible in 1946 the front of the Church was cleaned up and from the rest of the building worn stones were removed and replaced, the thick grime and soot was taken off and repairing, renewing, cleaning and painting had to be done. The Canongate crest on the apex, the Royal Arms of King William and the Arms of Thomas Moodie were all now cleaned and painted, making the front of the building take on a new dignity and beauty.

That same year we started the Boys' Choir. Three hundred years before that there had been "singing boys" in Canongate and at Holyrood. So we began with nineteen boys at first, in purple cassocks lent from St Giles'; but soon these were changed to our own scarlet cassocks as befitted a Royal Foundation. As the years went on the number of boys in scarlet cassocks increased to fifty-six.

The outside of the Church having been done, we then began to tackle the restoration inside. This at first was not very easy because of the still standing war-time conditions regarding licences and the like. But the first attack was made on removing the large galleries which blocked a great deal of the light from the Church, and a great deal of the technical troubles were thus removed. Her Majesty Queen Elizabeth at the beginning of the renovation of the interior of the Church graciously and kindly came to see the work being done, accompanied by Princess Margaret, on 17th July 1947. Princess Elizabeth was to have come too, but by this time she had become engaged to Prince Philip.

Immediately after the Queen's visit I set off with 100 boys representing the British Boys of The Boys' Brigade under the leadership of Douglas Pearson Smith, a son of the Founder and an old friend of mine who frequently stayed with me when he came to Edinburgh, who had asked me to come for this special visit, as Chaplain. We sailed to Denmark and must have explored every corner of it; but the highlight was the great Camp of 1,000 boys from Denmark and Norway (most of whom spoke excellent English). It was interesting, so soon after the war, to meet quite a number who had been engaged in the Resistance Movement, and even some of the boys had acted as messengers, and to hear some of the stories of the German occupation. The one I liked most was that which was told me about their King—Christian—of Denmark, who had complained about a Nazi flag being flown on one of the public buildings of his capital. It was contrary to the treaty forced on Denmark by Germany. The German officer said that he took his orders from Berlin. But the old King was not going to be put off by that. "The flag," he said, "must be removed by twelve o'clock, otherwise I shall send a soldier to remove it." At five minutes to twelve, the King repeated his statement that he would send a soldier to remove it; to which the German officer replied "The soldier will be shot". Then the King replied "I am the soldier". The flag was lowered.

The Queen's visit in 1947 was a memorable occasion and was the first visit from the Royal Family since the erection of the present building. In 1937 King George VI had kindly sent a Christmas tree to the Church, a custom that has been maintained ever since, and is greatly appreciated; and in so many other different ways the Royal Family have shown great interest in its Parish Church. A Royal pew had always stood within the Church except for a short time after the 1882 restoration, and when the Church was again restored, a Holyrood pew was again set aside, as well as one for the Governor of the Castle; but the Queen's visit was the first personal visit during all these years and it did more than anything else to encourage us in the restoration.

The next task was a fairly easy one which was to make a centre aisle. It was easy because it didn't mean getting any new material or licences but only cutting through the very long pews and opening up a decent sized centre aisle for processions and the like, where married couples could walk out side-by-side without parting at the first pillar! But what really was the main task was the removal of the "dummy" wall which had for over 100 years covered the apse, and so also the removal of the rather ancient organ which was almost falling apart. In 1950 the wall was removed and with it that old organ, and once more with the apse displayed the Church was seen in its rightful proportions. And on the floor were placed flat stones bearing the names of all the Ministers of Canongate since the Reformation, beginning with John Craig. Various gifts were given to adorn and beautify the newly opened up building with all its renovations. The complete story is told in *The Kirk in the Canongate*.[1]

[1] See especially pages 140-144.

We owed much to our architects Ian G. Lindsay and George Hay (and later to Esmé Gordon) and some of the various Trusts that helped, and not least, and by no means the first or the last time, the Russell Trust; and of course the interest and enthusiasm of the congregation; for even those previously most doubtful and critical "could scarce forbear to cheer".

We were most grateful to the Duke of Buccleuch for his contribution of choir stalls from Bowhill and seats for the pews for Holyrood and the Governor of the Castle. Of the two main stalls one was given by the Dukes of Hamilton, Buccleuch, Argyll and Montrose, and round the stall in Latin I had the words inscribed "Behold how good and pleasant a thing it is for brethren to dwell together in unity"—a reference to the days when the ancestors of these four Dukes would certainly not have combined to give a stall, or for that matter, to do anything else together!

The other main stall was given by the Duke of Roxburghe whose ancestors were superiors of the Canongate until 1636. The main lamp hanging in the chancel was given by Lord Beaverbrook. I had never met him but I knew that he was interested in the Church, and not least in the Church of Scotland, and so I wrote and asked him if he would give this particular lamp, and he wrote back immediately and said he would be only too pleased to do so.

The obtaining of the pulpit was interesting. I had read that Thomas Chalmers' pulpit was in what had been his Church in the West Port and which was now a furniture store, and was still placed there where it had originally stood. The Home Board had been offered it and immediately I got in touch with the Board to ask if I could have it for the Canongate. Harry Richmond and I went along with a barrow and took the pulpit, by this time in pieces and looking very ragged and disreputable (we paid only £5 for it!), and pushed it all the way from the West Port into the Church. Its appearance hardly gave encouragement to those who saw it. It was set up again and painted in the same colours as the rest of the Church and fitted in very well, and it was good to know that Dr Chalmers' pulpit had been rescued. There was a time (in 1819) when he had asked permission to come and preach in the Canongate and was refused!

162

Perhaps one of the most daring parts of the whole restoration was the painting of the Church in a light blue colour with white walls, a change from the rather dull brown pews and equally dull walls; a break that has been followed by so many other Churches since, not least among the extension Churches. It made the Church look bright and cheerful and clean, and after all that is what the "House of God" should be.

Then there is the story of the organ. When the dummy wall that hid the apse was removed in 1950 the organ, of course, had to go too. It had been a second-hand instrument when placed in the Church last century, and was in a bad state of repair in any case, and its only value was now the lead pipes which we sold. A reed organ was bought second-hand to replace it and was placed at the back of the Church; but we hoped that this would be a temporary arrangement and that one day we would be able to find a suitable organ to place in the remaining back gallery. Well, it so happened that one day in September 1959 my friend Canon Cyril Taylor, who was staying with me at the Manse, and I were walking up the Canongate when Mr Notman, the antique dealer, came across the road to tell me that there was a large house in Kinross-shire that was being taken down, that there was a big sale there, and that the house contained a fine organ. Now Cyril Taylor was at that time Principal of the Royal School of Church Music and is one of the greatest authorities on Church music in the country; (I shall never forget how once, when staying with him, his playing over to me on his piano one of the tunes he wrote which has become famous—"Abbots Leigh"). We decided that we must go and see the organ that afternoon before it was too late, and he suggested that we ask Eric Routley, another great authority on Church music, who happened to be staying in Edinburgh at that time, to join us. The three of us set off; they saw and tried out the organ, and decided that it was just what we wanted for Canongate. To dismantle it and set it up again I was told would cost £1,750, so I offered £250 for it and to my amazement the offer was accepted. I now realised that I had bought an organ which would cost £2,000 without a penny to pay for it! All this happened on a Saturday and I said nothing about it on the Sunday. And then on Monday morning I received a telephone call from my friend and lawyer James P. Shaw: "You are hoping to get an organ one day," he said, "well, I have the Misses Legget here in my office and they have offered to give £2,000 towards an organ for Canongate in memory of their brother" (who had been one of our Elders). I said, "Well, as a matter of interest, I got it on Saturday and he said, "What"! And that is how we got our organ—surely another "miracle"! At the "opening" of the organ by Mr Michael Lester-Cribb the choir and orchestra of Fettes College also attended.

Chapter 2

In addition to the Restoration of the Church, the Order of Service was also "restored" in a way more in keeping with the old Scottish Reformed tradition.[1]

The Order of Divine Service was printed first in 1947 and reprinted with some additions and alterations several times since, and is still used each Sunday morning. The congregation were now able to participate more in the worship, repeating together a prayer of Confession, the prayer of General Thanksgiving, the Apostles' Creed (or the Nicene Creed at Holy Communion) as well as the Lord's Prayer. All this the people accepted, as they did when the whole service was no longer taken from the pulpit, which was used for preaching only. It wasn't until our service was first televised on 20th November 1952—the first ordinary service to be televised from Scotland (the only previous service being televised was an afternoon service to mark the beginning of Television in Scotland from the then Moderator's Church, St Cuthbert's)—that some opposition was raised in letters to the papers, and elsewhere, accusing us of Anglicanism and even Popery. It was left to Gordon Donaldson, later Professor of Scottish History at Edinburgh University, to have the last word in a letter to *The Scotsman* of 8th December, 1952:

Sir, since "D.N." finds it difficult to understand "under

[1] See *The Morning Service on the Lord's Day* (Blackwood, 1961).

164

what sect of Christianity" the Canongate Church is held, he might profitably consult the *Book of Common Order* of the Church of Scotland. This would convince him that everything in the Canongate service has the full authority of the General Assembly behind it. He might also turn to an earlier *Book of Common Order*—that used by John Knox. There he would find a service of similar structure.

If, on the other hand, he looked at the Order of Morning Prayer in the *Anglican Book of Common Prayer*, he will find a Service that in structure and content has not the remotest affinity to the Canongate service.

If he cares for historic studies, let him investigate Scottish worship in the seventeenth and eighteenth centuries. He will, I suspect, discover that "the Presbyterian service we all love" was the creation of the late Victorian era. Or does he want to revert to such earlier practices as the exclusion of hymns, the standing posture for prayer, and the absence of Scriptural lessons—all of which were features of the Presbyterian worship at one time?

The Boys' Choir came too under criticism; boys were evidently regarded as "Popish" while I presume women were "Protestant"! When we were offered wax candles on either side of the Communion table there was, from outside, nearly an uproar, so we put electric candles in their place, and peace reigned: candles were "Popish" but electric bulbs were "Protestant"! Such is the nonsense with which some people will argue.

Fortunately full support came from the congregation and I was greatly blessed by having a Session Clerk like John Inglis and a Treasurer like John Sellers, both from old Canongate families, and with them the backing of the Kirk Session. I was fortunate too in having some splendid Assistants who gave me all support and encouragement—in addition to some already mentioned, men like David A. R. McGregor, William Morris, now of Glasgow Cathedral (who in 1978 succeeded me as Senior Chaplain-in-Ordinary to the Queen, when I became again an Extra-Chaplain on my seventieth birthday), Robert J. Henderson (who won a D.S.O. when he was nineteen) now of Melrose, and Hugh Mackay, now Minister of Duns. I was greatly supported too by Deaconesses like Miss Edith Macbeath, Miss Gardiner and Miss Grant, and by so many of the Divinity Students living in Russell House, like Tom Crichton, Jim Colquhoun, Colin Douglas, John Miller, Gordon Haggarty and Gordon Currie. The various Assistants from the United States were too a great blessing to me and to the whole Parish, beginning with Amandus William Loos before the war and Jack Cooper, Wallace Jamieson, Wade Huie, Bob Evans, Andrew Sorensen, and Donald West after the war—some of whom lived with me in the Manse. Of the "laymen" none did more than Harry Richmond—but of him more anon—and our organist David Laidlaw. And of the women, apart from the Deaconesses, none did more than Miss Helen Nimmo.

Without the help of all these, and too many others to mention, it would not have been possible to carry on at the rate we did.

Another "innovation" was to start on each May Day a sunrise service on the summit of Arthur's Seat which has continued ever since, with a congregation of at least 1,000 people of all ages.

It should be needless to add that what matters above all is the spirit and truth of the worship. Sincerity in worship, without which all else is empty, should mean, as we ourselves receive, giving of our best in words and actions, in music and art, in beauty and care, in order and discipline, in devotion and dedication, if we are to "worship the Lord in the beauty of holiness". In the Reformed Church the whole sea is ours, not just a small shallow pond in our garden—all the richness of our Catholic heritage, of the Universal Kirk, of Ecclesia Scoticana Reformata et semper Reformanda.

Chapter 3

Though I have been Minister of only one Church, I have had four Manses. The first was at 3 St John Street which had been one of the Minister of Canongate's Manses since about 1816.

166

St John Street was built in 1768 as a kind of ":suburb" in the midst of Canongate, and had housed in the past many distinguished residents, including the Earls of Wemyss, Hopetoun, Hyndford, Lord Blantyre, and many of the old Scottish nobility who had left their Edinburgh tenement houses to enter the more "respectable" self-contained houses in St John Street. Lord Monboddo when he lived in No. 13 had Robert Burns as a welcome and frequent guest, and it was there that Burns met some of the most distinguished people in Scotland, and also Monboddo's beautiful and accomplished daughter Eliza Burnet, about whom at her death at an early age he was to write one of his loveliest poems:

"We saw thee shine in youth and beauty's pride,
    And virtue's light that beams beyond the spheres;
But like the sun eclipsed at morning tide,
    Thou left'st us darkling in a world of tears."

The poet Campbell lived there and at No. 10, where his printer and friend Ballantyne had his home, Sir Walter Scott was a frequent visitor; in fact every house had some name of distinction living in it. At No. 5 Dr Gregory of Gregory's Mixture fame lived.

Most had moved from the town tenement dwellings. The Earl of Hopetoun, for example, lived in a tenement fronting the Canongate itself with access by the turnpike stair on the West side of St John Street, and it was in that flat where later Mrs Telfer lived, who was the sister of Smollett and where he resided for some time.

Right up to nearly the close of last century the street "maintained its character for respectability" but when I went there the Manse at No. 3 was the only house not divided into flats, and the rest of the street was either demolished or grossly over-crowded.

As mentioned before, in No. 1 157 people lived up one stair, and the whole street was in a very bad state of repair. When I went to the Manse at No. 3 in December 1936 they had to put electricity into the house, since my predecessor had only had gaslight; and though I was delighted to have such a central Manse, it was really in a very poor condition with an old sink and rather leaky roof and general signs of having been

167

neglected for a considerable time, even though the congregation had so kindly not only given me electricity but had it all painted for the arrival of the first new Minister for nearly fifty years.

Though much had been done to help make the Manse as habitable as possible for me, and though I was very happy to settle down there, it soon became clear that sooner or later some other place would need to be found. Largely, I suppose because of the state of the roof and the neglect of past years, the whole place was very damp, and indeed the unused old kitchen in the basement became at times a pond in which rats had swimming galas. I was fortunate to have staying with me Bill Loos from the U.S.A. and Jimmie Dalgleish who had stayed with us previously in Saxe-Coburg Place, one of the finest boys one could ever meet, and my two dogs, Bruach, an Old English Sheepdog, and Nobby, a Sealyham. But clearly another Manse would have to be found for all of us.

Now it so happened that Acheson House in the Canongate had just been beautifully restored by Robert Hurd for the Marquis of Bute, and had been opened for a year to the public, and indeed visited by Queen Mary, and that I heard that its future use was undecided. So I immediately got in touch with Lord Bute's lawyers and Robert Hurd, the Architect, to see if I could get it as a Manse and Clergy House for the Parish. Acheson House had been built in 1633 for Sir Archibald Acheson who had been one of the Secretaries of State for Scotland in the reign of King Charles I. Before it was restored by Lord Bute it had become, like so many old Canongate Houses, divided up into rooms for houses—a then typical congested slum. After considerable negotiations Lord Bute allowed me to rent it during my time as Minister of Canongate, for £140 a year. I wrote to all the people and firms I could think of to ask if they could help, and with the promise of many donations, from the Lord Provost "downwards", I felt able to go ahead in November 1938 and we were able to move from 3 St John Street (which we then decided to use as the Boys' Club) early in 1939. Bill Loos and Jimmie of course came with me, and so did the dogs. Acheson House was a most wonderful place to have, beautifully restored and just opposite the Church—a residence not only for the Minister

168

but for the Assistants and various helpers in the Parish. "Munich" was over and it looked as though there would now be no question of war, and that there were glorious days ahead. I drew up a programme for all the residents as follows:

07.15 a.m. Rise
07.45 a.m. Morning Prayer in Chapel
08.00 a.m. Breakfast
Time for letters, morning paper, etc., walking
10.00 a.m. Service in the Church
10.30 a.m.-01.15 p.m. Reading and study (preceded by a cup of tea)
01.30 p.m. Lunch
Afternoon visiting until, say, 5.45, funerals, weddings, etc.
06.00 p.m. Supper
07.00 p.m. Evening services in Church, weddings, etc.
Evening—lectures, Clubs, etc., study
10.00 p.m. Tea, etc.
10.30 p.m. Compline
Minister on duty does not visit, but stays in or around the House. . . . A Meeting will be held once a week to discuss formally the week's work.

Everything turned out well and even the "ghost" made one or two "appearances". I never "saw" him but Bill Loos did one night in his bedroom, and on the other times when he was "seen" by others, he bore the same description. I did, however, hear him—or his colleague!—on more than one occasion from my bedroom which looked on to the courtyard. I would hear the outer door under the Crest open and footsteps crossing the courtyard and proceeding up Bakehouse Close; I thought that it must be the man who looked after us at the time (who had been one of "Monty's" batmen) going out for a midnight stroll. But one night on hearing the door open I rose from bed to see—and the door was still shut! I changed my bedroom out of interest to see if the new occupant would have the same experience without, of course, mentioning anything to him; and he came and told me the same story. Indeed on one occasion two of them (I think Peter McEwan and George Wilkie) set a watch, heard the door open (although it remained shut), heard the footsteps, though no one was visible, and remained baffled. But it didn't worry us at all. And so the rest of 1939 continued well until on 1st September while I was having a late afternoon bath I heard Walter Scott on the telephone tell me that the "magic word mobilisation" had come and to report to the Drill Hall at East Claremont Street at once. Three days later I left with the Battalion. By this time Jimmie had joined the Royal Horse Artillery at Woolwich, Bill Loos had returned to America and I had got someone to take both Bruach and Nobby; and by November George MacLeod and the Iona Community had kindly taken over the running of Acheson House, which they did until after the War, though I kept my room there.

After I came back from the War three reasons made me decide, very reluctantly, that I should need to leave Acheson House. First the Iona Community had, quite naturally, to seek other accommodation which they found in Candlemaker Row, second the expense of running the house was getting too much, and third the House was rented to me only during the time I was Minister of the Canongate and therefore the Church would not have a permanent Manse for any future Minister; so I decided that we would try to find a Manse for the Church and my successors.

For long I had had my eye on the old Manse in Reid's Court and began to make enquiries about obtaining it; but I soon realised that though it was to be my ultimate objective, it would take some years to negotiate, so in 1947 I managed to get a new Manse at 17 Regent Terrace, overlooking the Parish, and there I remained for the next ten years, and there too Harry Richmond happily came to stay, who has done so much for me ever since. Indeed he has been to me all these years very much what Ambrose St John must have been to Cardinal Newman, for he too "has never thought of himself if I was in question".[1] I brought my golden cocker Goldie with me and soon added Dougall, a golden setter, to our happy "family" which for a time included also Norman Davidson when studying for his medical degree, which he successfully combined with playing for Scotland at both rugger and cricket.

[1] Cardinal John Henry Newman: *Apologia pro Vita Sua*, p. 252 (Oxford Clarendon Press).

We spent ten very happy years in Regent Terrace, during which time Harry was called up for National Service and obtained a Commission when I proudly went to see him passing out as an Officer Cadet at Aldershot. From 1950 to 1952 I had rather a bad time with my spine. Indeed the doctor told me in 1950 after an X-ray that he "would give me four more years if I didn't leave Canongate". I told him that I'd stay on for the "four more years"—and risk it (I actually stayed on for another twenty-seven!) I was motored to the Infirmary twice a week for some time for deep-ray treatment on my spine and had a plaster-cast to sleep in at night. I had to lie on my back most of the day and wasn't able to do anything in the Church or Parish for over two months, and was so glad to have the considerable help of the Rev. David McGregor, so well-known and loved during his six years as Assistant at St Giles', who came for a while as Deputy Minister. For some time before and for many years after, I had hardly a day without considerable pain; but I got used to it, and at least it was better, I'm told, than having a "nagging" wife!

Meanwhile I was still negotiating to get Reid's Court, and in 1957 it eventually became possible.

Chapter 4

Though I had had my eye on Reid's Court as a Manse since I first went to Canongate as Minister, the real "battle for Reid's Court" lasted from 1947 till 1957. It was a battle with the Town, the Presbytery, and with constantly rising estimates and costs. Regent Terrace was found to be full of dry rot and, largely because of that, was sold for the ridiculously small price of £2,200 (recently a similar house was sold there for £45,000!). We were helped by many people, including the Ivory Trust, and not for the first or the last time, by the Russell Trust. The first estimate for the restoration of Reid's Court was for £5,000, then it rose to £9,000 and then to £13,000. But at last the money was found and it was all paid for, with the splendid result that can be seen now.

171

The house in Reid's Court was built at about the same time as the Church, the East and West wings being added to it later—the West being for a time the then Countess of Home's town house. It was for a time, I believe, a Coaching Inn, and was certainly for over forty years the Manse of Dr Buchanan who, helped by his wife, had private means and did so much for the parish, not least for its education. He died there in 1832. The house was later used for various other purposes, the most important probably being the first Kindergarten School in Edinburgh—if not in Scotland. For a time too, later, the Manager of the Edinburgh Gas Company lived there, and when I first saw it, it was largely used for storing gas equipment, the West wing had become derelict, housing itinerant beggars, and the East wing had been divided up into houses. The whole place was badly in need of restoration and the two side wings were joined to the main building. But the main structure of the building was as it had always been; and, though the garden had been greatly reduced since Dr Buchanan's time to make room for the Gas Board, a sufficient garden remained to turn it into the delightful oasis of trees, roses and shrubs, which it became.

Harry Richmond, my beagle Map, and I entered the new Manse at the end of 1957 when it was dedicated by Dr George MacLeod; and another new chapter was to start in the history of Canongate. It was wonderful now to have such a lovely old house in the centre of the parish, with its own courtyard and front and back garden, and its delightful sunny rooms. Many receptions were now held there. Each year the Lord High Commissioner came for lunch on the Sunday preceding the General Assembly, to which other guests were invited, including the Cardinal and the Anglican Bishop, the Keeper of Holyroodhouse, and the successive Governors of the Castle. Dr Warr, who had joined the Canongate after retiring from St Giles', was always a most welcome guest, and the Secretary of State for Scotland came too on more than one occasion. A special afternoon tea reception was arranged in October 1971 for my friends Anthony and Elizabeth Chenevix-Trench, when he came from being Head Master of Eton to being Head Master of Fettes College, and I invited almost everyone I could think of to meet them!

But by far the most memorable visitor was H.M. The Queen who came to the Manse for coffee one morning in May 1969, the year she came in person to the General Assembly. I arranged for some members of the congregation and a number of leading local Canongotians to be presented to her, whom she met in the Hugh Blair Room, before meeting others while she drank coffee in the drawing room; the coffee made by my sister-in-law Clare and her daughter Diana, was especially appreciated! In the small sitting-room off the drawing room some of her suite also drank coffee, among them Sir Martin (now Lord) Charteris, her Private Secretary, Commander Jock Slater, her A.D.C. (whom later I was to assist in marrying at St Columba's, Pont Street, and later became the youngest Captain in the Royal Navy), and Alastair Blair, the Purse Bearer, one of our Elders, who was to be knighted the next day. There too was Seumas, the young Marquis of Graham, who happened to be staying with me at the time. He had deliberately tried to "hide" himself because his father, the Duke of Montrose, was then in the Government of the U.D.I. Rhodesia, and he didn't want to cause any embarrassment to the Queen. When the Queen unexpectedly entered that room and Seumas was presented to her, she asked later why he had not been on the list of presentations; and when this was explained to her, a phone call came from Holyroodhouse inviting him that night to a dinner-dance in the Palace!—just another typical, thoughtful act of the Queen.

Before she left to a rapturous reception from the crowd outside, and not least the children of Milton House School, she planted a tree in the front garden to commemorate her visit.

Among those who came to tea none gave my mother and me more pleasure that Sir John Betjeman, whose poems we both loved so much, and who is such a lovable person himself; and a number of informal supper party meetings were held by a group of friends who called ourselves the Pentagon Club, with such guest speakers as Sir Compton Mackenzie, Sir Iain Moncreiffe, Lord Cameron, Chief Constable Merrilees, Tom Fleming, and the delightful Lord Birsay.

I got to know Compton Mackenzie fairly well when he came to stay in Edinburgh and he kindly invited me to his small eightieth birthday party celebration at Prestonfield

House. He told me once that he was tempted to write a book on the greatest liars he had known, and when I asked him who they were he said "Well, people like Ford Maddox Ford, Axel Munthe and T. E. Lawrence of Arabia!" When John Betjeman came to Holyroodhouse as a guest of the Earl of Wemyss during the Assembly of 1959, he found he had forgotten his evening dress shirt, and we motored from the Palace to Drummond Place to borrow one from Monty Mackenzie's housekeeper, he himself being in France at that time.

Some years later I sent him a note to say how much I had enjoyed re-reading *Sinister Street* and he wrote to me:

Pradelles, Les Arques,
Par Cazals, Lot,
France Les Arques 4.
1st May, 1966.

My dear Doctor,

Your letter about *Sinister Street* gave me the greatest pleasure. It is encouraging to hear that a book over fifty years old still has life in it. Just before your letter came I had a letter from a young woman in New York who had just read it for the first time. When the book was first published I never had any letters from women but they started to come in about twenty years ago—a sign of the times.

We shan't be back in Edinburgh until the end of November but we shall be there over the winter and my wife and I very much hope you will look in on us. I am just about to start on Octave 7 of *My Life and Times*.

With all best wishes,
Yours very sincerely,
Compton Mackenzie.

While we were in Reid's Court, in March 1967, Harry got married, but still continued, as he has always been, such a great help and encouragement to me.

Among those who stayed with me as members of the "family" were Peter Thompson who came, after leaving Fettes, for over two years before leaving for the Far East; Charles, the young Earl of Cassillis, who came to do extra studies, and two outstanding Divinity students, Norman Drummond and Henry Kirk. It was in the Manse that Norman, who was a Cambridge rugger Blue and later captained the Army XV, met his future wife, Lady Elizabeth Kennedy, Charles' sister. All these, and others too, did so much to help in the work of the Church and Parish, and by no means least, in the Boys' Club; and each in his own way gave much help. So the old Manse at Reid's Court was yet another dream come true.

When my beagle Map was killed, run over by a van in a quiet lane near Skateraw and was buried there beside Barney (dear Barney, Dougal's and Goldie's son, who had been with me for nine years before being run over by a skidding taxi when out for an evening walk with Harry in Regent Terrace), another beagle called Happy succeeded him at Reid's Court. Happy was a great favourite too and he died from a heart attack one Sunday before the morning service, and was buried that afternoon in the Manse garden by some of the Royal High School boys from the Boys' Choir, when many tears were shed. He too had been with me for nine years and I felt that I could never get another dog again. But after another year came Gen, then eight weeks old, a Ware black and white Cocker Spaniel who had been given to me by General Sir Derek Lang, then Governor of the Castle (hence his name "Gen") for assisting at the wedding of his daughter Sarah to the Head Master of Roedean, John Hunt. Gen too was much known and loved by everyone; he came in 1969, spent the last years with me at Reid's Court and came with me to Moray Place and was my constant companion until his sad death in October 1979. All my dogs have meant so much to me, and to Harry, and to many others; but none more than the last one!

But there was to be yet another dream come true also in Reid's Court—Russell House. My then doctor—Alastair McLaren—(not the one who in 1950 had given me "four more years"!) had his eye on the empty mid-eighteenth-century house that stood within the gates of the Court; but after much negotiation with the Town he found that it would not be suitable for his purpose and offered it for a small sum to the Canongate Kirk Session for—what I had always wanted—a Church House where Divinity students and others could live

175

and help the Minister in the work of the Parish.

Once again Dr David Russell and the Russell Trust, though unasked, came to our help and not only acquired the House for us but restored it in memory of his father, Sir David Russell, who also had been so kind and generous to us all in the Canongate. I once asked Sir David why he was always so good and kind to the Canongate and me and he said "Because I like to—and you never ask!" David Russell in kindness and generosity has followed in his father's footsteps; and we can never be too grateful to them both and the Trust which had been set up in memory of David's brother who had been killed in the Desert battle of the Second World War.

At first Russell House, which too was dedicated by Dr George MacLeod, was taken over by the New College Missionary Society under the leadership of Tom Crichton who, with four splendid students from New College, did much to help the work of the Parish. The four main rooms were called after Ministers whom Sir David knew well, and who in their turn owed so much to his help and kindness—Dr Charles Warr, Dr George MacLeod, Dr Nevile Davidson, and myself. We were able to start again early morning and evening daily services in the Church—Prime and Compline—and while some visited, others helped in the Boys' Club and the Camp site at Skateraw. When some years later the Missionary Society pulled out and went to Craigmillar, we were still able to keep Russell House going, as it does to this day. Later there was even talk of turning the House into a "Dower" House for the retired Minister, but by that time the Queen had most graciously and kindly offered me Queen's House, her Grace and Favour House in Moray Place.

Chapter 5

The interest shown by the Royal Family in their Parish Church, which was started by the gift of a Christmas tree by King George VI in 1937 (a very much appreciated custom that has been maintained ever since), by the King and Queen,

176

Queen Mary, and other members of the Royal Family contributing to the Appeal for the restoration of the Church, and by the Queen and Princess Margaret visiting the Church to see the beginning of the restoration in 1947, was continued further by the gift from the King of antlers from Balmoral to replace the old antlers given by Dr Lee when he was Minister in 1824, for the apex of the front of the Church. In 1951 the Princess Royal attended morning service, the first member of the Royal Family to do so since the present building had been erected in 1688. She came at her own request since I had got to know her well as Colonel-in-Chief of the Royal Scots—and a very wonderful and much-loved Colonel-in-Chief she was for forty years, taking such a personal interest that she knew the names not only of the officers and N.C.O's but of their families too. Each year I would receive from her a personal card at Christmas to "Dear Mr Selby Wright" with a personally signed book or calendar; and it was at her own request when she attended the morning service again in 1957 that she opened Panmure House after the Service. This new Headquarters of the Boys' Club, which had been restored for us by Mr Roy Thomson (later Lord Thomson of Fleet), was to have been opened by the Duke of Hamilton, the President of the Club, and a plaque had been prepared and set up to that effect, and he and I the day before the opening had to remove the plaque—with some difficulty—to have it altered when we heard that she intended to perform the opening herself.

Great was the excitement and the pleasure when we heard that our new Queen intimated that she would visit the Church on the first morning of her official visit to Edinburgh. And so it was that on the 25th of June 1952 the first reigning sovereign on her first morning in Edinburgh as Queen entered the Church. As her Mother, now the Queen Mother, and her sister had done at their visit in 1947, the Queen planted a tree after she had seen the restoration of the Church.

A further tree was added when the Duke of Edinburgh visited the Church in the following year, and in 1970 a fifth Royal tree was planted by the Prince of Wales after a similar visit. The large Church Bible was signed too by each member of the Royal Family. In addition to his visit to the Church in 1953, the Duke of Edinburgh visited the Boys' Club in

Panmure House in 1958 and the Queen was to return to the Church in 1965 to unveil a plaque giving the history of the Church from the days of David I, which had been presented by the last ten Governors of the Castle from 1945-65. The plaque was dedicated by Dr Warr, Dean of the Chapel Royal and of the Order of the Thistle, and the then Governor, Lt.-General Sir George Gordon Lennox, was present, accompanied by some of the former Governors. By this time I had been appointed first an Extra-Chaplain to the Queen in 1961 and then a Chaplain in 1963—an office I was very privileged to hold until my seventieth birthday in 1978, when once again I became an Extra-Chaplain.

The Sovereign's interest in the Church could be seen too in the Queen's gracious gift of a silver chalice to mark the occasion of my Silver Jubilee as Minister of Canongate in 1961, which was presented to me for the Church by Dr Warr on behalf of the Queen, at a short but notable ceremony in Canongate Tolbooth at which Professor J. S. Stewart spoke so well—notable not least because it was the last appearance of my dear mother before she went south to stay with my sister and her family at Richmond in Surrey, never again to return to Edinburgh.

The beautifully restored Church now became often used for special services and a popular place for weddings. Among the former can be numbered the Memorial Service for King George VI to which the garrison troops marched from Edinburgh Castle, and the Lessons were ready by General Sir Gordon Macmillan, the Governor; the Service to commemorate the Centenary of the Canongate becoming a part of the City of Edinburgh, in 1956, in which year the University of Edinburgh, largely, I heard later, through the Principal Sir Edward Appleton, Professor John Macmurray and Professor John Baillie, awarded me an Hon. D.D. when I was further honoured by being capped by the Duke of Edinburgh as Chancellor of the University, and as the Principal pointed out "one of his own parishioners".

It became the custom for some years for the Lord High Commissioner to attend the Church on the Sunday preceding the opening of the General Assembly, and in 1976 the Duke of Gloucester invested the new Duke of Hamilton as Prior of the

Order of St John, as successor to David, Marquis of Aberdeen, whose early death had so saddened us all, at a great service held in the Church. But possibly the most outstanding service of all was held in May 1976 when the King's Own Scottish Borderers laid up their old Colours, handed to me for their safe keeping by their Colonel-in-Chief Princess Alice, Duchess of Gloucester, because, added to the significance of the Service itself, among those who took part was the much-loved Cardinal Gray, the first Scottish Cardinal since the Reformation, who gave the Blessing. This was especially significant since at the time the Regiment was serving in Ireland and indeed the officers and men present had come from Ireland for this special occasion, and returned there the following day. It was good to see my good friend Brigadier Frank Coutts, now Colonel of the Regiment, accompanied by the Commanding Officer, Allan Alstead, who had been married by me in the Church, and their former Colonel, Sir William Turner, and to have taking part in this memorable service, Dr Nevile Davidson, Farquhar Lyall, the A.C.G., James Gardiner, our Hon. Assistant for many years, and, from the Manse, Norman Drummond and Henry Kirk. Sir David and Lady Scott-Barrett were, of course, present too, for since he had become Governor of the Castle, they had regularly attended our Services.

Two notable School Services in the Church too deserve special mention. In 1968 a "Farewell to the Old Town" service was held when the Royal High School had to leave its long, distinguished and historic connection with the old town of Edinburgh to go to its new buildings at Barnton. In many ways 7th June 1968 was a sad day because for over 800 years "Schola Edinensis" had been situated in the old town of Edinburgh and its first Rectors were the Abbots of Holyrood. The very future of the School was, largely for political reasons, even then in doubt. I gave the Address[1] and Dr Warr the Blessing; and as we watched the long procession of boys and masters returning up the pathway to the fine building that they were soon to leave ("the finest setting for any School in Britain" Dr Lionel Smith once called it) Dr Warr turned to me and said "the end of another chapter in Scotland's history".

[1] *Schola Regia*, Volume 64, No. 185: July 1968.

Then there was the great Centenary Service of Fettes College on 31st May 1970, an evening service in memory of the Founder Sir William Fettes, when, at the close, a wreath was laid by the Head Master and the Head of School on his tomb in the Churchyard.[1]

On both these occasions the Church was filled with members of these two Schools, and in the preparation of the Address I was able to learn much of their notable history.

I was asked too to preach the sermons at the 150th anniversary of the Edinburgh Academy in 1974 at the Academy, and the 150th anniversary of Loretto School in 1977 in Loretto Chapel[2] and so was able to learn, to my great benefit, more of the fine history of another two of our great Scottish Schools.

Chapter 6

That Edinburgh Castle is a part of the Canongate parish, though separated by the High Street, the Lawnmarket and Castle Hill, may seem rather strange. This dates from the foundation of the Abbey of the Holy Rood (or Cross) in 1128 by King David I "in honour of the Holy Cross, the Blessed Virgin, and all the Saints". Before occupying and controlling the Abbey, the Canons of the Order of St Augustine had lived within Edinburgh Castle, which at that time was not only a fortress but also a Royal Palace; and when the Charters of the Abbey were drawn up a part of the Abbey's revenue came from the Church of the Castle, over which it had from then onwards superiority and right of Sanctuary; and to this day "The Castle and all its pertinent buildings is within this parish". So the Minister of the Canongate (the Kirk of Holyroodhouse) is also Minister of Edinburgh Castle; but he is not necessarily Chaplain to the Castle, which is an Army appointment.

When I became Minister the Chaplain was Dr Warr. On 2nd

[1] *The Fettesian*, Volume XCII, No. 3: Summer 1970.
[2] *The Lorettonian Magazine*, No. 4: January 1978.

May 1938 I had been appointed a Chaplain in the Territorial Army to the 7/9th (Highlanders) Battalion, the Royal Scots (known as "The Dandy Ninth") and on Dr Warr's resignation as Chaplain of the Castle I was appointed Chaplain in March 1939; but when war broke out and the Battalion was mobilised in September of that year, I had to give up that Chaplaincy. It was not until after the death of the then Chaplain, the Rev. W. W. Morrell, that I was again appointed Chaplain in October 1959, and in 1971 at the request of the then Governor, General Sir Henry Leask, became, too, Chaplain to the Governor of the Castle, which offices I retained after my retiral as Minister (along with Honorary Membership of the Officers' Mess) and as such, accompany the Lord Lyon and Heralds with each Governor in procession into the Castle after his Installation.

My connection with the Castle both as Minister and as Chaplain has brought me into close relationship and friendship with the General Officers Commanding in Scotland, in their capacity as Governors of the Castle, since 1937, but chiefly from the time of the first post-war Governor, my old friend General Sir Neil Ritchie, whom I had had the honour and pleasure of serving as Senior Chaplain in 1942-43 when I shared a Mess with him, Lt.-Colonel James Cassels (later Field-Marshal) and Lt.-Colonel Tom Craig. It was then that I was able to see for myself the true greatness of Neil Ritchie, who had just returned from Commanding the 8th Army in the Desert. It took a great man to be posted from being an Army Commander to a Divisional Commander without bitterness or excuse. But then, Neil Ritchie was a great man[1]—as the 52nd Lowland Division was quickly to see; and later 12th Corps, South-East Asia Command and Washington were later to learn. It was through him that a special pew was placed for the use of the Governor of the Castle in Canongate; and he and his wife Sunny were as welcome in Canongate as they made me welcome at Gogar Bank which I began in their days frequently to visit and where I baptised their daughter.

[1] When, thirty-seven years later, I went as a guest of Michael Gow to the Tattoo at Edinburgh along with Prince Edward and Field-Marshal Sir Gerald Templar, two months before he died, who was taking the Salute, at dinner Neil Ritchie's name was mentioned, "I can't tell you", said the Field-Marshal, "how much I admire that man!"

All the Governors I have known have been, without exception, outstanding men of great faith, ability and kindness, with the most delightful and charming wives. To mention some and not others would be invidious, but I cannot help but mention a few as typical of all those who, like Neil Ritchie, became special friends. There was General Sir Gordon Macmillan who opened our War Memorial Chapel in the Church in 1951, who too brought the Garrison from the Castle for the Memorial Service for King George VI, and who started the practice which continued as long as they were held on Sundays, of inviting me and the Boys' Choir in their scarlet cassocks to take the Epilogue at the Tattoo in the Castle. His very able A.D.C. was Captain Colin Mitchell, later to win fame as "Mad Mitch", the outstanding Commanding Officer of the Argylls at Aden. There was "Tiny" Barber—who on his attendance on his last day as Governor wore our Boys' Club tie.

There was General Sir Horatius Murray who, with his artist wife Beatrice, hardly ever missed a morning service in Canongate, and who were both so kind to my mother. When we unveiled a memorial to her (and my father) in the Church—the beautiful "Penitence of St Hubert" by my friend Josephina de Vasconcellos—it was he whom we asked back to do so. "Nap" Murray was also Colonel of the Cameronians, his dearly loved "poison dwarfs", and had, previous to coming to Scottish Command, commanded the Commonwealth Forces in Korea, and after leaving Scotland became Commander-in-Chief Allied Forces, North Europe. I shall always remember his answer to a rather pompous lady at the time of the Suez crisis who said to him "But you know, my dear General, oil is so important". "Yes ma'am, but there is something more important than that—people, ma'am, people!"

Then there was Lt.-General Sir William Turner and his wife Nancy, whom I had first known as a Major, always so cheerful and unpompous, a much loved Colonel of the K.O.S.B., before the equally cheerful and unpompous Frank Coutts succeeded him. As a prominent member of the Royal Company, the Queen's Bodyguard for Scotland, I still meet him frequently as their Chaplain, and, though a Lord-

Lieutenant and all the rest of it, he never changes—always the same old "Willow".

General Sir Derek Lang and Elizabeth have always remained among my best friends. I first got to know him when he was Chief of Staff at Scottish Command, then later as Commander of Highland District—then a Major-General held that office—before he came as a Lt.-General to Scottish Command. It was he, as I have already mentioned, who gave me my beloved dog Gen (called after him!) when I assisted at the wedding of his daughter Sarah, who had for a time been such a wonderful hostess at Gogar Bank. Later he did so much, as Chairman, for the Veterans at Whitefoord House, and all his life has been concerned to help other people.

Lt.-General Sir George Gordon Lennox, with his wife Nan, brought a touch of Guards polish to Scottish Command, and their kindliness and friendliness will long be remembered. They both did much for the Church and the community, as well as for the Army. After they left I have spent some very happy days with them at Gordon Castle, needless to say so beautifully restored by Nan; for wherever she went she restored. Government House at Sandhurst, where I have stayed on seven occasions when preaching at Sandhurst during the terms as Commandants of General Sir John Mogg and General Sir Peter Hunt—two of the greatest men one could ever meet—was completely restored by Lady Gordon Lennox while Geordie was Commandant there; she restored the Commandant's House at Tidworth, and, on coming to Scottish Command, both Gogar Bank and the Governor's House at the Castle, where they sometimes lived, were completely restored by her; and his term of office as Army Commander and Governor left a marked impression. They kindly invited me to lunch with the Queen when she came to Gogar Bank on the morning after she had unveiled a plaque in the Canongate, giving the story of its foundation from David I, and presented by the Governors since the end of the War. Though a Grenadier Guardsman, in which Regiment his sons are following so successfully, he made an outstanding Colonel of the Gordon Highlanders, only retiring from that office in 1978 after Prince Charles had become Colonel-in-Chief, which gave both Geordie and the Prince of Wales, and the Gordons, so much pleasure.

I owe a special debt of gratitude, too, to Lt.-General Sir Henry Leask and to his wife Zoë for all he did for me while I was Moderator. No one could have given me more help and encouragement. During the Assembly he gave me an excellent Army Orderly, Lance-Corporal Alasdair Hope, who stayed in the Manse and looked after me there and at the Assembly, and who later became an officer in the K.O.S.B. before returning to Rhodesia. He allowed Tommy and Mary Nicol, while he was my Senior Chaplain, to stay in the Governor's House at the Castle throughout the Assembly. Tommy, whom I had known since he was five years old, was at that time Assistant Chaplain-General and destined to be the Queen's Domestic Chaplain at Balmoral, and when he was succeeded as Senior Chaplain-Scotland by W. G. A. Wright, it was again largely due to Henry Leask that such excellent arrangements were made for my visits to see the Black Watch in Hong Kong and the Royal Highland Fusiliers in Singapore, with the Royal Air Force taking me there and back, and with Willie Wright as the Chaplain accompanying me on such a memorable journey.

No one did more to help and encourage the Church than Lt.-General Sir David and Elise Scott-Barrett. His term of office coincided with my last years as Minister, and also "saw in" my splendid successor, the Rev. Charles Robertson. They were most regular and appreciative in their attendance at Church and entered into the life of the Church and Parish in the most practical way. Lady Scott-Barrett, a Roman Catholic, always attended with him; and often when he had other Sunday Army services, would attend on her own. When the Church appealed for cleaners, she came and helped to dust and scrub, and at any function she was the first to be found washing the dishes! Even after I left the Canongate, and during the rather long vacancy, they still kept up their attendances and their interest; and on two occasions I was invited to stay for some days at Gogar Bank as their guest—even to Christmas dinner with them and their three sons. Canongate can never be too grateful to them; and indeed the whole of

184

Scotland will ever be thankful to them for all they did during his term of office. They made a wonderful team; and it was typical of him that before he left in January 1979 he shook hands and spoke to every member of Scottish Command.

David's successor, Lt.-General Sir Michael Gow, also a Scots Guardsman and a fine Churchman too, occupied the Governor's pew in Canongate each Sunday, and even joined the Choir! I spent very happy Christmas and Easter days with him and Jane and their charming family; and, though their time with us all was shorter than others, they will be greatly missed. As I write he has had accelerated promotion before his full term of office is over to be Commander Northern Army Group and Commander-in-Chief B.A.O.R. and the next Governor is another friend—Lt.-General Sir David Young, which will give particular pleasure to the Royal Scots since he is at present their Colonel. How lucky we are to have such really outstandingly good and kind men of faith as the Governors of Edinburgh Castle!

Before I leave the Castle I should add a word about St Margaret's Chapel—its oldest building.

Though services were always held in the Castle and from the time of the Reformation Elders of the Canongate Kirk were appointed to assist the Ministers and Chaplains to watch over its spiritual welfare, it is sad to think that after the Reformation the little Chapel itself was practically forgotten and that as recently as 1845 it was used by the battery of the Castle for storing the gunpowder with which salutes were fired on special occasions. The small round-headed window on the South was built up, and the central window was blocked up and long forgotten and misused and it was almost unrecognisable as a Chapel. Of the few historical remains of Edinburgh which have escaped the destroying hand of time and conflict, the Chapel of St Margaret is the oldest and, in many respects, the most interesting. The interior presents much the same appearance as it did in the days of Queen Margaret.

Sir Daniel Wilson brought it to the country's notice in 1845. An effort at restoration, which was supported by Queen Victoria, was carried out under his supervision in 1853 when the five small windows were filled in with stained glass, later replaced as we have them now by the beautiful windows by Dr Douglas Strachan. But it was not until 1929, by the vision, action and generosity of the late Sir David Russell, that a start was made to restore it, not only to its former glory, but to something of its former use. After much negotiation by Sir David with the Secretary of State for Scotland, the Home Secretary, and even the Prime Minister, and with the support of the Ministry of Works and the late Dr Charles L. Warr and Dr George F. MacLeod (now Lord MacLeod of Fuinary), on the 16th of March 1934, the restored and refurnished Chapel was dedicated.

In 1942 the St Margaret's Chapel Guild was started under the patronage of H.R.H. The Princess Margaret and the enthusiastic leadership of the late Lady Russell, to arrange that those with the name of Margaret should supply and place flowers in the Chapel of St Margaret in Edinburgh Castle each week of the year, to keep the life and principles of St Margaret of Scotland before Scottish women and girls as an example of good and Christian womanhood, and to encourage the use of the Chapel as often as possible for public and private devotions.

And so now this old Chapel has been restored to something of its former beauty and each week Margarets of Scotland are responsible for the flowers in it throughout the year. The first to do this, by gracious permission of another much-loved Scottish Queen, was the Princess Margaret; and Margarets from the richest to the poorest now follow the Princess in making this offering to the greater glory of God and to the beautifying of this Chapel built so long ago by their saintly Queen, whose name they bear.

In 1957 I produced a booklet with contributions from the Right Rev. Monsignor Ronald Knox and Dr Lucy Menzies which is sold in the Chapel and brings in several thousand pounds a year for various charities, having by 1980 sold a million copies. I was especially glad to have Ronnie Knox as one of my fellow contributors for I always admired him so much as a man and as a writer. He contributed to *Asking Them Questions* and I have a number of letters from him in his own handwriting, and one that I especially prize since it was written shortly before he died:

Mells,
1st July 1957.

Dear Dr Selby Wright,

Thank you so much for your exceedingly kind letter; it's a great consolation to know that anything one's written has, by God's Disposition, been of use to somebody. I haven't anything to complain of; more than I'd any right to expect. I've been allowed to write the books I should have wished to get written—but the nearer approach of death drives one back, more than ever, on the formula "Nothing in my hand I bring". Really nothing; no *lively* sentiments of faith, hope or charity, only an obstinate capacity for *trust*. I shall greatly value your prayers for my perseverance in that attitude; the disease from which I'm suffering produces a kind of languor in the mind which makes me feel terribly dependent on the prayers of others. With all my best wishes.

Yours very sincerely,
R. A. Knox.

Chapter 7

The Palace of Holyroodhouse has a close relationship with the Canongate since it is within the Parish; and, indeed, as the Parish Minister, I was invited not only to all the Royal and Lord High Commissioners' Garden Parties, but, thanks to the Hereditary Keeper of Holyroodhouse, the good Duke of Hamilton, I was also invited from time to time to most interesting dinners and teas at the Palace. At dinners I met men like the Presidents of India and Pakistan, of France and Italy, and, at tea, the King of Nepal ("he doesn't like 'small talk' " I was warned), and the Russian leaders Bulganin and Khrushchev, who visited Edinburgh under the greatest security precautions I have ever seen. I remember remarking to General "Nap" Murray that I preferred Bulganin, but he answered, "Ah, but did you see his eyes?"

Another memorable time at Holyrood was the dinner-dance given for King Hussein of Jordan who was very keen on Highland dancing. I had a not uncommon bad attack of arthritis that evening and so was, thankfully, not able to join in, and sat beside his then English wife, the charming Princess Muna, who was too tired that evening to dance. We were joined by the then Air Force Commander's daughter who had been in the same hockey team at school, and they talked of their schooldays together. During the Queen's visits to Holyrood I had the pleasure of meeting the Kings of Norway and Sweden. The King of Norway greatly pleased me by saying how much he had admired the Manse when passing up and down the Royal Mile!

One of the most interesting dinners was when Prince Charles was staying with the Duke and Duchess of Hamilton and for the first time at Holyrood in 1964—full of life and fun. This was the third "first time" that I had met him. In 1957 when I was staying at Balmoral I had seen him setting off to school for the first time when, with the young Princess Anne beside me, I saw him leave with his father and the Queen to go to Cheam; and that evening I went with Princess Margaret to have dinner with the Queen Mother at Birkhall. The second occasion was when he came to see me at Gordonstoun, a rather homesick small boy in his first term there. Then in 1967 he invited me to a small dinner-party consisting of a schoolboy friend and his detective—the first time he had been the host at Holyrood. Although it was a private visit, to which he had invited me by phone, somehow some of the papers heard about it and produced a garbled and inaccurate account next day to my embarrassment. He too had seen it and sent me a typical charming letter from school in which he wrote:

. . . It was a great pleasure to see you again on Sunday evening and I was glad that you could come to dinner and weren't I hope too busy. The papers seemed to think that I had tried to go to the Canongate on Sunday morning, but that you had advised me not to go because of the footballers. Apparently I had invited you to dinner as an alternative to going to Church! I hope the press didn't bother you afterwards.

The short stay in Edinburgh went all too quickly and the

brief change to civilisation in Holyrood was short-lived by a rapid return to Gordonstoun. Thank you once again for two such splendid books (I had sent him the *Jerusalem Bible* and John Buchan's *Montrose*, since we had discussed them that evening) and for the useful advice as to whom one might ask to speak here. I do hope I shall see you again before too long,

Yours very sincerely,

Charles.

This was the kind of personal letter that I was to receive from him from time to time, and also each year a personal Christmas card—typical of his thoughtfulness, kindness and courtesy.

Quite my most memorable times at Holyrood were the three occasions when I stayed there as Chaplain to the Earl and Countess of Wemyss when he was Lord High Commissioner, in 1959 and 1960. No one could have been a greater or more suitable Lord High Commissioner than David Wemyss with his great knowledge of Scottish history and tradition. These days at Holyrood were among the happiest days of my life, not only because of the gracious kindness of Lord and Lady Wemyss but also because of their suite which included the Purse-Bearer David Scott-Moncrieff, Bailie of Holyrood, steeped in the romance and knowledge of Scotland's history, the Lady-in-Waiting, the Countess of Ellesmere (later the beloved, Diana, Duchess of Sutherland), sister of the Duchess of Hamilton, and one of the most charming and gracious people of all time whose funeral and memorial service I took when she died after a courageous illness in 1978. The Maids of Honour included Lady Caroline Douglas-Home, Lady Elizabeth Charteris and Miss Robina Dallmeyer. They all, with the A.D.C's, made one of the happiest "families" you could ever meet; and added to them were the many guests who included John Betjeman (whom I took one day to visit the Zoo), Sir Arthur Bryant who was quite thrilled by the Assembly, and especially by the singing of "The Lord of Heaven confess", Sir Bernard Lovell and others like Lord Hailsham and Lord Maclean, then the Chief Scout.

Of the many guests at Holyrood through the years there

189

were none that gave me more pleasure to meet again than Field-Marshal "Bill" Slim (who came the year that General Sir Richard O'Connor was Commissioner in 1964) unless it was Lady Astor, the first woman M.P. I happened to be sitting beside her at lunch during the Assembly of 1957 when she suddenly turned to me and said, "You look tired. You need a holiday. I shall send you £25 to get one. . . . No, I'll make it £50!" I thanked her but said I didn't need a holiday—or the money (both statements being hardly true!); but sure enough some months later on 19th August, when I had forgotten all about it, a cheque for £100 with a note in her own handwriting, "I hope you will spend this on a good holiday for yourself. . . . Nancy Astor", arrived.

In 1963 I note in my Journal, which I began to keep daily from then onward, a conversation at Holyrood with Lord Elphinstone about his experiences as a prisoner-of-war, when he told me how greatly helped his fellow-prisoners had been by my Radio Padre broadcasts and not least by the "coded" ones from M.I.9; and a talk I had with Eric Linklater suggesting that he wrote the life of General Hector Macdonald in which he showed great interest, but which, alas, was never written.

On one occasion in 1960 when getting out of our car as we reached the entry to Holyrood the driver said to me "Excuse me sir, but isn't that General O'Connor?" I said that it was and that that year he was a guest at the Palace. "Oh," he said, "I should love to meet him again; you see I was General Neame's driver when he and General O'Connor were captured in the Desert in 1941, along with me, and I haven't seen him since." I immediately ran after the General and told him and the two shook hands and had a long talk together. To see the much-beloved and respected "Dick" O'Connor and his old driver meeting together after all these years was for me a never-to-be-forgotten sight. . . . I remember too David Scott-Moncrieff and myself in May 1960 watching from the dining-room the Cameron Highlanders guard led by their pipes and drums marching out of Holyrood for the last time before the Regiment was amalgamated with the Seaforth Highlanders in February 1961. . . . But then Holyrood is full of memories of past and present history; for there was yet another historical occasion when in July 1978 I baptised Alexander Douglas, Marquis of Clydesdale, the son and heir of the Keeper of Holyroodhouse and probably, as the Earl of Selkirk was to point out at the Reception in the Palace later, the first baptism in the old Abbey Kirk since 1687.

Chapter 8

My most memorable stay at Holyrood was also in 1960 as Chaplain when in October the Queen and the Duke of Edinburgh came for the celebration of the quarto-centenary of the Reformation in Scotland, and Her Majesty attended the General Assembly in person, the first Sovereign to do so since 1602 when King James VI, in an era of less happy relations between Church and Throne, bent a suspicious eye on the doings of the Scottish Churchmen.

The Queen and Prince Philip had among those staying with them, the Lord High Commissioner (the Earl of Wemyss), the Countess of Wemyss and four members of His Grace's suite—the Lady-in-Waiting, the Countess of Ellesmere, later Duchess of Sutherland, David Scott-Moncrieff, the Purse-Bearer, an A.D.C. and myself. Prince Philip had obviously "done his homework" about the Scottish Reformation, and made us all wish that we had done likewise, and I was amazed how the Queen was able to talk about all the many people who had been presented to her at the large Reception held in the Palace, as she sat talking round the fire after they had gone. Holyrood cannot be such a comfortable place to stay in for the Royal Family, and lacks the homeliness of Balmoral. Balmoral is a real home where the Royal Family can relax and be at comparative peace. Holyrood is quite different.

I was the Queen's guest at Balmoral on three occasions. The first I have already mentioned when Prince Charles went to school, and the previous evening we had sat round the fire and played "consequences"; the second occasion was in 1972 when I was Moderator and on the first evening we had a film show and the second we had a picnic in Queen Victoria's cottage

191

beside the Loch where Prince Philip, Prince Charles and Princess Anne did the cooking; the Queen set the table and the singing round the fire was led by the Queen Mother and Princess Margaret. "Why didn't you have a Paraphrase this morning?" Prince Philip asked me. I explained that I hadn't chosen the hymns. "Well," he said, "I like the paraphrases; let's sing a paraphrase now." And sure enough we all sang "O God of Bethel"! Apart from myself the only other non-Royals present were the Queen Mother's Lady-in-Waiting and the charming Patrick Plunkett who died shortly after of cancer.

My third visit to Balmoral was in 1977 when I was due to retire as a Chaplain-in-Ordinary and become again an Extra-Chaplain. On the first night we had a small dinner-party with the Queen and Princess Margaret, presided over by Prince Edward, and then after dinner, as on the second night when Prince Philip, Prince Charles and Prince Andrew were also present, we sat round the fire talking, and I was able to see again for myself what a really happy family the Royal Family is. I was able to thank the Queen personally for letting me have The Queen's House in Edinburgh and gave her a specially bound copy of my new book *Seven Sevens* and gave too a similarly bound copy to Prince Charles who had so kindly allowed me to dedicate the book to him. Earlier and before dinner, and after I had had tea with Tommy and Mary Nicol at Crathie Manse, I had visited the Queen Mother at her request, when she was pleased too to accept a specially bound copy of my new book, and where, as usual, she was so happy and relaxed at Birkhall.

This may seem a strange diversion from the Royal Visit to Holyrood in October 1960—but I couldn't help comparing life at Holyrood and Balmoral!

There was one rather amusing decision that Sir Thomas Innes of Learney, the Lord Lyon, was called upon to make at the October 1960 visit, though few knew about it. The Lord Provost's department pointed out that since the Queen was there in person the Lord High Commissioner had no "status" as such and that therefore the Lord Provost as the local Lord Lieutenant took precedence over the Earl of Wemyss as long as the Queen was present. But the Lord Lyon, who knew more about precedence than anyone else, gave his ruling: since the Queen was present the Lord Lieutenant had no "status" either and since Lord Wemyss was an Earl and the Lord Provost a Knight, Lord Wemyss took precedence!

When the Queen took leave of the Fathers and Brethren her place in the Throne Gallery was immediately taken by the Lord High Commissioner, and the Lion Rampant took the place of the Royal Standard on the flagpost at Holyroodhouse. It was in more ways than one an unique visit.

Before leaving Holyroodhouse I would mention the Services of Holy Communion held on the earlier part of the Sunday morning halfway through the Assembly. These were started when Lord Wemyss was Lord High Commissioner and I was not only his Chaplain but also the Parish Minister; and it was in the latter position that I conducted the Services there. The 1959 Service was the first Celebration of Holy Communion according to the Reformed rite to be held within the ruins of the old Abbey Kirk of Holyroodhouse since 1687, and it was significant that the Communion Cups used were these still in use in the Canongate which had come out of the old Kirk at Holyrood. A dozen or so of our choirboys in their scarlet cassocks, white frills and light blue girdles, led the singing and four of the Canongate Elders assisted me. Their Graces with their suite and household guests, as well as any of those who worked in the Palace, including the Guard, were invited to attend. This Service was to continue for the next thirteen years; and all who attended these Services found great peace in the old Abbey with the sun coming through the old windows and, especially noted by all present, the birdsong—a gracious oasis in the midst of a busy week. In 1964 owing to the bad weather, the Service was held in the East drawing-room—the first time that a Service of Holy Communion had been held within the Palace itself; and in 1965 the Service had an added significance and interest since the Cameronians formed the Guard of Honour that year and before the Service could start, the Captain of the Guard came up to me and saluted and said that I was now able to proceed with the Service since no enemy was in sight and the pickets were posted—shades of the days of the Covenanters!

193

Chapter 9

I had hardly got settled down again to work in the parish when I was asked in 1946 if I would become the first Chaplain in Aberdeen University. The request was completely unexpected; but so strong was the pressure put on me by so many people, and not least by the Principal, the much-loved and respected Sir William Hamilton Fyfe and my good friend Dr William Neil, that after much consideration I accepted, only to cancel my acceptance by telegram the same day—so that the refusal came before the acceptance! It wasn't that I wanted to leave the Canongate, but the unexpected challenge to start something new and with so many men recently demobbed from the War, as well as the younger students, made me feel at first that this would be like the days as a padre again, since, being demobbed myself, I was still feeling rather lost without them. But then the Vision I had for the Canongate returned, and with it went the telegram of refusal. In any case Allan McArthur who was appointed in January 1947 and whom I had known when he was Chaplain of the Scots Guards in Italy, made a much better Chaplain than ever I would have been.

It was when I was staying with the Principal (just after my refusal) that he told me how Dr Nathaniel Micklem, whom we both knew so well and respected so much, phoned him one evening to ask him how he was enjoying Karl Barth's Gifford Lectures at Aberdeen, and to ask what they were about; to which the Principal replied: "I think that what he is saying is that few are called and none are chosen!" Some years later, in 1956, when Barth was getting an Hon. LL.D. at the same time as I was getting an Hon. D.D. from Edinburgh University, I told him this to his great amusement. He was, of course, the greatest theologian of our time and a man of great kindness and humanity. He was, too, a great lover of music and made us laugh by telling us how "when the angels were playing before God they always played Bach, but when they were on their own they played Mozart".

Some years later I received an even greater challenge—this time in 1954—when I received a letter from Sir David Russell, then the Accessor to the Chancellor of St Andrews University, dated 2nd January 1954, asking if I would accept the

Principalship of St Mary's College, since there was a very good chance that I would be offered it. And this was my reply dated 28th January:

My dear Sir David,

I have been thinking a great deal about your kind letters to me and the visits I have paid to you about the Principalship of St Mary's College, St Andrews. As I have mentioned more than once, the very suggestion of it has come as a very real shock to me for I have never seen myself anywhere else than in the Canongate, where I am so very happy and where there is so much to be done. I went there when I was young and I have made a lot of mistakes, and I should like to do better. It is all so very much a "family", e.g., of the forty-eight boys in the choir at least forty I baptised as babies! Then there is the Boys' Club which I have run now since I went to St Giles' in 1927, and where I spend still four evenings a week and where now some of the sons of former boys are members. To me, as a bachelor, the Canongate Church is like a wife and the parish, the choir, the club and the others, like my family. And I have had no higher ambition—for I feel that there is none—than to do my best for that "family".

In my most ambitious moods—though it may seem to you to be rather conceited of me—I have tried to model my ministry on that of Arthur Stanton of Holborn, who shortly after his Ordination wrote to his mother that the most real way of working a parish was to give up time and money and even health and life, if need be, to work in the "most glorious work ever given to men—that of saving souls; working to displace vice by purity, hatred by love, despair by joy". St Alban's was his only charge, and he was a curate there for fifty years. As with Stanton at St Alban's so has Canongate been my ambition. I put my hands to the plough and haven't got very far.

On the other hand One greater than Stanton did tell us that there may be times when a man had to give up things he held dear for another field of service, and that there is no "wall" to the field that needs to be ploughed.

That you should have thought of asking me if I would accept the Principalship of St Mary's I count a very high

195

honour indeed, and because it came from you and came unsought, I feel that if St Andrews want me I could not easily turn aside.

I am not in the least bit interested in the stipend—my present stipend is £550 and I have been able to live on that; but I would be concerned to know how much work there would be to do—and the more the better. Since there is no Chaplaincy at St Andrews would the Court be prepared to include in the Principalship the Chaplaincy and the responsibility of the Chapel?

Having made my position then clear, St Andrews approached me again, this time to invite me to be the first Chaplain at the University. The Principal wrote and offered me the post and great pressure was put on me; and what made it all the harder to make up my mind was the knowledge of nearly all my friends urging me to accept. Sir David went as far as to ask me to approve of a flat for the Chaplain at 1 Gillespie Terrace—a delightful situation looking on to the sea and the Royal and Ancient Clubhouse. It was a very anxious time for me since the pressure was so strong and the offer so attractive. But in spite of all that, I decided to refuse the offer and wrote to the Principal; but before posting the letter I had informed the congregation on the Sunday morning, taking as my text J. B. Phillips' translation of I Corinthians, verses 1 to 5, where St Paul says that while ministers should be faithful, the right to judge them of their faithfulness or of the decisions they make, doesn't lie with other people. "As a matter of fact", he wrote, "it matters very little to me what you or anyone else thinks of me—I don't even value my opinion of myself." The right to judge doesn't even lie with our own conscience, he says, but with God whose ministers we are. Therefore, as long as we are here on earth, it is never really possible to criticise with praise or blame. I told them that I hoped therefore they would pardon me for making a personal statement that morning, since some of them knew the situation I had been in and the difficulties I had had to face as to whether or not to stay on in Canongate where I had now been for almost twenty years, and for the nine preceding years before that working in the Canongate, or accept a very pressing call to fresh fields; a very special call, a more serious call than I had ever had before—and that for several reasons.

(1) This was the second "call" to go to St Andrews in a short space of time. (2) I had made no approach myself and indeed had opposed it, yet 95% of my friends whose opinion I most valued, had advised me to accept. (3) There was obviously a need for such an appointment, especially in a residential University of students who were potential leaders of the future. (4) I would be returning to my happiest days as a padre. (5) I would have two beautiful Chapels. On the more material side it would now be easier to work in a more concentrated way when relieved of financial worries and be less tiring both physically and mentally, and I would have five months a year to travel, lecture, run camps and conferences. Then, too, there was an ideal Manse looking on to the sea in a delightful student town. Then from the Canongate's point of view I should remember the advice given to me by my predecessor in the Canongate, before he knew that I would ever succeed him, "Don't do what I did and stay on too long". If I should go surely now is the time, before I am too much older and before the new people come to the Parish and the new Clubrooms and Halls are up, and the new Manse ready with a new start for a Minister fresh and able to do better what has been done so badly—the pastoral work. The two sides—St Andrews and Canongate—would seem to cry out that if there is time to go it is now—and to this new field of wonderful opportunity that has been offered to me. I said that I had tried my best here in Canongate, but that much had yet to be done, and a fresh mind was no doubt needed to get on with it. These, I said, were some of my arguments. And then I paused and looking round the Church that has now been so beautifully restored, and on the faces of the dear people in front of me, I said, "And after much thought and prayer, restless days and nights, I have decided . . . to stay in the Canongate!" I explained again that it had not been an easy decision to make and I only hoped it had been the right one; "But you can make it easier or more difficult. WE have work to do and WE must all unite in it." And here is part of the letter I wrote to Principal Knox:

15th January 1956.
I have thought over most carefully—almost at the

expense of everything else I have been trying to do—the very kind offer that you have made me and I feel that . . . I have most regretfully to decline. In many ways this is a very real sorrow to me, not least because of the very great kindness I have had from you and your colleagues—kindness which has been so little deserved and which I appreciate more than I can say. I also am tremendously aware of the great help and encouragement and all too frequent kindness of Sir David Russell in this as in many other matters. . . . It is not simply a matter of leaving a Parish—that has been done by hundreds of very much more able men than I shall ever be—but I am involved in so many other activities here—running a Boys' Club, which I have done now since I left School and which were I to go would mean its closing down and with it the buildings which are in it's, and not the Church's name; acquiring new Halls since the Town are turning us out of our present Halls; building a new Manse beside these Halls for which I am solely responsible for raising money; my permanent Camp site beside the sea which is in my name and which, were I to go, would be left almost derelict, since I can get no one to take it over; the clearing off of the Church's overdraft; plus countless other commitments from which I would need to break myself more gradually. The fact is that I have built up a monster (though a very pleasant monster) here and this challenge from you has made me see that I have to spend some time in trying to get everything put on a more permanent and less personal basis and that, as I see it, may take a year or two. I have discussed this matter with very many good and wise people, and nine out of ten have told me to go, and that has not made the decision any easier:—Truly I

> did eagerly frequent
> Doctor and Saint, and hear great argument
> About it and about; but evermore
> Came out by the same Door as in I went!

The terms of your offer, I need hardly add, are most kind and generous and indeed by staying here I shall have half the stipend that I would otherwise have had, and I have been more and more aware of the vital importance of the Chaplaincy. Yet the words of Gregory in 596 come back to me:

> Forasmuch as it had been better not to begin a good work, than to think of desisting from that which has been begun, it behoves you, my beloved sons, to fulfil the good work, which by the help of our Lord, you have undertaken. Let not therefore the toil of the journey . . . deter you; but with all possible earnestness and zeal perform that which, by God's direction, you have undertaken . . .

so I hope you will appreciate, and not think the worse of me when I tell you, that my conscience tells me that I really ought to consolidate in the next year or two what I have been trying to do during these last twenty years. It has been a very hard decision to make, as I hope you will appreciate; and I hope you appreciate too my reasons for it. . . .

I am writing a private note to Sir David and will take the liberty of enclosing a copy of this letter to him, and I shall also write a note of thanks to those who have been so kind in writing to or seeing me.

It has been a great joy to meet you and your colleagues and I hope that I shall be able to renew this happy acquaintance from time to time—indeed as soon as next month when I have the pleasure and privilege of coming to preach.

With kindest regards to you and your wife and with great, though I hope you appreciate, understandable regret.

The response of the congregation was quite wonderful, and the kindest possible letters came even from those who never usually write letters. Even those who were strongest in advising me to go wrote that, though they regretted my decision, they were sure I had made the right one. I especially valued at the time the letters I had from Forbes Mackintosh, the Head Master of Loretto, Melville Dinwiddie and Professor James S. Stewart—three of my friends whose advice I valued so much.

That, I thought, was the end of a difficult time; but I was

wrong. It so happened that I was due in any case to preach at St Andrews on 19th February, and Sir Thomas and Lady Knox asked me to stay with them that weekend. They were, as they had always been, extremely kind and friendly. The Principal suggested that I might think it all over again, not immediately of course; but since I had made it clear that one of the chief reasons I had given for not accepting was to see through the completion of the opening of Panmure House and the restored Manse at Reid's Court, perhaps when that was done I would re-consider the offer? He would wait for two years if necessary.

A new, and even more attractive, offer came from the Principal on 19th September, asking too if in the light of this new offer we could meet again and discuss it, and on 27th September 1956, I received a letter from the Duke of Hamilton, as Chancellor of the University:

I hope you will not think I am presumptuous in writing to you, but I feel very much torn between loyalties to the University, of which I am Chancellor, and to the Canongate Kirk and district, as Hereditary Keeper of the Palace of Holyroodhouse. I do, however, know how much the University would like you to go to St Andrews and I believe you could very greatly help the students. At the same time I am much aware what a loss this would mean to the Canongate, and how difficult it would be for anyone to follow you. I cannot help feeling, however, that it would be an opportunity of a kind that should not be missed, and it is possible that you may feel that a change at this juncture is right and that you would be able to fulfil yourself in a different, but possibly an even more effective sphere. Whatever your choice is may I wish you Godspeed and every blessing.

After again being advised by many good friends to accept and further pressure from both the Principal and the new Principal of St Mary's College, Matthew Black, I again refused, though it had been even harder for me this time, and on 4th May 1957 and in a further letter from the Duke of Hamilton I was grateful when he wrote:

200

I am grateful to you for letting me know your decision about St Andrews. I have no doubt that you have acted wisely.

As a kind of postscript to all this I was put under pressure again at St Andrews to apply for the Chair of Practical Theology, and wrote to the Principal on 30th April 1958 to tell him that I would not wish to be appointed, adding "in any case I have been doing my best to sponsor Stuart Louden of Greyfriars who is a first-class fellow".[1]

And, though I have been back there to preach again more than once, here endeth my rather large file on St Andrews!

Chapter 10

I did, however, accept another Chaplaincy which this time didn't involve leaving the Canongate; for in the summer of 1957 Donald Crichton-Miller, the Head Master of Fettes College where I had often preached since the latter part of Dr Ashcroft's time, called to ask me if I would be prepared to come as Honorary Chaplain, since their present Chaplain was leaving, at the beginning of the winter term. He had previously asked me if I could help him to find a full-time Chaplain for the College, and not having been able to do so, this was the result! I said that I would be very pleased to come for a term or two until a full-time Chaplain was appointed, provided I had transport to and from the School, came on a voluntary basis if they gave a donation to the Church, took morning prayers, some classes in Divinity, and had a room where boys could come and see me. All this he agreed to, and the term or two at Fettes turned out to be for me three very happy years, which would have been longer had it not been that I began to find that my work as Chaplain was beginning

[1] Stuart Louden was not appointed, nor was he later nominated as Moderator of the General Assembly—truly a double loss to the Church of Scotland.

to take up too much time and so have a detrimental effect on my work as a Parish Minister. Donald, himself an Old Fettesian, had been at an early age Head Master of Taunton before succeeding Dr Ashcroft at Fettes, and did a tremendous amount for the School. The boys, but not all the Masters, liked him tremendously and were very sorry to see him leave in 1958 to become Head Master of Stowe. Everyone was most friendly and co-operative. The Staff was excellent—men like Freddy Macdonald, Tom Goldie-Scott, Ian Sutcliffe, Dick Cole-Hamilton and Charles Whittle; and some of the more junior members of the Common Room were quite outstanding—men like Eric Anderson, now Head Master at Shrewsbury, where he and Poppy give you such a good welcome and soon to go to Eton as Head Master; Patrick Crocker who later went to Eton, and Michael Lester-Cribb, a quite brilliant musician.

The boys were all most friendly and responsive—indeed had they not been so I should have been able to stay longer at Fettes! So many latterly came to talk to me, make their "confessions" and pour out their troubles, whether of School or home, that it became more than I could tackle along with a busy Parish.

While I was still Chaplain, Ian McIntosh, then Head Master of George Watson's College, became Donald's successor. I found Ian equally easy to work with, although on the whole his approach was somewhat different. The masters, but not quite all the boys, liked him, and indeed, though greatly respected, some boys found him a little difficult to talk to and confide in; but he was a man of great ability, an excellent after-dinner speaker and a good friend.

My visits to Fettes were made even all the more pleasant when Anthony Chenevix-Trench was appointed Head Master in 1971. When he was Head Master of Eton I had twice stayed with him and Elizabeth when preaching there, and got to know them and their delightful family well. He was one of the great Head Masters of our time, and indeed twenty-six of the Head Masters of the Public Schools attached to the Headmasters' Conference, were once "under" him, which must surely be a record! A brilliant classical scholar at Oxford, he had been for nearly four years a prisoner-of-war with the Japanese, and before being Head Master at Eton he had been an outstanding Head Master at Bradfield. Though he sent both his sons, Richard and Jonathan, to Eton, he himself had found that it was too impersonal because he liked to know all boys individually. He brought a different "climate" to Fettes.[1] Boys were free to come and see him at almost any time; he would call them "my dear", and even those whom he had to punish were among the first to regard him with affection and respect. Nothing and no one was ever too much trouble to him, and the Head Master's Lodge was an ever open door. His wife Elizabeth, a descendant of Thomas Chalmers, was the ideal Head Master's wife. They both must have been very tired at times, but they never showed it. As mentioned, they had a most delightful family and always made one feel very much a part of it, and I was always invited to join the family for Christmas dinner.

So my Fettes connection has remained very strong through the years and I was glad to know that it would continue when my friend Cameron Cochrane, with his charming wife Rosemary, his two daughters and David, was appointed as Tony's very worthy successor in 1979, who kindly asked me to return as Chaplain for his first—and for me a most enjoyable—term in the autumn of that year, when George Buchanan-Smith, who had succeeded me as Chaplain in the autumn of 1960, was taking a term off.

When I gave up the Fettes Chaplaincy in 1960 Forbes Mackintosh, the retiring Head Master of Loretto, whom I had known for many years, asked me if I would come to Loretto and take the Church of Scotland Confirmation Classes there, which he had always taken himself, and, to keep the matter right with the local Presbytery, be Honorary Church of Scotland Chaplain. His successor, Rab Bruce-Lockhart, had welcomed this and so I gladly agreed to come for a year—and have continued now for over twenty years! These classes, and preaching for at least once a year since 1945, have been to me a great pleasure and benefit. I have always had a very high regard for Loretto which is a deliberately small School of about 250 boys where everyone knows everyone, which does

[1] See my obituary of him for the Royal Society of Edinburgh 1980, and *The Fettesian* of September 1979 for part of my Memorial Sermon.

much to help to make it the very "healthy" School it has always been. The boys are always most friendly, tidy, and polite, and I have made many good friends there and felt greatly honoured when in 1976 I was made an Honorary Old Lorettonian and presented with their tie.

Forbes Mackintosh was the son of Professor H. R. Mackintosh, one of our greatest Scottish Theologians and a greatly beloved former teacher. Forbes had succeeded Dr J. R. C. Greenlees whose reputation as Head Master of Loretto almost equalled the great Dr Almond's, and so his job was not an easy one. But Forbes was a man whom you had to know well to appreciate and admire. Sometimes to the boys and masters he may have seemed rather unpredictable at times, but he had in his way a great influence for good on the School—an influence that he never fully realised himself. His presence "filled" a room and he had only to walk into Newfield for everyone to know he was there! His letters, full of wit and wisdom, would be worthy of publication. I was very fond of him and grateful to him for putting his trust in me; and his charming wife Betty was a power of strength to him and to Loretto. His successor in 1960 was Rab Bruce-Lockhart, a former Scottish rugger international, who was "quieter" and more restrained, and was too a wise and memorable Head Master as befitted one whose grandfather, father and brother, were all themselves distinguished Head Masters. His father I had known when he was Head Master both of Cargilfield and Sedbergh, and as mentioned before, once when I was staying with him when preaching at Sedbergh I asked him if he were a parent who found he could afford to send a boy either to a good Prep School or a good Public School, but not both, which he would advise to choose. His immediate answer was "a good Prep School" because by that time, in most cases, they would have learned the basic ideas of right conduct which should ever remain with them, good manners, discipline, loyalty, responsibility, fair play, and a kindly faith. From my much less knowledge and experience I think I would agree with him. Rab's successor in 1976, David McMurray, who had been a distinguished House Master at Fettes, is the best type of Old Lorettonian and there could be no higher commendation than that! And in Philip David the School had a most helpful and co-operative Anglican Chaplain.

Though still continuing my evening classes at Loretto, I was invited in 1966 to be Honorary Chaplain of the Edinburgh Academy. I gladly accepted the Rector's kind invitation, since it only chiefly involved conducting the service and preaching (shortly!) at the beginning and end of each term, and conducting the monthly morning service in the Hall, when I was free to invite guest preachers. Some like Dr Charles Warr, Dr George MacLeod and Dr Leonard Small, were quite outstanding; some were good and a few quite appalling, for they either talked down to the boys, which is a fatal thing to do, or talked above their heads—including mine! Dr Mills, the Rector, who had won a good M.C. at the D-Day Landings and had previously been a Master at Sedbergh and was an excellent sportsman and mountaineer, was always very kind and friendly; and I used to enjoy my visits and talks over a cup of coffee at the end of each Service. He did a great deal for the boys at the School, though he probably wasn't quite so good with some of the parents! He at least didn't go as far as the late Mr Beamish, one of the Fettes Masters who is said to have written in a boy's report: "This boy is unimaginative, dull and stubborn—will make a good parent!" Or the great and good Dr Lionel Smith, Rector from 1931 to 1945, who, with his twinkle and friendly smile, remarked in an impromptu speech at the City Chambers, "When I see these fine-looking boys whom I meet daily it saddens me to think that hour by hour they are going to resemble their parents!"[1]

I remained as Honorary Chaplain of the Academy until the close of my year as Moderator, when, as I had so often suggested, a full-time Chaplain was appointed. As a parting gift I received my personal Moderator's pennant mounted on a silver pole, "from the Directors of the Edinburgh Academy in appreciation of his happy connection with the School as Honorary Chaplain 1966-73". In that same year I was made an Extraordinary Director of the Edinburgh Academy, which gave me extraordinary pleasure.

When I retired from Canongate in 1977 I still retained, with my Chaplaincy of the Castle, my Chaplaincies of the Royal

[1] See *Arthur Lionel Foster Smith*, edited by Leonard Hodgkin (1980) and my Essay there on his Edinburgh days.

Company of Archers (the Queen's Bodyguard for Scotland) whose company at the monthly Match Dinners and bi-annual Mess Dinners held in the beautiful Archers' Hall, I have always so much enjoyed; and of the Merchant Company of Edinburgh where I lunch at the meetings of the Master and his Court and say the old Company prayer at the beginning of their meetings in their splendid Hall. These two Chaplaincies, along with that of the Order of St John of Jerusalem, give me special pleasure, since all at one time had been held by Dr Warr.

The most striking Service of the Order that I can remember was that already referred to held in the Canongate Kirk in 1976, when the Grand Prior, the Duke of Gloucester, installed the new Duke of Hamilton as the Scottish Prior; and of the Annual Investitures was that held within the Banqueting Hall of Holyroodhouse in 1978 when the Prior of Scotland, who is also Hereditary Keeper of Holyroodhouse, invested, among others, the Duke of Roxburghe, the Marquis of Graham and Tony Chenevix-Trench, as Officers of the Order, and Harry Richmond as a Serving Brother. It was unique too in that the English Prior, Lord Caccia, was also present—so that young Guy Roxburghe, who had been Captain of Cricket at Eton and won the Sword of Honour at Sandhurst, was delighted to find that both his former Head Master and former Provost were present together, for Tony had been Head Master of Eton and Caccia Provost of Eton when Guy was a schoolboy there.

Before finishing this Chapter on Chaplains it might be worth noting that I belong to that small group of Royal Chaplains who have twice been Extra-Chaplains, since I was appointed an Extra-Chaplain in 1961, a Chaplain-in-Ordinary in 1963, and an Extra-Chaplain again on my seventieth birthday in 1978.

Chapter 11

The "vintage" years of the Boys' Clubs in Edinburgh, and certainly of our Club, were, in my opinion, those from 1927 until 1939 (I saw little of the Clubs during the war), and from 1946 until the mid-sixties. In the pre-war years all the Boys' Clubs were run entirely on a voluntary system with sometimes a small honorarium for the Club Leader. These were the days of men like "Nunky" Brown, who ever remained a "guide, philosopher and friend" to Leaders and boys alike until his death in 1977, and of an equally legendary figure, Stanley Nairne. What men they both were! And they gathered round them for longer or shorter periods men like Jack Tait, Tony Beilby, who was killed in North Africa and recommended for a V.C., Roy Sanderson, Arnot Fleming, "Gig" Macmillan, Neil Campbell, Sandy Somerville, and so many others.

The Voluntary system was always the way our Canongate Club was run from the time it first started in 1927 as the St Giles' Cathedral Boys' Club, until it ceased in 1978. No Leaders were paid, and all came as a voluntary act of service from which they all would admit they gained as much as they gave; men like John B. Logan, James Shaw, Alastair Blair, Cyril Jones (who took over from me as Warden for a time when I went to Glasgow Cathedral), George Thomson, and my brother "Pip", before the war, and after the war the same James Shaw (who took over as Warden during the war years), Hugh Mackay, Peter Thompson, various Assistants of Canongate, and a number of former members like Harry Richmond, John Hood, David Croft, Billy Nicoll, Pringle Fisher, Stuart McFarlane, and latterly Charles, the young Earl of Cassillis, who stayed at the Manse with me. We also had the help from time to time both at Club and Camp, of two doctors —Professor Ellis and my own doctor Alastair McLaren.

Another man of the post-war period who was always helping people was John Loudon who became Manager of the Pleasance Trust, as well as an Elder in the Canongate. In addition to running a very good Boys' Club in the Pleasance, he did much for the old, including the housebound, for whom he showed too, great care and compassion. After his first wife died of cancer he married my sister-in-law Clare in 1976. Though far from well himself for several years, no one did as much to help "Nunky" Brown in his last sad years of illness than he.

207

Probably the most colourful and certainly the most eccentric of all our helpers was Father H. T. Coles, who came and went for years, and whose visits, especially to the Camps, was always greatly appreciated. I could write at least a chapter about him alone, for he was quite unique. He had run away from home when a schoolboy at George Watson's, and joined the Gordon Highlanders, became later a Sergeant-Major ("never swore, smoked, or drank"), later an officer in the Seaforth Highlanders at the Somme and Ypres, where he was one of two officers left who had not been killed or wounded ("acting Lt.-Colonel") and from which he had never really recovered. In addition he had gone to Canada ("was a cowboy"), been a missionary in India ("walked through the jungle alone in bare feet") and returned to this country where he had for a time a Mission Church in Comely Bank. I first met him in 1927 through my father whose first introduction to him was meeting him in a heavy rainstorm, and he suggested that he ought to have an umbrella to receive the answer "Christ never had an umbrella"! He was in many ways a saint and could hold the boys spellbound with his stories—chiefly about the First World War. He could easily take offence but quickly repented. If you gave him anything he almost as quickly gave it away. The stories about him are many, and mostly true. In his innocence he would sometimes come out with the most startling remarks. Once on a very wet day when a number of us were sitting round the fire he suddenly said "Let's have a game: I'm thinking of a four-letter word beginning with 'F'", and stunned us all into silence. Another time I overhead him telling some small boys a story which began "There was a man who lived all alone except for a horse and buggy . . ." but once again he confused the word "buggy". He would say to the toughest boy "My son, you are a child of God—we are all God's children". The hymn he loved to hear best at prayers round the Memorial Cross at Camp was "Fairest Lord Jesus", and more than once it brought tears to his eyes. He loved Skye and the Pentland Hills where he often used to wander by himself, for he was a great walker; and he was a great swimmer too. A saint with all of a saint's eccentricities, and certainly a "child of God". Once when I took him into the Manse garden to see the roses which

208

were at their very best that year. He looked at them for a while then stretched out his hands and said: "Isn't God good!" We weren't quite sure how old he was, since he was never quite sure himself, but when he died we think he was eighty-six.

Of some of the boys themselves during these "vintage years" I have already written.[1] Cyril Taylor always used to be amused when I spoke about the men in the Army as "grand chaps"; well, most of these boys really were "grand chaps"! I always insisted—and insisted is the word—on good manners; for good manners, apart from being pleasant in itself, fosters the right sort of friendship between younger and older people and teaches a boy to have self-respect as well as respect for others. The boys and Club Leaders always had their own way of shaking hands on entering the Club each evening, and on leaving each boy would again shake hands and say "goodnight sir". Today, when manners are not so common, that may seem rather old-fashioned; but that is how we started and we kept it up to the end of the Club's fifty years. It became a natural tradition, and the boys were proud of it. Visitors too were greeted the same way and it made them feel at home. I believed too in a fairly strict, but I hope always kindly, discipline; and sometimes the "ping-pong" (table tennis) bat had to be administered! (I remember once at a Kirk Session Meeting when six of the former Club boys were then Elders, one of them saying "We'd just better agree with him otherwise we'll get the ping-pong bat"!)

On more than one occasion I was accused of expecting too high a standard of the boys, and so one day I got them together and told them what had been said. I told them that all I expected was that we should all try to do our best, and that though we, all of us, often failed, at least we could always try, since I wouldn't insult anyone by expecting their second-best. And on that we were all agreed! After the war, for twenty years, nearly every boy was for some time a member of the Boys' Choir, which for a time numbered over fifty boys. Not many were very good singers, but it meant that they came to Church each Sunday, many both morning and evening—nor were they put off by not having "the right sort of clothes"

[1] *Our Club* (Oliver & Boyd).

for they processed in scarlet cassocks, white ruffs, and blue girdles, and so were all dressed the same. The Choir helped too to make us into a family, and it was especially noticeable at, for example, prayers at Camp, when for a time, under the leadership of Hugh Mackay, we even sang Compline.

Every boy needs at least four things: the sure knowledge that he really matters and that one cares for him; a sense of security, so that however long the "chain" there is always an anchor; discipline which really means—in the long run what General Sir Neil Ritchie defined to me once—unselfishness; and, perhaps hardest of all, example. So naturally every Leader had to strive after these attributes too. In any good Boys' Club it is not only the boys but also the Leaders who are helped; and indeed just because they are Leaders the heavier strain has to be carried by them. A Boys' Club, in the words of one of the greatest of all Club Leaders, Sir Basil Henriques, "is a gymnasium in which to learn to make the whole of life supremely good".

I think we all tried our best, but I know that we, boys and Leaders alike, often failed. But what was it that Sir J. M. Barrie once said when speaking to the students of St Andrews: "When you reach the evening of your days you will, I think see with, I hope, becoming cheerfulness, that we are all failures, at least all the best of us!"

Chapter 12

Now, I saw in some of these Club and Choir boys, especially in the post-war period, the kind of fellows who seemed to me to be of the stuff of the early Church and the kind of men that the Church needed today as Ministers to add to its ranks. But since most of them had to leave School at fifteen (indeed in the earlier days it was fourteen) and had very often dead-end jobs at that, there just wasn't a hope for them. So when I read in July 1950 that there was an "alarming" decrease in the number of candidates for the Ministry, and that this was not least due because "the supply of war service candidates students was now ceasing altogether" my thoughts turned to Kelham. Dr Caldwell, the Convener of the Committee for the Education for the Ministry, had stated in the article I had read that the number of probationers or men available to take up vacancies in 1949 was fifty as against 205 in 1938. Yet here in these boys and others like them, if given the chance. . . . So I wrote to Dr Caldwell on 7th July, 1950:

For a considerable time now I have been troubled by the fact that so many of the best potential manpower in the Church has been lost from the ministry. For example, in so many of our Churches year after year some of our finest young boys in our Boys' Clubs, etc., are having to leave school at the age of fifteen. If only their vocation could be tested they would, I feel sure, in many cases make most excellent ministers in the Church. What I should very much like to see would be a vocational centre set up in Scotland where these boys could spend the years before National Service in preparing not only for entrance to University but for the whole life and work of the Church. At the present moment in most cases this is denied just the kind of people I feel we need, and certainly the kind of people who formed the backbone of the early Church. It is strange but true to think that it is doubtful if any one of the early apostles would have been accepted as a candidate for New College! Several things recently have emphasised the need of a test school for prospective divinity students; and not least this notice I got from Kelham the other day which I enclose with this letter. I have seen "The Cottage" at Kelham where these young fellows are tested and have been tremendously impressed by it, and even more impressed by the type of man they have eventually turned out for the Church—I venture to think, the type of people we want in the Church of Scotland. I should very much like to discuss this matter with you and your Committee and I would be quite prepared myself to do everything I could to foster it. . . . I think there is an extreme possibility of being able to get the backing of the Church of Scotland. In view of the desperate situation and, to me more important, in view of the fact that I am certain

211

we are losing some of the best men, I do hope that it will be taken seriously. . . .

He replied, showing an interest, as did Roy Sanderson who was at that time Convener of the Youth Committee, and Dr Warr, to both of whom I had sent copies of my letter. Roy wrote that "it looked as though I had something here" and that he would bring it before the Youth Committee, and Dr Warr wrote: ". . . You have got hold of a big idea, but just because of that you must expect many obstacles to be surmounted. . . . Remember that any help I can give you will gladly be forthcoming. . . ."

My first connection with Kelham had been in the early '30s when attending a Students' Conference in York and had got to know Father Giles Ambrose, a young member of the Society; and in 1940 I was able to visit Kelham myself for a few days as the guest of its beloved Founder, Father H. H. Kelly, and was able to share to my great benefit something of the life there of The Society of the Sacred Mission, and meet the members in residence at that time, not least the Kelly brothers and Father Gabriel Hebert, all of whom welcomed a young Church of Scotland padre as though he were one of themselves. It was then, and through Giles Ambrose, that I learnt more about "The Cottage" where boys were trained to test their vocation for the Ministry of the Church of England, and felt how good a thing it would be if we could have something similar for the Church of Scotland.

Well, I duly met Dr Caldwell and with him the Vice-Convener Dr George Gunn, and they seemed hopefully interested. But the next meeting of the Committee was postponed and didn't meet for some time later. When it did eventually meet it did, what all Committees seem to do, set up a Sub-Committee that would "report back". It in turn set up a Sub-Sub-Committee; and so it went on! In the meantime, in order to hasten things up a bit, I tried to have something more tangible to put before them. With the usual considerable encouragement from Sir David Russell and his son, I looked for a suitable place, drew up suggested daily programmes, worked out possible costs, and approached those who would agree to help as tutors and in the general running of the place. I

212

approached the Duke of Roxburghe, who had helped me before in the Canongate, about Broxmouth House, near Dunbar, visited Beil House near Dunbar, part of which was soon to be demolished and which had a lovely small Chapel (I had spent my first school Corps Camp in its ground as a very young Lance-Corporal in charge of a tent of older boys) and had written to my good friend Jamie Stormonth-Darling about the possibility of getting Hill of Tarvit near St Andrews. Jamie was particularly encouraging. As Adjutant of the 52nd Reconnaissance Regiment to Jack Hankey as Commanding Officer, before he himself became Commanding Officer, they made the best C.O./Adjutant team I have ever seen, and no one has done for the National Trust as much as he. He said he had privately (for the whole idea was yet in a very "private" state) mentioned it to the Earl of Wemyss "whose initial reaction was much in favour of your scheme" and also to Mr Arthur Russell, the Law Agent and Sir David's cousin, and he too thought that the Hill of Tarvit was a real possibility. And so the correspondence, including further very helpful letters from Kelham, went on. I was later summoned to meet a very powerful Sub-Sub-Committee which made me feel that I was being tried by the Inquisition for heresy!—and put the whole case before them. At last the suggestion was put before the General Assembly of 1954 and turned down. It had taken the Church four years to come to any conclusion! The main reason was not, alas, far to seek, and I had been aware of its possibility from the beginning. I had had kindly "warnings" of it too from men whose opinions I valued and respected, and who had been in favour of my idea: for instance, two who were later to become distinguished Professors and Churchmen. Robin Barbour wrote on 20th July 1950: ". . . I'm very glad you have taken the matter up with the Committee on Education for the Ministry—though whether you have any luck is of course quite a different question! I think the idea in general is excellent, and, as you say, the question is vital. It seems to me that the main danger to guard against is that of segregating boys so that we have something like an esoteric priesthood of people. . . . That of course would be particularly fatal to Presbyterian methods and the Presbyterian spirit in general, but with yourself at the helm at any rate there wouldn't be much danger of that happening. . . ." And J. K. S. Reid, too, was aware of the danger of the scheme being suspect. On 1st December Jack wrote:

> . . . I want now to say that time has not altered my view but only confirmed it. It seems to me really possible that you are on something big here.
>
> You must be as aware as anyone that the scheme involves the greatest of difficulties for at least certain elements in the Church. What in fact appeals to some of us to some degree will be precisely what sticks in the throat of many of our colleagues. The "seminary" idea is held suspect, and will at once incur entirely unfounded charges of—you know what—Romanism and Anglicanism. I foresee the danger that the scheme will not be heard on its merits but be settled upon what are finally extraneous and adventitious grounds like these.
>
> The important thing seems therefore to me to be to build strongly on those points in the scheme which manifestly commend it to as wide a public or as many of the clergy or presbyters as possible. My judgment is that the strongest card to play, in addition to the shortage of men, which is certainly important, is the *type of man* such a scheme might make available to the Church. For years now the Church has drawn and has regretted that it drew from too exclusively the "lettered" classes for its recruits to the clergy. A scheme like this, were it to succeed, would inject a dose of new blood of a virile and valuable kind, from the so-called working classes. I believe that many people would be quick to see the manifest advantage of this.

Well, many people did, including such Church Leaders as Professors John and Donald Baillie; but, as has been seen, not enough.[1]

[1] The wording of section 7 of the Education for the Ministry Report on 21st May 1954, read: "The General Assembly note the account of a proposal received by the Committee for the establishment of a Training College for Boys. . . . They suggest that this section of the Report be considered by Presbyteries in relationship to the main endeavour which the Church is making to secure candidates for the normal (sic) course, and that comments on it in that context (sic) be forwarded to the Committee." The first Amendment was to delete the second sentence and that was carried against; the second Amendment was to substitute that sentence for "They suggest that the Committee give further consideration to this proposal and bring a recommendation to the next Assembly" and that was voted against. And that was that!

But at least having "cast the bread upon the waters" some good seems to have come of it at last, and a more simplified course made available. Of course it is important that we should have an educated ministry, and the Church needs its scholars; but that surely need not be the only criterion, else though no doubt St Paul and St Luke would have got into our Divinity Halls, I doubt if any of the Apostles would have been accepted for the Church of Scotland ministry until they were, at least, forty years old or over!

Fortunately one does not need to be a Minister to be an Apostle! But, oh, what a very clumsy system our Committee system can be in the Church of Scotland—and to think that the Assembly can so easily dismiss something that they haven't even studied!

PART V

Chapter 1

I have never been a "Committee man", and least of all a
Church Committee man. The only Committee I have really
enjoyed was that established in August 1968 by Mr Edward
Heath, then Leader of the Opposition, to examine the
proposal for the creation of a Scottish Assembly under the
Chairmanship of Sir Alec Douglas-Home (previously the Earl
of Home and later Lord Home). In neither composition nor
intention was the Committee a Party-political body, else I
would not have accepted Mr Heath's kind invitation to join it.
The full Committee with Sir Alec in the Chair included Lady
Tweedsmuir and Sir David Milne, Viscount Dilhorne, Sir
Bernard Fergusson (later Lord Ballantrae), Professors A. L.
Goodhart, J. B. M. Mitchell, Sir Charles Wilson and Lord
Polwarth, with Sir Robert Menzies and Professor Kenneth
Weare as Advisers. It met on seventeen occasions between
September 1968 and March 1970, in Edinburgh, Glasgow,
London, Inverness, and Peebles; and many smaller meetings
were also held. Over 1,000 people were consulted from
Industry, Trade Unions, Church, Law, Journalism, Universities, Economists and Politicians and, since the evidence was
given in confidence, it was not possible to list all those who
helped. We felt that the findings of the Committee gave the
best answer to the whole question of Scottish Devolution; but
unfortunately the recommendations were never followed up,
either by the Heath or the Wilson Governments. I made little
or no contribution except to get the Committee to agree, with

the strong support too of Bernard Fergusson, that the name "Scottish Convention" rather than "Scottish Assembly" should be used so as not to confuse it with the General Assembly of the Church of Scotland.

It's two chief aims were to keep the United Kingdom united and to make an effective effort to improve the machinery of Government as it effects the people of Scotland. It was a great privilege for me to work under Alec Douglas-Home and to be associated with such wise and friendly people. As mentioned before Alec Home and his father had always been so kind and friendly and I had been the guest of each on more than one occasion at the Hirsel—on three occasions accompanied by the Canongate choirboys. On one visit we practically "invaded" the Hirsel when he was Prime Minister, and were fed on strawberries and cream, cakes and buns, under the kindly care of his daughter Caroline. His brother Henry, the "Bird Man", not only came to the Boys' Club and spoke about birds, but took us all, too, to the Hirsel to give us a practical demonstration.

This has, thankfully, taken me away from grousing about Committees, though I have to admit that I enjoyed the Scottish Constitutional one as I have enjoyed few others. I was too a member of the Kilbrandon Youth Committee to which the Secretary of State had appointed me, and though I much enjoyed and benefited from Lord Kilbrandon's Chairmanship, and meeting the people on the Committee, I felt slightly out of place; for I am still old-fashioned enough to believe that "voluntarily" means what it says, and have always regretted the professionalism that has now dominated so much of the work that used to be done, and it is still done in The Boys' Brigade and the Boy Scouts, on an "amateur" basis.

From 1956 to 1969 I was Chairman of the Edinburgh and Leith Old People's Welfare Council, during which time Lamb's House in Leith, Margaret Tudor House in Edinburgh and Dalry House were acquired, and a large number of new Luncheon Clubs were formed. I was also able to see the beginning of Stockbridge House. Work for the old and the young go closely together, since both depend much on the

218

help that is given by the middle-aged, who should be able to stand on their own feet.

I was also from 1960 to 1970 a member of the Edinburgh Education Committee and learned something of Local Government; but latterly I felt there was far more interest taken in party politics than in education, and not always the better side of politics at that. I was especially annoyed at those who attacked the "fee-paying Schools" and who had either benefited from them themselves or even had their own children at them. There were many fine people on the Committee like Mr Sellers, the Depute Town Clerk, Melville Dinwiddie, Craig Richard, Freddy Macdonald, Graham Fraser, Mrs Mansbridge, Dr Reith, the Director, and, for too short a time for the benefit of the Committee, Cameron Cochrane, who later was to become Head Master of Fettes College. Though I had enjoyed it at the beginning, I was glad to resign when I did.

As for Church Committees, I have been on few of these, and then only for the required four years.

It came therefore as all the greater surprise to me when I was asked if I would allow my name to go forward as a Nomination for the Moderatorship of the General Assembly. It is true that I had been Moderator of the Edinburgh Presbytery in 1963, and in spite of my ignorance of procedure—motions, counter-motions, amendments, and amendments to amendments, points of order, and all the rest—I rather enjoyed it. Everyone was so kind and helpful and understanding.

At the Meeting of the Moderator's Committee (there's that word again!) in October 1970, I heard later (for the procedure and findings of the Committee of eighty members was in confidence) that I had been proposed by my good friend Roy Sanderson (who had first approached me) and seconded by my equally good friend Melville Dinwiddie (who had persuaded me to be Radio Padre) and that the final voting had resulted in a tie between Andrew Herron and myself; and that, quite rightly, the Convener had given his casting vote to Andrew.

I was honoured to be asked again to stand the following

219

October and again accepted, though by this time I wasn't so keen about waiting to see what the result would be! Yet to refuse after a tie would have seemed rather churlish. I learnt later that Roy Sanderson had again proposed me and that Professor James S. Stewart (too a former Moderator, our greatest preacher, and so much-loved and respected by everybody—and certainly not a Committee man) had seconded; and the upshot was that I was nominated as Moderator in October 1971, but only just, the runner-up being my second-cousin George Reid, then at Aberdeen, who was, thankfully, nominated the following year.

I received literally hundreds of letters of congratulations and good wishes which greatly cheered me and gave me more confidence. Two of the telegrams of congratulation and good wishes I especially appreciated—one from the Roman Catholic Cathedral in Edinburgh, and the other which read "G.O.C. and all ranks in the Army in Scotland and all Scottish Regiments world-wide send their heartiest congratulations and deepest respects on your nomination as next Moderator stop We are all delighted—H.Q. Scotland".

I didn't relish too much some of the Chairing of the Assembly for the reasons that I have already given, but I did look forward to the time when the Assembly itself would be over and I could begin the visits and journeys that lay before me—shades of the Army and Radio Padre days! The Lord High Commissioner was that fine man Lord Clydesmuir whom I had known in Army days, and we were privately and somewhat irreverently known in some quarters as "The Two Ronnies".

In my opening remarks I explained to the Assembly that (to paraphrase Archbishop William Temple) my ignorance of administration was so profound as to be almost distinguished! Partly because of this "confession" everyone was most kind and helpful and made it all so much more easy for me than ever I could have hoped. In Tommy Nicol, then just ceasing to be Assistant Chaplain-General Scotland, to become Minister of Crathie and Domestic Chaplain to the Queen, and Hugh Mackay, Minister at Duns, I had two excellent Chaplains. I had known Tommy since he was five years old and had greatly admired his father, and he and his wife Mary, along with my

The memorial to my mother and father in Canongate:
"The Penitence of St Hubert"
by Josephina de Vasconcellos

Morning Service in the restored church

17

Duke of Edinburgh, 1953
(Duke of Hamilton and the
Rev. David McGregor behind)

Lord Baden-Powell, 1934

The Queen at the Manse, 1969

19

Scotsman Publications

With His Royal Highness The Prince of Wales, 1970
(at the back Major J. H. Duncan, Commander "Jock" Slater, D. S. W., Sir Alistair Blair, and Harry Richmond)

Moderator, 1972

Dr Minto, Mrs Pandit and the Head Boy, Kalimpong, 1972

Madras, 1972

22

Dartmouth, 1972

Royal Marine Commando, 1972

23

Outside Canongate Manse, 1966
Lt-Gen. Sir George Gordon Lennox, Governor of the Castle, Lord Grant, Lord Justice Clerk, Self. Front row Dr Charles Warr, Bishop Ken Carey, Cardinal Gray, The Earl of Wemyss

Outside The Church, 1971
Lt-Gen. Sir Henry Leask, Governor of the Castle, Gordon (now Lord) Campbell, Secretary of State for Scotland, Lord Clydesmuir, Lord High Commissioner, and the Duke of Hamilton, Keeper of Holyroodhouse

sister-in-law Clare, who acted as my hostess, except for three days when my sister Ray came up, were of the greatest help to me. Hugh Mackay had been a member of the Canongate since his days as Vice-Captain of Daniel Stewart's College, and had always given me great help in the Church, where he was for a time Assistant, and also at the Boys' Club and Camp; moreover he was an expert in administration, to my great relief.

As mentioned before, General Sir Henry Leask gave me an excellent orderly from the Army in Lance-Corporal Alasdair Hope; and with James Longmuir as the Principal Clerk and Roy Sanderson as the Convener of the Business Committee, I had little or nothing to worry about. I had to swear in the new Procurator, Mr C. Kemp Davidson, Q.C., since his predecessor, Lord Grieve, during the Assembly had become a Senator of the College of Justice, and on behalf of the General Assembly, and indeed of the whole Church, to thank James Longmuir since, having given great service, this was his last Assembly. He was succeeded some months later by Donald Macdonald who too was a very great help to me, his first Moderator. So somehow I got through the Assembly itself and really rather enjoyed it.

I gave my closing address "In Christ we are all one", a copy of which, thanks again to the generosity of David Russell, was sent to every Minister of the Church of Scotland. I think it was a bit too long, and probably contained too many quotations but, thankfully, it was well received.

I think it was George MacLeod who said that for one year a Moderator is "IT" and after that "Ex-IT"! He takes precedence in Scotland over the Prime Minister and the Dukes, wears (when he has to) 18th-century clothes, has a car and a chauffeur and is treated wherever he goes as a V.I.P. Now he has a flat in Charlotte Square. He is not just "Chairman" of the Assembly, but for a year he is the Representative, without powers, of the Church of Scotland, and is received everywhere with the greatest courtesy and kindness; so what is really a very hard and exhausting year doesn't at the time seem so. When not travelling he is speaking and preaching; and his sometimes very ordinary and pedestrian words are listened to and noted as never before in his

Ministry. He is blessed by the prayers of the Church and therein lies the secret that keeps him going.

Chapter 2

Almost as soon as the Assembly finished and I had attended a lunch given by Edinburgh Presbytery and a dinner by the High Constables of Holyroodhouse, I flew to London for the funeral of the Duke of Windsor, for the Queen had especially asked that the Moderator should be invited to take part at this Service along with the two Archbishops.

On the eve of the service at St George's, Windsor, the Dean, the Right Rev. Launcelot Fleming with whom I was staying, took me to see some of the wreaths lying in the Cloister—a most wonderful sight—from every corner of the world and from every head of State.

But what impressed me most were not the great wreaths from the Emperor of Japan or the Shah of Persia or the Aga Khan, from Kings and Presidents, and all the others, but some of the little wreaths with their little affectionate inscriptions— for example: "On behalf of my grandparents, my grand-uncle and grand-aunt who are among the poorer people of London who loved you so much."

The funeral service itself was remarkable and one I will never forget for its simplicity and its beauty. To see the coffin of the former King carried by tall handsome young Guardsmen from the Prince of Wales' Company of the Welsh Guards and laid so gently down as the congregation was singing:

> And on his shoulders gently laid
> And home rejoicing brought me:

to hear the Garter King at Arms reading the late King's titles—"The High and Mighty Prince"—it was all so gracious, so moving and so memorable.

It was a "private" funeral which, in addition to the Royal Family and their relatives, was attended by, among others, the

Prime Minister (Mr Heath) and the Cabinet, the Leader of the Opposition (Mr Wilson) and the Shadow Cabinet, and of course the Knights of Windsor. The Choir, surely one of the finest in the world, sang beautifully. I thought that the Duchess of Windsor looked old and tired and frail, and very sad. The Dean told me that on the evening before he had seen Prince Charles walk with her round the Chapel, taking her by the arm, and how he had joined him at the little service of prayer round the coffin later that evening. On several occasions I have stayed at Windsor with the Deans who have been most kind and friendly hosts—Robin Woods, whom I had got to know well during the war in Italy, Launcelot Fleming, and Michael Mann—all such lovely people; but it is that funeral service for the once King Edward VIII that shall stand out ever in my memory.

From Windsor I flew to Belfast to join the other members of the Church of Scotland party who were attending the Irish Assembly with me—Dr Nicol, Dr Sawyer, who was standing in for me at Canongate, and Major J. H. Duncan, my quite excellent Session Clerk (all incidentally holders of the M.C).

In addition to addressing the Irish Assembly and presenting them with a Bible belonging to their first Moderator, Dr Chalmers' son-in-law, Dr Hanna, which I had long had in my possession, I was also able to go to Portadown and speak at an Assembly meeting there.

I visited Campbell College and saw too some of the great work being done by the Gordon Highlanders and, as previous Moderators had been, was the guest during my stay of those hospitable host and hostess, Lord and Lady MacDermott. I saw some of the terrible destruction that is going on in Northern Ireland and heard of, and witnessed, the courage and discipline and compassion of our own British troops there, and the anxious time that so many of the good folk in Northern Ireland were having. I doubt if people realise sufficiently what a wonderful job the Army is doing under the most difficult possible conditions, and often in the most uncomfortable circumstances. We should all be very proud and grateful to these young men for the very high standard they set, and remember them all daily in our prayers, as we always did in Canongate.

My first Presbytery visit (for a part of the Moderator's duties is to visit six Presbyteries each year) was to Kirkcudbright; and with Eddie Marr's help, I could not have had a kinder Presbytery to visit if I had chosen one from the whole of Scotland. The weather was good, which helped a bit, but the whole great kindness and friendship I received everywhere I went would have made even a wet day seem bright. All the Presbyteries had taken tremendous trouble to make my visits easy and happy for me, and there they greatly succeeded.

I was able to visit the Churches, schools, homes, hospitals, farms, and even the cattle market, and everywhere I went I met with nothing but kindness. I am deeply grateful to the Presbytery Clerks and the Moderators and all the Ministers of the Presbyteries for the wonderful friendship they showed and the encouragement they gave me.

It is sometimes difficult to know what the Moderator does if one only "reads the papers". I read, for example, that I attended and spoke to the Royal High School in Edinburgh—which I had and, as usual, greatly enjoyed. But no mention was made of all the other Schools I had visited and spoke to and enjoyed—George Watson's, Fettes, Loretto, Edinburgh Academy, Rannoch, Melville College, Queen Victoria School, Dunblane—to mention but a few!

Mention of the last makes me think of all the various Army units I was able to visit: the Junior Band Leaders at Dreghorn where I presented the prizes; the Freedom of the K.O.S.B. at Duns; the Queen's Guard at Ballater; the Army Range in Kirkcudbright; the Passing-Out Parade at Glencorse; and various functions at Edinburgh Castle; the Bridge of Don Barracks, Aberdeen, as well as more mentioned later.

I cannot speak too highly of the help I had from the Army, beginning, as I have already mentioned, with the orderly whom General Leask arranged for me to have during the Assembly and shortly after, Lance-Corporal Hope. I would like here to pay tribute to the help I have had from all H.M. Forces and their very real desire to do all they can to assist the work of the Church.

Among the many other visits I have had the pleasure and privilege of making, was one to Abbotsford, the first time that the Moderator visited there officially since Sir Walter Scott

224

built it, where I was most graciously received by Miss Patricia and Miss Jean Maxwell-Scott.[1]

My visit to the Abbey of Pluscarden, accompanied by Hugh Mackay, was certainly a highlight. I had the privilege of not only addressing them in the Chapel, but also taking a prayer, and, at the gracious invitation of the Prior, gave the Blessing at the close of the Service. Accompanied by the Parish Minister, we lunched with them all afterwards. Since that month marked the 400th Anniversary of John Knox's death, I gave them a presentation of a fine old copy of his *History of the Reformation*, which they received with great pleasure as "a token of the more friendly times in which we all now live".

My visit to Balmoral, which I have already mentioned, was especially notable since this time all the Royal Family were present at Church, and all of them in residence at Balmoral itself. What a very happy family it is and what a wonderful example they set to us all in the country. How lucky we are to have them.

It was a great pleasure, too, to see Tommy and Mary Nicol so happily settled in Crathie Manse and so much appreciated by everybody.

The Army kindly sent a car to take me from Balmoral back to Edinburgh via Ballater, where I had the privilege of inspecting the Guard of Honour there, and also of meeting the officers and men of the Company of the K.O.S.B. who were that year forming the Queen's Guard during Her Majesty's stay at Balmoral, and I wished them well before they started their third term in Northern Ireland.

I had the pleasure of staying at the home of the Lord High Commissioner and Lady Clydesmuir, and also with the Secretary of State and Mrs Gordon Campbell at their lovely house near Cawdor—two very happy and gracious homes, again setting a standard for us all.

I much enjoyed preaching in a number of Churches throughout Scotland, and it was a special pleasure to preach at Dunfermline Abbey for the 900th Anniversary of Queen

---

[1] Their father Major-General Sir William Maxwell-Scott, Bart., who died in 1954 was, like the rest of the family, a Roman Catholic, and long before the days of the good Pope John had been a keen advocate of Christian Unity—so much so that I amused (and pleased) him by saying he was really an Honorary Elder!

Margaret, and at St Mary's, Haddington, where such wonderful work is being done for its splendid restoration, for which both Elizabeth, Duchess of Hamilton, and John McVie, their Town Clerk, had done so much.

I was privileged too to dedicate the splendid new hall at New Kilpatrick, and the striking new Churches at Kilmarnock and Cumbernauld, and to open and dedicate the Netherbow next to John Knox's house in the High Street, so beautifully and imaginatively built, which is now a great asset.

Chapter 3

The initial main purpose of my visit to India was to attend the 25th Anniversary of the Church of South India at Madras on 26th September 1972. On the previous Sunday evening, 24th September, I had attended a memorable service in St Paul's Cathedral in London where all branches of the Church were represented and messages conveyed to the C.S.I. by Dr Michael Ramsay, the Archbishop of Canterbury, the President of the Methodist Council and myself, and over 1,000 received Communion in a packed Cathedral.

On the next morning I set off at 7.30 a.m. from St Columba's Manse to fly (first class!) to Bombay by Jumbo-Jet and was met there by Dr Chris Wigglesworth, rested for a few hours, and then flew on to Madras to be welcomed there by Bishop Lesslie Newbiggin, Murdoch Mackenzie and others. What wonderful work these missionaries do! One has only got to see for oneself the sacrificial way they live and the tasks they perform to appreciate this—they not only preach the Gospel, they live it. The warmth of the welcome matched the heat—100°+: as someone put it, "I felt like a fish *in* water"!

I read a message from Dr Nevile Davidson who had been there at the beginning; and the services each day were unforgettable—2,000 communicating—as were the evening meetings. Murdoch Mackenzie and his wife were so kind and helpful, and put me up during my week's visit, which included Vellore, Chingleput, the slum clearances, the leprosy patients, Madras Christian College (where I preached), and was the first Moderator to preach in the very fine old St Andrew's Church, Madras, in the gardens of which I planted a tree to commemorate my visit, which I understand is growing already to a great height!

From Madras I flew to Calcutta in the evening and was so glad to see John Nelson's welcome face at Dum Dum Airport; he did such wonderful work in Calcutta and it was a very great pleasure to be with him.

It was a great privilege to preach in St Andrew's Church, Calcutta, to a full congregation (with, as at Madras, the British High Commissioner, the Roman Catholic Archbishop and the Bishop present) and afterwards attend a most delightful Scottish evening in the Hall—an hour or so after a fierce "demonstration" of over 20,000 people had taken place quite near, which I am glad to say had nothing to do with my visit! John Nelson accompanied me to a most enjoyable visit to the Governor of Bengal and his wife in the old Viceroy's house, and I was able to meet also a number of the British Community. But it was so hot—and the slums so terrible—worse, if possible, than Madras. There is in India no unemployment money and no sickness benefits—no nothing in fact, and very sad with so much unemployment.

I was so glad to have John Nelson's company from Calcutta to the hills where we were met at Badroga by Miss Scrymgour and motored in a jeep, which fortunately had good steering and brakes, by the winding, twisting, I would have *thought*, dangerous road to Kalimpong, where, by way of security check at Testa, we arrived in time for tea on the lawn, a delightful welcome and sweeter air, at Jubilee House—the house of the great and good Dr Graham. I was especially interested to visit Kalimpong because when Dr Graham contemplated retiring in 1941 he wanted me to succeed him—a kind and challenging offer which (for various reasons) I could not consider, but which, as so often happens in one's life, left the question of "what might have been" had I done so, and no regrets that I hadn't!

I shall never forget my visit to, and reception at, the S.U.M. Boys' School. To come from the humid heat of Bombay, Madras and Calcutta to Badroga Airport and then along that long, steep and winding narrow mountain road for miles and miles into the cooler, clear air and into the heights of the land around Darjeeling and Kalimpong, with its glorious views of the snowy mountains, is an exhilirating and never-to-be-forgotten experience. But it is not just the surroundings but far more the people who make a country—and what lovely happy people they all are. Here "by God's kindly grace are they not blest" to live in such a countryside amid the green hills and white hills and rivers, streams and valleys, and to be encompassed about with so much care and loving kindness?

Surely I shall never forget the graciousness, happiness and kindness of the people there, and not least that address made to me by a Bhutanese boy of seventeen—himself a Buddhist:

Respected Sir,

It is with feelings of utmost delight and very great gratitude that we . . . welcome you. . . . As you are representing the Church of Scotland we would like to let you know the naked fact that the people of Kalimpong and the surrounding places are greatly indebted to your Church. The pioneer missionaries of your Church, constrained by the love of Christ, came to this place and engaged in humanitarian activities for over a hundred years among all sorts of people, irrespective of caste, creed, colour or nationality. We are indebted to the Church of Scotland . . . and Moderator, Sir, you have today had an opportunity of seeing with your own eyes. . . . We pray to God almighty to keep you and guide you throughout your life and make you a channel of blessings to many. We sincerely wish you a very nice time in Kalimpong and wherever you go in this great land of India.

Well, I *had* "a very nice time in Kalimpong" and saw "with my own eyes" that love of Christ that Dr Graham had radiated to "all sorts of people, irrespective of caste, creed, colour or nationality"; and it is that love that shines there still.

I visited too the Girls' School, where I dedicated and unveiled a plaque, the Charteris Hospital, the Leprosy Centre and so many other places. Nor will I forget the kindness of the Principal of Dr Graham's Homes, or Mrs Pandit—as much

228

respected in Britain as she is in India—of Dr Minto and of so many others.

I was especially glad to meet Mrs Pandit, one of the great ladies of India. She had been a Cabinet Minister, a State Governor, an Ambassador to Moscow and Washington, High Commissioner in London, and President of the United Nations, sister of Nehru and aunt of Indira Gandhi, who she quite obviously didn't approve of or like much!

She looked after me well and spoke now with a new affection for things British, with special admiration for Mr Harold Macmillan and Lord Home.

At the invitation of the Chaplain, Mr Webster, I had the pleasure of conducting the service in the Church filled with young people, with the procession of colours, band and uniforms, and later preaching, with an interpreter, in the rather "tatty" Macfarlane Memorial Church. The kindness was matched by the glorious scenery—not least the snowy mountains.

I should have gone on to see Miss Ritchie at Sikkim, but by this time my back was showing signs of tiredness and so I went straight to Darjeeling, stayed a night with the Brodies, visited and spoke to the Schools, etc., and unveiled and dedicated a plaque for a new wing in the Girls' School run by the indefatigable Miss Dorothy Wallace.

A few days' stay at Ging near Darjeeling among the beautiful tea plantations with Mr and Mrs David Little from where, rested and sustained by their kindness, and having visited, among other places, Darjeeling Zoo and St Paul's School (the "Eton" of India)—more "English" than the British!—I set off once more for Calcutta on my way to Delhi. At Delhi, where I was most hospitably housed and fed by the British High Commissioner and Mrs Male, I preached in Delhi Cathedral, the first Moderator to do so, met some of our good devoted missionaries—who had come from far and near—at the home of these wonderful people the Cambridge Brotherhood whose very presence is a rich spiritual experience, visited the Red Fort at Delhi and Agra, the Taj Mahal, and so many other places. Everywhere I went there was nothing but kindness and a deep appreciation of all that Scotland meant: "Did you know?" or "Do you know?" and then out came the names—Boyd, Macphail, Carstairs—and so on.

From the time I had left London until I returned over three weeks later, I had landed and taken off by plane fourteen times and travelled many miles by car and train—an exhaustive and exhausting but so well-worthwhile journey, which showed me how greatly our Church is still loved and remembered in India.

Chapter 4

My journey to Caithness by train took nearly as long as the journey to India by plane! But it too was well worth it. I was taken to nearly every corner of Caithness and everywhere received the greatest possible welcome and the kindest hospitality.

There were many interesting highlights of the visit—Dounreay, the Caithness Glass Works, the various schools and Receptions, not least by the Town Councils of Wick and Thurso, and the large number of large and small (especially the small) meetings throughout the County; and tea at the Queen Mother's Castle of Mey was a delightful experience. I was glad to see a leather-bound copy of *The Kirk in the Canongate* on a shelf among the Queen Mother's books!

After ten days in Caithness, including two memorable Remembrance Day Services, I returned to Edinburgh and had the pleasure of visiting Linburn, where such wonderful work is being done for and by those who were blinded in the Wars, where I was accompanied by the Senior Chaplain, Scotland.

At East Kilbride I received a cheque for £20,000 from The Boys' Brigade in Scotland to help with missionary work; that they should raise so much money so quietly and unobtrusively and for such worthy causes—*here* is "modern youth".

My visit to the Presbytery of Meigle was "interrupted" for the 25th Wedding Anniversary of H.M. The Queen and Prince Philip

My diary for that day—Monday, 20th November—reads:

"London at 6.30 a.m. and met by Miller Scott who motored me to Dean's Yard, Westminster. The Dean's housekeeper gave me a very good welcome, put a room with bath at my disposal, and gave me an excellent bacon and egg breakfast. The Dean (Eric Abbott) who hadn't been too well came at 9.15 a.m. and was kindness itself. He took me through the Abbey and showed me where I was to sit and the Lectern, etc.; couldn't have been nicer. Later I met the others who were to be in the procession with me—the Archbishops of Canterbury and York, the Bishop of London, Cardinal Heenan, Dean of Windsor, Dean of St Paul's, General of the Salvation Army, etc.—all so friendly, as if we had all known each other for years, though I do know some of them. I sat in the Sanctuary immediately opposite the Queen, Duke of Edinburgh, Queen Mother, Prince of Wales, Princess Anne and Princes Andrew and Edward, and all the rest of the Royal Family, and read the Lessons—the only one to do so. It was a wonderful Service, 2,000 there, Prime Minister and all the Government and Opposition, etc. We lined up at the end and the Royal Family thanked and spoke to us, the Queen Mother thanking me especially for coming so far! Drove from the Abbey to the Guildhall for the magnificent lunch given by the Lord Mayor for the Queen and Royal Family. I was at the Queen Mother's table with the Duke and Duchess of Norfolk, the Gordon Campbells and Field-Marshal and Lady Hall. The Queen spoke so well in answer to the good speech by the Lord Mayor. (The Queen began "We—and I mean by that, both of us"!) She was at the small table beside us and the Prince of Wales just opposite. A truly wonderful occasion. I motored back to the Athenaeum and had a long talk with the Archbishop of York (Dr Coggan) and got the 22.30 train from Euston to Perth.

Heard that Bill Grant (one of our Canongate Elders and the Lord Justice Clerk) had been killed this afternoon in a motor accident near Kingussie. He was driving alone but some of the others were killed or badly injured. Very sad for Margaret and wrote to her from the Athenaeum before I left."

So, I returned to continue my visit to the Presbytery of Meigle.

These Presbytery visits, as ex-Moderators know, can be very tiring and exhausting but also very well worthwhile, because of the tremendous interest there is in the Church of Scotland. Each Presbytery is visited only once in ten years by a Moderator.

In Edinburgh I attended the Service in St Giles' to honour the Fourth Centenary of John Knox, and in the same evening took the Confirmation Service at Loretto School. (Someone wrote to *Life and Work* to ask why I only went to certain schools. The answer is—and this may seem strange to some people—that I only go to schools to which I am invited!)

One morning in October Lord Balerno called to see me to tell me that I had been elected by the Council as a Fellow of the Royal Society of Edinburgh, and that the actual election would be in March 1973. I was both surprised and delighted since I had not been nominated in the usual way, and the announcement came as a great surprise to me. Alick Balerno was shortly to retire as Treasurer of the Royal Society. I had known him and his delightful family for years; Robin had been a help to me at Canongate when he was a Divinity student; George had come and helped at some of our Camps and had done such good work with Geoff Shaw in the Gorbals before succeeding me as Chaplain at Fettes College, and Alick Jnr. as well as being a distinguished M.P. did so much for the boys of Currie.

Chapter 5

MODERATOR'S LONDON AND FORCES VISITS

Perhaps the best way to describe my Moderator's London visit and the visits to H.M. Forces is to take some extracts from my 1972 Diary and let them speak for themselves:

Monday, 27th November

At 9.15 p.m. arrived at the Sergeant-at-Arms Residence in Palace of Westminster where I was greeted most kindly by

Admiral Sandy Gordon Lennox and his wife and given a very nice bedroom and bathroom overlooking the Thames, which I shall have until Friday. Big Ben is just above me. I had a talk with Sandy Gordon Lennox about the Crypt service on Wednesday. It was started last year but very few attended and is not really wanted, and I have to go in any case for Lord Reith's Memorial in Westminster Abbey—so decided to have it cancelled.

Tuesday, 28th November

Very nice cup of tea in bed and then breakfast with Sandy Gordon Lennox who took me round Parliament, etc. Our decision to put off service in Crypt tomorrow not well received by J. Miller Scott! Visited the Speaker—Selwyn Lloyd—very nice talk about Fettes. Lunch at Lancaster House presided over by Gordon Campbell (the Secretary of State for Scotland)—about thirty there. Then to House of Commons to Distinguished Strangers' Gallery to hear Question Time, etc. Received by the Lord Chancellor (Lord Hailsham) in his room and he spoke, very friendly, for some time about Holyrood, etc. Went from him to 10 Downing Street for a cup of tea and talk with Ted Heath, the Prime Minister—he was very friendly and interesting and saw me to the door—couldn't have been nicer. We met in the Cabinet Room. Then to the House of Lords for the Scottish Peers' tea for me, run by Lord Ferrier: Geordie Selkirk, Alick Balerno, Kay Elliot among those there. I was then taken by Black Rod to the Lords—a very good seat beside him, and spent the evening at Caledonian Christian Club—supper there and concert by some of the young men. I spoke for fifteen minutes—very nice crowd of chaps.

Wednesday, 29th November

Early tea then breakfast with Sandy Gordon Lennox and then went with Miller Scott to Westminster Abbey to attend unveiling of stone to Lord Reith, walking in procession (in Moderator's kit) with the Archbishop of Canterbury. Service taken by the Dean (Abbott) and all the Reiths there. Talked with Lord Hill, the former Radio Doctor (when I was Radio Padre we once did a broadcast together) and others in the

Jerusalem Chamber, before motoring to St Paul's Cathedral Chapter House for lunch with the Dean and Chapter, the Provost of Southward, the Religious Director of the B.B.C., etc. Good to see Sam Woodhouse again, now Archdeacon of London, and Canon Collins. I made a reply to the Dean's very nice speech. Went from there to the Bishop of London at Fulham Palace (the last time a Moderator will visit there for the Bishop is giving it up) and had a very enjoyable tea with him. Both he and Collins said that Harold Macmillan was our greatest Prime Minister. Very nice party for M.P's, mostly Scottish, at the Sergeant-at-Arms House; Alec Douglas-Home, Fitzroy McLean, the Earl of Dalkeith, Woolridge-Gordon, etc.—a large company. Very nice dinner party later—the Gordon Lennoxs are so kind—Alick Buchanan-Smith, the Duke and Duchess of Richmond and Gordon, Betty Harvey-Anderson.

Thursday, 30th November

Visits to Toc H etc. and later also to the Dean of Westminister—always so nice. David Edwards joined us. Lunch with the Bank of Scotland—Ronnie Clydesmuir's (who presided) K.T. just announced today; all very welcoming and kind. Went to Buckingham Palace to sign Visitor's Book and then on to the Lord Mayor of London to have tea with him and the Lady Mayoress—both so nice. Then visited Dover House, the charming house of the Secretary of State for Scotland, and taken all round to meet the typists, officers, etc. George Younger and Nicola Campbell were "guides". I met a fellow called Banner who over forty years ago was a member of the Fet-Lor Club and said that when he was fourteen I gave him £1 to go with some of his friends to the Carnival! Dinner at Grosvenor House with the Royal Scottish Corporation. I sat beside Betty Hamilton and Lady Cathcart. Betty a bit worried about the lack of support at Haddington Abbey.

Friday, 1st December

John Goudie (the Principal Naval Chaplain) called at 9.15 a.m. to take me to the Admiralty. Said goodbye with grateful thanks to the Gordon Lennoxs; they have been so kind. Very interesting visit to the Board, Nelson Room, Admiralty

House and the Defence Ministry where I saw the Second Sea Lord, the Navy Secretary, the General Commanding the Royal Marines, etc. Each so nice. If only the country could be governed by men of such integrity and concern! They gave me lunch in full Naval Uniform on the *Discovery* in Captain Scott's own Cabin—quite delightful and all so well and thoroughly arranged—a great honour to the Church of Scotland really. Back to car and then to Miller Scott's Manse. Then to the Royal Caledonian School where the children gave a performance. I spoke and we had a very well-arranged supper-party. Very good to see Ian Lorne there. The children charming—just need affection and security.

Saturday, 2nd December

Breakfast at Crown Court Manse and from there car to Westminster Cathedral for coffee and talk with Cardinal Heenan who was very friendly and kind, deploring the modernism in all the Churches (including William Barclay!) I told him the story told me by the General of the Marines yesterday who asked a Marine Sergeant-Major "Are there more Catholics or Protestants in the Unit?" and answered, "No sir, we are all Marines!" and the Marine who was asked by the Prime Minister, Mr Heath, "Have you any troubles?" and received the answer "That's not my department sir!"

Sunday, 3rd December

Preached at St Columba's, Pont Street, at 11 a.m.—a packed Church—on Advent: "What I say unto you, I say unto all 'Watch'". Very nice to meet Niall Livingstone there with his parents—such a nice chap, and old Loretto Confirmation candidate who lives when in Scotland, at Lismore. Fraser McLuskey in bed with bronchial trouble; glad to see him and have lunch with Ruth before going to St Columba's again for the St Andrew's Day Service, where I spoke on St Andrew. Gordon Campbell read the Lessons. Tea afterwards, when again I spoke, and then back to Crown Court where there was a Social Meeting of Crown Court and Elders.

Monday, 4th December

Went to see the United States Ambassador at Grosvenor

Square: very friendly and showed us pictures, etc. Then on to Press Lunch at Crown Court where Iverach Macdonald of *The Times* took the chair and I spoke and answered questions, etc. From there to 1A Lennox Gardens. Fraser a little better and Ruth made me a cup of tea before I set out for Harrods to get my hair cut, and then on to Wigmore Street to Bassinos for photograph, and then back to St Columba's Manse. Later met St Columba's Kirk Session and wives and saw Highland dancing, etc. Have a bit of a temperature tonight and not feeling too fit.

Tuesday, 5th December

John Goudie, Principal Chaplain R.N., called for me at 1A Lennox Gardens and we motored in R.N. car to Paddington and caught the 9.30 a.m. to Plymouth, lunching on the train. Met by Glyn Williams, and in Admiral's car with R.M. Corporal driver to Admiralty House, and got a warm welcome there from Vice-Admiral and Mrs McKaig. Went from there in same car to *H.M.S. Raleigh* and *H.M.S. Fisgard* where I saw round these two training centres for young sailors; had tea and returned by Ferry to Admiralty House for dinner. I have really splendid rooms! And everyone so kind and friendly. A nice dinner-party at night. Mrs McKaig tells me that I am sleeping in the bed the Prince of Wales slept in a fortnight ago and at dinner sat in his chair! Got to bed after 11 p.m. and slept well after a hot bath. Mrs McKaig said that Admiral McKaig is soon to go to a new and higher appointment—I think to do with entry into Europe. Wrote some letters.

Wednesday, 6th December

Plymouth. Cup of tea brought to me at 7 a.m. Addressed the R.N. Engineering College, Manadon, at Divisions at 7.50 a.m. after leaving Admiralty House and taking leave of Admiral McKaig at 7.45 a.m. Breakfast with Commanding Officer, Captain and Mrs Gibson, at Manadon House. Then off to R.N. Hospital Storehouse and back to Manadon House for coffee with some of the students, including Stephen and Fergusson from Fettes and Kirkwood from Kirkcudbright. Then visit to *H.M.S. Penelope*—piped aboard and on leaving!

And then on to *H.M.S. Drake*. Visited 42 Commandos in the afternoon—a *very* enjoyable visit. Then motored to Dartmouth where I stayed with Captain and Mrs Forbes who gave me a very nice dinner in my honour and once again I had a lovely bedroom.

Thursday, 7th December

Took Divisions at Royal Naval College, Dartmouth—a very fine parade. I spoke on "Port, left: Starboard, right!" "Come to Church on Sunday and avoid the Christmas rush!" Breakfast afterwards with Captain and Mrs Forbes. Captain Forbes took me round the College and I met a number of Midshipmen and Students, including Steel of Loretto. I was taken a "sail" in a boat up the Dart—very enjoyable—and had lunch in the Wardroom. I saw round all the College and everyone most kind. On leaving the Captain, Commander, etc., saluted me from the deck—the first time the Chaplain had seen such an "honour"! John Goudie and Vass accompanied me to Exeter where I got the train to Westbury where the Army collected me and took me to Tidworth, where I stayed with the Royal Scots. A very nice buffet supper and met Peter McIntyre, ex-Fettes, and Jim Johnston, ex-Loretto, and so many others. Very nice to be with the Royal Scots again (of which I am an Honorary Member).

Friday, 8th December

Breakfast at Tidworth at the C.O's House and then spoke to the Royal Scots—the whole Battalion—military band playing, and saw round the Barracks. Then on to Aldershot where I met the new C.O. etc. and had lunch at Government House. Then on to Pirbright where I had an excellent visit to the Guards. "Chips" Maclean's son took me to "K" Company where the young Scots Guards from Scotland were there to meet me "sitting at attention" until told to "sit at ease"! Went on to Boys' Wing—1,300 boys of Guards and Household Troops. It rained very hard, not good for my stockings and brogues! Very nice tea at the Mess, spoke to some good Scots Guards officers, including Nicol and Ramsay. Then motored to Bagshot where they had a big dinner in my "honour". I occupied the Chaplain-General's fine quarters. Many there

237

including John and Margaret Mogg (soon to go to be Deputy Supreme Commander at Brussels), General Dunbar-Naismith, the Chaplain-General, Macgregor of Macgregor, the C.O. Camberley, Willie Wright, David Whiteford, etc. The C.G. made a nice speech and I replied and afterwards we all visited the very good Chaplains' Museum. A good long day!

Saturday, 9th December

Left Tidworth with Jim Harkness for Watford where we had lunch with the R.A.F. padre and the Mansells. After lunch the Mansells motored me to the R.A.F. Cranwell—two-and-a-half hours by car—where I visited St Andrew's Church and then on to the Lodge where I am staying with the Commandant and his wife—both charming people—in another excellent room. They gave me a splendid dinner-party in the Lodge at night and some very nice people present: dinner jackets.

Sunday, 10th December

Early cup of tea and then breakfast at the C.O's House at Cranwell. Preached at the morning service on Advent. Lunch with the padre and his wife, with the Commandant and Mrs Austen-Smith, and the Mansells. Rested for a little in the afternoon at the Lodge, and then motored to Nocton Hall where I saw round the Hospital. Among those I saw there in bed was Brewster, Jock Slater's cousin. Tea with the C.O. and his wife and then preached in the Hospital Chapel on St Andrew—the Church of England and Roman Catholic padres both present—in a full Chapel. A very good dinner party in the beautiful Mess—wives present—with roast duckling, etc. Motored back to Cranwell in a very fierce rain storm: I nearly lost my personal pennant, blown off by the wind; but we managed to find it on the road in the dark! Got back to the Lodge after 10 p.m.

Monday, 11th December

The Lodge, Cranwell. Had early tea and then a very good breakfast. The Commandant arranged for me to see the M.O. who gave me some tablets for my head and throat before I set out to see round Cranwell. I was taken all over the place and was able to meet some of the students and talk to them before lunch in the Staff Mess. I was very impressed with all I saw and everyone, as usual, most kind and courteous. Left at 2 p.m. for Connington, the home of the Phantoms—a very powerful striking force. Met by the Station Commander and taken round the whole Airfield. I was very impressed with the way so many of the Airmen were making toys, etc., for the children in hospital, e.g., 41 Squadron who had made about fifty really excellent teddy bears! I was allowed, as in other places, to see a lot of "secret" rooms, etc., and taken to the Observation Tower and too was very impressed with the Simulation Room. I was billeted in the V.I.P. Wing of the Officers' Mess—private sitting-room, bedroom, and bathroom. A special dinner given for me by the C.O. in the Mess at night, with the various Commanders etc. present, including the padres—all so friendly and kind. MOON LANDING!

Tuesday, 12th December

A Mess waiter brought my tea to my room at 7 a.m. and a very good breakfast to my private sitting-room at 7.15 a.m. I left at 8 p.m. in the C.O's car with three "stars", as throughout the whole Forces' visit, and drove to Grantham Station for the 9.38 a.m. train to Edinburgh with the Chaplains seeing me off. Got to Edinburgh at 2.30 p.m. and met by Willie Wright and Donald Macdonald and drove to the Manse in Army car and had an hour's consultation with Donald Macdonald. A huge pile of letters waiting for me! Went to the Harry Younger Hall and to the Church for Toc H Service with tea later at Panmure House. Phoned dear Ray: she said that Leonard Boden is painting the Queen again and he and Margaret mentioned my name, and she said that she and all the Royal Family were very fond of me! Dear Ray seemed quite cheerful.

Wednesday, 13th December

Gen home! Motored to West Calder to collect dear Gen who was so excited to see me, as well as glad to be home again!

So ended my London and Forces visits, full of interest, enjoyment and kindness, which all helped to make it less tiring than it might have been.

Chapter 6

But there was no rest to follow. I had another huge correspondence to attend to personally. During my absence from home Alick Sawyer, whom I was fortunate to have as Interim Moderator at Canongate during that period, helped, as usual, by Mrs Taylor, had dealt, and was still to deal with as much as possible, but much had still to be attended to personally; and all this had to be combined until the end of the month, with more local Services and engagements, such as the Memorial Service for Lord Grant, the 50th Anniversary of the Royal Naval Reserve in Scotland, the Dedication of Holy Trinity Church, and the welcome to the new G.O.C. Scotland—Lt.-General Sir Chandos Blair, as Governor of the Castle, as well as the Christmas Services at Canongate.

From the beginning of the year I had preached in the Universities of Glasgow, Dundee, St Andrews and Aberdeen, and in a large number of Schools, and I was particularly pleased to have addressed the boys and girls of St Augustine's Roman Catholic School at their invitation, where I was presented with a beautiful leather-bound edition of the Jerusalem Bible. This friendship with the Roman Catholics has never been so important as today, not least because of the troubles in Ireland; and Cardinal Gray and I on more than one occasion shared in the same activities, one of them being our joint visit to the *Daily Express*. The visit to Nunraw, too, was a memorable occasion where once again I was asked by the Abbot, as I had been at Pluscarden, to take part in the Service, give the Blessing and address the Community.

I remember with particular pleasure preaching in Perth in the beautiful St John's Church, in Glasgow Cathedral, where I had for a short time been an Assistant, and where Dr Morris, a former Assistant of Canongate, is doing such notable work as Minister, supported by another former Canongate Assistant, the Chaplain, the Rev. David McGregor; the 200th Anniversary at Kelso Parish Church, and the Services at Clifton Hall and Cargilfield. For more years than I can remember I have preached at the beginning of each session at

Clifton Hall School and on the last Sunday of each session at Cargilfield School. A year for me would not be quite the same without these two fixtures!

But possibly the most memorable Service of all was that in St Giles' Cathedral in January—a Memorial Service for the Scots Guards killed in Ireland and attended by not only the Guards themselves but by the relatives of those who had been killed.

Sometimes I was exhausted by the kindness I received; though it was a nice kind of exhaustion which made me sleep well at night and look forward to the next morning.

I have several times been asked, because of the heaviness of the Moderator's programme, whether Moderators should not be chosen either at a younger age or else for a two-year period. The usual age for a Moderator is in his early sixties; but against a younger age one has to remember that one of the liveliest of all our Moderators, Dr A. C. Craig, was elected at the age of seventy! As for the two-year period in office, I cannot really see how this would help, since the pressure, though considerably eased, would still be there: but it is true that it takes a month or so to settle down and one is really getting into one's stride during the last months of office. There is a lot to be said for one year only and it allows more to succeed to the highest honour and responsibility that the Kirk can bestow on its Ministers.

Chapter 7

The main object in going to Hong Kong and Singapore, to which I was flown by the R.A.F., stopping at Cyprus, to meet the padres there, and that wonderful little island of Ghan, was to see our Scottish troops; and it was a great joy to meet the Black Watch under Lt.-Colonel Tweedy, their Commanding Officer; to be shown round the Unit and to meet so many of our soldiers there; to go into the New Territories and see more of them in training; to go even farther into the New Territories and see beyond the Border into China and meet Scotsmen from the Royal Horse Artillery and even from the Gurkhas;

and to visit Scottish people in the Royal Air Force and in the Royal Navy.

The kind hospitality from General Sir Richard Ward, the Commander of the British Forces, was quite outstanding, and I was so grateful to him and to Lady Ward for all they did to make my visit comfortable and worthwhile. The General kindly put one of his Staff cars at my disposal for the week, as well as the use of his motor launch, Corporal Leung Chung Yuen, who drove the car, was a most charming and delightful fellow, and nothing was too much trouble to him. Willie Wright and I got to know him well and have since seen him twice in the U.K. when he was on courses, and each year he sends me still a Christmas card. I was told that he became a Christian after we left. He certainly always behaved as one.

I was also grateful to the Governor and his wife for their invitation to Government House; and to all the other people I met who gave me such a welcome as a representative of the Church of Scotland. And it was an added comfort to have Padre Wright (Senior Chaplain, Scotland) with me all the time.

Among many memorable visits I recall especially one we paid to Hay Ling Chau—"Isle of Happy Healing"—a centre for leprosy patients. A fast boat takes an hour to get there but it is well worthwhile to see the great work that has been done for so long by the late Dr Fraser and by his successors in their cause to help to cure leprosy. Indeed, the island which at one time held 500 leprosy patients had then well under 200; and the school which used to have forty children now had only two. There are now no more leprosy patients there, and it has been taken over by H.M. Forces.

It was a great inspiration, too, to see the work done by Padre Hynd, the Chaplain to the Black Watch, not least among the soldiers' families, some of whom quite naturally sometimes feel homesick, especially when the men have to go into training, jungle-fighting, or up to the New Territories.

The Black Watch has its own Kirk Session and it was a great joy to address the regiment and be entertained by the Kirk Session afterwards. It gave me a thrill to see in this British Colony the kilt and the red hackle—and possibly an even

242

greater thrill to go into the New Territories and see Scottish troops and hear the Scottish tongue in a land that didn't look far from Loch Lomond, although it was only a few miles from the Chinese border.

It is good to know that the present Chaplain of the Black Watch, as I write, is Norman Drummond where he and Elizabeth are rightly so much appreciated. They had bought from me the house I had at North Berwick—"Farend"—as their "home" before I moved into another holiday home there. "Farend" had been the home of dear Pip and Clare when he retired, and I had bought it from Clare after Pip died, having sold the little National Trust flat I had in The Lodge.

From Hong Kong, Padre Wright and I flew the four hours' journey to Singapore where I was the guest of the Commanding Officer of the Royal Highland Fusiliers, Colonel Mackay, and his wife; and there too I conducted a service for the battalion, and met them and many other Scottish men and women from the Navy, Army and Air Force. It was a special pleasure for me to meet Miss Macbeth, a former deaconess of the Canongate, who did wonderful work for the Huts and Canteens and was then carrying on so much valuable work in Singapore. I saw, too, the fine service given by the Padre, Peter Meager. I cannot be too grateful to the Chaplains I met out there and I cannot emphasise too much their wonderful work.

Both Hong Kong and Singapore have grim and vivid memories of the war with Japan when so many were killed or captured. In the War Memorial Cemetery at Kranji in Singapore one sees the thousands of graves of men in their late teens or early twenties who fell in 1942 when Singapore was taken.

Among the highlights of my year of office, the visits to Hong Kong and Singapore stand out as probably the greatest of all; and one would like to feel that the Moderator's visit to places like these is so well worthwhile and obviously appreciated as, for example, in the letter that I received later from the padre of the Black Watch:

"After almost two years away from Scotland it is very reassuring to know that the Church does not forget. The advantages of Moderators' visits cannot be exaggerated. They create an interest, underline the importance of the Chaplain and even influence the Chinese soldier.''

Nothing on this visit seemed too much trouble for the Services in the help and encouragement they gave the Moderator and the Senior Chaplain, and the Church is very grateful indeed for all that the Services do to show their appreciation of the Church of Scotland in this so vivid way.

So happy had been my visit to the Far East that I didn't realise until I got back how exhausting it had all been; for never for a moment, except for sunburn in Singapore, did I feel exhausted during the time I was there. But after the return journey, again so comfortably by an R.A.F. VC10, and stopping once more at Ghan and Cyprus, my feet swelled so much I couldn't get my shoes on and my throat became so sore I couldn't swallow. But it was all tremendously worth it.

Shortly after the return to Scotland I preached at the most moving Service of Thanksgiving for the life of the Duke of Hamilton, that great and good Scotsman who did so much for our Church and for the community—a memorable service indeed in St Giles' Cathedral. Following that there was a Centenary Service for David Livingstone at Blantyre, a visit to the Presbytery and the College of Education in Dundee, and then the first United Reformed Church Assembly in London, where it was good to see my old friend Eric Fenn again.

I was suffering again from very painful arthritis during this London visit where I was accompanied by Hugh Mackay and John Hood, and found great difficulty in preaching at Oundle and Uppingham Schools on the return journey to Edinburgh—though I greatly enjoyed my visits to these two great Schools and can scarcely ever have had a more appreciative audience than that of the boys at the evening service in Uppingham Chapel.

It would be impossible to thank everyone for the kindness and courtesy I received during my year of office, but I would specially like to mention not only the various Presbytery Clerks and Donald Macdonald, the Principal Clerk, but also all those connected with Her Majesty's Forces in the Navy, the Army and the Air Force for the help they gave me on so many occasions, which afforded me an opportunity to meet and talk with many people individually.

I had already expressed at the opening of the Assembly my views on the Moderator's dress! And never did I take it with me when I went overseas, whether to India or the Far East, and never did I find that a disadvantage. My only "distinctive" dress was a purple stock and a silver Celtic cross which the Scottish Chaplains had presented to me, and a light scarlet cassock at services.

It had been for me a most wonderful and memorable year. I am so grateful to the Church for having put this trust in me and sustained me by their prayers. I can only add what I said in my final words to the Assembly—that the Church must, while learning from the past and being able to distinguish between prejudice and principle, live in the present and look to the future, and that a Church that boldly preaches and teaches the eternal truths, however unpalatable they may sometimes be at the time, shall ever stand in the time-honoured words *et nunc, et semper, et in secula seculorum.*

Like the beloved Robert Louis Stevenson in his self-chosen epitaph, "I have meant well, tried a little, failed much". But at least I tried!

PART VI

Chapter 1

I have always felt it is of real importance that a clergyman's life (or indeed anyone's life) should embrace as many interests as possible. When a boy I was given by my mother a small book called *Being and Doing* I had looked up the page for my birthday, 12th June, and what I read there, written, I think, by Professor Huxley, had a great influence on me:

"Then learn as much as you can about all sorts of things, and so make this world, whilst you have to live in it, a perpetual source of interest and surprise and gratification. That will keep your *mind* from stagnating. And then get into the way of feeling for other people's troubles, and doing what you can to help them away, and that will keep your *heart* from stagnating. You may live until you are five times sixty-five if you can, you will never find the world a bit too weary for you."

It is important that one should never become too parochial. A parish Minister should not only know the people in his parish but as far as possible something about the many different interests that its many different members have; about the various football teams and their places in the league table, the names of the jockeys (though probably not their horses!), the various cricketers and the places of the Counties in the Championship, some knowledge of music, including even "pop" singers under that category! He should know how to

247

cook and to camp—indeed to learn "about all sorts of things", to be at home with young and old alike. And he should also try to show that there are other points of view in any argument, so that one can think more fairly. . . . I shall always remember General Denys Reid complaining to me once about the attitude at one time of some of the officers and men in the Division, and when I began to put their point of view against his to him, he turned sharply to me and said "Here, whose side are you on, padre?" And I said "When I'm with you I'm on their side and when I'm with them I'm on your side, as I have been already today". Then he looked at me with a smile and said "Well done padre, I wouldn't have it otherwise".

In party politics too he should usually be the "umpire" rather than a participant, and try there too to let people see the other man's point of view, while keeping his own point of view to himself. He should never preach party politics from the pulpit, unless it be to give both sides of the argument in as an unbiased way as is humanly possible.

I feel too that a minister should be able to mix quite naturally with all sorts of people: "Remember," my mother once said to me, "a gentleman is someone who is at home in any company." For that reason too, and so that I did not become too "parochial" and "short-sighted", I found my membership of the New Club in Edinburgh, which I joined in 1942 (before the University Club was amalgamated with it) and of the Athenaeum in London, to which I was elected in 1947, where one can meet all sorts of people with many different interests, a most valuable complement to the Canongate Boys' Club.

I had, for example, what was for me a most interesting and rewarding conversation one evening with Mr Harold Macmillan, shortly after he had resigned as Prime Minister, when I found myself alone with him in the Smoking Room of the Athenaeum. I told him about the great changes for good that had taken place in the Canongate during his term of office, and how true the words he had spoken in 1957—that most of our people had "never had it so good". He smiled and told me that these words were so often misrepresented because he had spoken them more as a warning than as a boast, for he had gone on to say "isn't it too good to last" and warned about the problem of rising prices and inflation. He spoke about the horrors he had witnessed during the First World War, where as a Captain in the Grenadier Guards he had been wounded three times. And then he talked of the appalling conditions he had seen at Stockton of which, during his first Parliament from 1924–29, he had been their M.P.; men without work or wages for years, some almost now unemployable, and unemployment in the country of nearly three million people. I told him how I had seen similar conditions in Canongate when I first started the Boys' Club in 1927, and how greatly changed for good it all was now. But he added that his often quoted words were spoken as much as a caution since it was important to realise that there would be teething troubles, that it was up to us all to see that these bad old days were never to return, and that we should never be complacent. I thanked him for all he had done for us; he said that, well, he had tried his best but that there was yet so much more to be done, not only for the physical but too for the spiritual benefit of mankind. It was a privilege to be able to sit and talk quietly with one of the few great statesmen of our time.

I remember too, also in the Athenaeum, having breakfast with T. S. Eliot who, because I happened that morning to be wearing a Royal Scots tie, took me to be Wykehamist, and I was able to point out to him that "Pontius Pilate's Bodyguard" (a name for the Royal Scots) is a much older institution than even Winchester College! So there too, as in the New Club, one could meet and talk with and learn from men of all sorts of different interests.

Of the many conversations I have enjoyed in the New Club none gave me more pleasure than those I used to have with Lionel Smith, when he would sit beside me and reminisce about his days in Oxford or in the Middle East. I asked him once if Dr Jowett was before his time at Oxford. "Jowett," he said, "why he was a godfather": and had he ever met Spooner? "Oh yes," he said. "I knew Dr Spooner quite well. I have many stories of him. I remember once walking down the High at Oxford and we passed a lady clothed in black from head to foot, to whom Dr Spooner doffed his silk hat. 'Poor woman,' he said, 'she lost her husband you know. Very sad. Eaten by missionaries.'" He would quote A. J. Balfour: "A religion that is small enough for our understanding is not great enough for our need"; or Raymond Asquith's essay on "The need of the wise to undo some of the harm done by the good".

A conversation I had with Sir David Hunter-Blair, the old Abbot of Fort Augustus, I had found so interesting that I wrote to him and asked him to tell me again what he had told me, and this was the letter I received from him:

7th September 1938.

Dear Reverend Sir,

The facts as to which you inquire are as follows.

After the death of my great-grandfather, Sir James Hunter-Blair (Lord Provost of Edinburgh) in 1787, his widow and some of her children, including my grandfather (afterwards Sir David) went to stay in Rome for a time.

Prince Charles Edward Stuart (b. 1720) was then in residence at the Palazzo Muti with his daughter Charlotte (known as Countess of Albany). He died in Rome in 1788, when my grandfather David was a boy of nine. I give these dates to show that David was staying in Rome in the last year of the Prince's life, and may often have seen him in the streets—his good daughter used to take him to Mass at the Church of the Holy Apostles, near Corvo in Rome.

When I was a child of four my earliest recollection is of having sat on my grandfather's, Sir David's, knee at Blairquhan Castle, my home in Ayrshire (he was then seventy-eight), of his stroking my curls, crooning out the old song "Wha wadna fecht for Chairlie?"—and then saying sadly, "Poor Prince Charlie. I remember seeing him walking about in Rome with a red nose and a big stick. Poor Prince Charlie! Far better if he had been killed at Culloden" (pronounced *Cullodden*).

This was in the autumn of 1854 when I was just four. Sir David died in December 1857.

Yours truly,

David O. Hunter Blair, O.S.B.,
Abbot.

All this, I feel sure, helps the work of a Minister; and not least in the work of his parish. A Minister is "An Ambassador for Christ" and no Ambassador is of any use if he sits all the time in his Embassy! When my father once told Sir Donald Tovey how much he envied and admired his breadth of interests, he replied, "Well, I suppose I've got a sort of blotting-paper mind!" There is something to be said for that; and at least it prevents "stagnation" and carried one into old age so that the world "never becomes a bit too weary for you".

Chapter 2

A "perpetual source of interest" too, if not of "surprise", has been the many visits I have had the privilege and pleasure of paying when preaching at Schools and Colleges, especially the Boarding Schools because there I have had too the added enjoyment of staying with the various Head Masters, and sense more intimately something of the spirit of each School. These visits have always been for me most refreshing and rewarding experiences.

No one, I feel, summed up better the benefits derived from these great Schools than Lord Lovat when writing of his old School, Ampleforth:

"What did school teach me? I reply without hesitation 'essentials not to be found in the Comprehensive system: to love God and serve the King. To learn a sense of responsibility and loyalty to superiors; to give of one's best and take a beating cheerfully; to feel, but not to show emotion; to lead and not be driven; and, above all, to show tolerance and consideration for others, to realise that authority can never be abused, to have good manners and never lose one's temper'."[1]

[1] *March Past* by Lord Lovat (Weidenfeld & Nicolson).

I have so many happy memories of these School visits through the years—of the various Chapels, of the fine singing, of the friendly courtesy of the boys, many of whom were invited to join us at meals, and the generous hospitality of the Head Masters and their wives. It would be invidious to single out one School from another, though I have already mentioned some elsewhere, but there are some special memories that will ever remain: on my first visit to Rugby looking from my bedroom window on to the pitch that started it all; the sight of seeing small boys dressed like Masters in gowns at Eton, Winchester and Radley; the great cricket field at Shrewsbury; the glorious Chapels at Lancing, Wellington and Eton; the Confirmation Services at Sedbergh; the two young Arabian Kings at Harrow; the three Schools at Sherborne—Preparatory, Boys' and Girls'; the "haunted" bedroom on my first visit to Repton; the beagles at Stowe; seeing the original "Mr Chips" at Leys—come at once to mind. But of all the memorable visits I have been privileged to make to the many Schools at which I have stayed and preached, perhaps the most memorable was that made in the summer of 1979 to Eton.

On my previous visits to Eton I had been the guest of Tony and Elizabeth Chenevix-Trench when he was Head Master and preached both in Lower Chapel and in College Chapel; but on this occasion I stayed with Martin and Gay Charteris on what was much more of an official occasion. Martin, now Lord Charteris of Amisfield, having retired as the Queen's Private Secretary, was by now Provost of Eton, and this time I stayed in the Provost's Lodge, and been motored there by David and Elise Scott-Barrett from their charming home in Woking where they now lived, he having in January of that year retired after a distinguished three years as Army Commander in Scotland. To stay in the Lodge was in itself a memorable experience with its drawing-room surrounded by the quite magnificent portraits of former Etonians—gifts, when they were leaving, by famous artists; but Martin had arranged a visit that would take in so much of the life at Eton, which included dining with the Provost and his guests, who included the retiring Vice-Provost F. J. R. Coleridge, and the Senior Chaplain elect, James Bentley, attending early

Communion in College Chapel at which nearly a hundred boys and Masters communicated (in spite of the fact that during the week the first class of the day started at 7.20 a.m. and Sunday is the only morning that they don't need to rise early), preaching in College Chapel at 10.40 a.m., followed by coffee with Michael McCrum, the Head Master, and being taken by the Provost to lunch in the beautiful College Hall where all the King's Scholars eat each day, their gowns over their tail coats and white bow ties, and where lunch is preceded by, and finished with, a chanted—and enchanting—Latin grace led by a small group of singers and a boy precenter. In the afternoon Johnny Chenevix-Trench called for me at the Provost's Lodge and took me to his room in his House where I had tea with him and two of his friends. Johnny was at this time in "Pop" and had been for three years in the Rowing Eight, an Oppidan Scholar and in the Sixth Form Select and yet, as usual, so modest about it all. I had dinner on the Sunday evening with the Conduct, Roger Royle, and among the guests were Johnny again, the President of Pop, and the Art Master J. R. Booth—a really charming group of people. On the following morning I watched the Eton Corps rehearsing for the Trooping of the Colour on the fourth of June, with an excellent Pipes and Drums Band with Lord Bruce as the Pipe-Major, as well as their Regimental Band. The Provost took me to lunch in Bekynton, the Assistant Masters' attractive Dining Hall, and was kind enough to accompany me himself to the Deanery at Windsor, where I was staying next with Michael and Jill Mann.

Among all the famous Schools, each with its own great characteristics, Eton is surely quite unique. After all, a School that can produce, according to J. M. Barrie, Captain Hook and, according to Ian Fleming, James Bond (before he went to Fettes!), and can also number among its Old Etonians the Duke of Wellington, Gray, Shelley and Fielding and twenty Prime Ministers, well, *is* surely unique!; and it is good to know that the new Head Master, an old friend, Eric Anderson, is the first member of the Church of Scotland to hold that office.

I was to return to Eton Chapel later in the year but, alas, this time for a different reason; for on the 5th of October a Memorial Service was held there for Tony Chenevix-Trench.

253

I went with the small contingent from Fettes College composed of Cameron Cochrane, Dick Cole-Hamilton and the Head of School; and since I was also representing Dr Robin Barbour, the Moderator, with typical courtesy I was asked to give the closing prayer and the Benediction. Patrick Crocker who had been an Assistant Master at Fettes from 1959 to 1965, and had been Assistant Master at Eton since, was our most hospitable host and gave us all lunch at Bekynton, and we had with us also some Old Fettesians, including G. P. S. Macpherson, Lord Fraser and Donald Crichton-Miller.

It was a moving service where the Choir sang most beautifully. The Lessons were read by Richard Chenevix-Trench and by Michael McCrum, the Head Master, and in the full Chapel along with Elizabeth and her family, were also the Provost of Eton; the Dean of Christ Church, Oxford; Sir William Gladstone, the Chief Scout, who had been Tony's best man at his wedding; Sir Robert Birley, and a number of Head Masters. Unlike the Memorial Service held at Fettes College at the end of the summer term in Edinburgh, no address was given. The service was conducted by the Conduct, James Bentley, and the Head Master of Bryanston, the Rev. D. I. S. Jones, who had previously been Conduct at Eton. The other School at which Tony had been Head Master, Bradfield, was too represented as was his old school, Shrewsbury. The whole service was a fitting tribute to a great and much-loved Head Master of three great Schools.

It was a memorable service and I personally shall never forget the beautiful singing by the Choir of "Thou shalt keep him in perfect peace whose mind is stayed on Thee".

In 1967 the Oxford University Press published a book containing thirty-three of my School sermons under the title (which I didn't choose!) *Take Up God's Armour*, which was, thankfully for me, well-received. In a personal letter from Sir John Betjeman, whose lovely poem "Advent" I had, with his kind permission, included, he wrote:

Reverend dear and Holy Doctor Ronald,
    I am immensely pleased and flattered to have your excellent book of addresses which I have been reading to the improvement of my mind, and much more important, with

enjoyment and interest. You say a lot, simply and shortly. . . .

Among other encouraging letters was one from Professor James S. Stewart, our greatest and most modest of preachers:

I am so glad to have this book; for often one is asked to recommend something relevant for people who are feeling bewildered and perplexed, and I shall know now what to give them.

The Reviewers, too, were on the whole kind. Donald Hughes, the then Head Master of Rydal wrote:

I recommend this book unreservedly to those who preach in Schools and Colleges. They will have much to thank the author for—and so will their congregations.

And Dr William Neil of Nottingham, whose friendship and whose books I have always so much valued, wrote:

He has a flair which amounts almost to genius for getting through to young people and holding their interest. . . . This is a moving, inspiring and wonderfully helpful book for people of all ages. As a gift for teenagers it could not be bettered.

In another book which was published in 1977, which Prince Charles kindly allowed me to dedicate to him, called *Seven Sevens*, I included seven more School sermons, making forty then in print.

But as well as the gracious encouragement, the publication of such addresses has too its disadvantages; one being that you cannot easily preach them again! A notable example of this was when I was Moderator and was asked to preach a radio New Year sermon, I used a talk called "Janus" from *Take Up God's Armour*. Some days later I received a letter from a young man who wrote that he had been travelling by car with his mother to Church and had listened to, and enjoyed, my sermon; but judge of his astonishment when at the Morning Service in their Church he heard, word for word, the same sermon! He thought that this was most dishonourable and wanted to know what source we got our sermons from. He couldn't sign his name for his father was far too well-known, so he signed the letter "Viator". Fortunately I saw the postmark and wrote to the local paper saying that someone had written to ask the source of my sermon; and I gave it. I received a most apologetic reply, saying both he and his mother both hoped that I would forgive them for their rudeness but that still, because of his father, he couldn't give his name; but I wonder if he ever said anything to his Minister!

I have never been able to understand the attitude of those who condemn our great Public Schools on the ground that because everyone cannot benefit from them then no one should, and that therefore they should be abolished, instead of trying to raise the standards of all Schools. It is, of course, true that mostly well-to-do—and let it be equally said—often self-sacrificing—parents that can send their boys (and girls) to these Schools; but it is equally true that through scholarships and the like an opportunity is given too from those of the poorest homes. One might as well argue that because everyone cannot afford to run a car then no one should; or else that we should all go about on bicycles!

Personally, though in no way against Public Schools or the Boarding School system, I feel that the best answer—unless there is a good reason—such as parents being abroad, in the Armed Services and the like—is a good Day School where the advantages of a good School can be combined with the even greater advantage of a life at home with the family: but I may be wrong!

As for preaching at Universities I, who am neither a theologian nor a scholar, nor a great preacher, have always been comforted by the words of the then Vice-Chancellor of Cambridge when I was Select Preacher there in 1947. I was his guest for the weekend, had a dinner given for me in Clare College, of which he was too, at the time, Master, processed with him in robes through the streets, led by a mace-bearer (by which time I had come to the conclusion that they must have invited the wrong preacher!) and then in Great St Mary's, having given the Bidding Prayer, and the choir having disappeared behind curtains, I preached a very simple sermon on "What is God like?" to a good congregation—because still by that time there were many ex-Servicemen at the University and the Radio Padre had not been quite forgotten. On the way processing back I apologised for preaching so simple a sermon to so distinguished an audience; and then came his comforting words which have stood me in good stead at similar functions ever since: "Most preachers when they come to a University seem to think that they have to give some learned theological essay, forgetting that most of us are spiritually and theologically really very simple people. Yours was one of the few sermons here that I could really understand, and we all thank you for it!"

Chapter 3

After my very exhausting, but rewarding, year as Moderator I should have taken at least one month's complete rest; but having been away from the parish for a year I felt that it was my duty to get back there immediately, so that the good folk who had looked after the Church and parish so well during my absence could be relieved.

Even during that one year the changing face of the Canongate had seen still further changes. The new houses in the Dumbiedykes area had been, and were still being, occupied by new residents, and even more younger people had left the parish for the new housing areas, so that the number in the Boys' Club began to diminish still further, though it must be admitted that what we lacked in quantity was more than made up for in quality; and my last few years of the Club and Camps saw some of the best members we have ever had. But the number didn't justify our keeping on Panmure House now, and the latter days of the Club were centred on the Harry Younger Hall. By 1974 for practical and economic reasons we gave up Panmure House to the Town for a different kind of youth work and retained the Hall, adding later a small annexe which we called "The Stag's Head" and which Charles, the young Earl of Cassillis, opened (with Angus, the new Duke of Hamilton, presiding) since, while staying with me at the Manse, he had done so much to help the work of the Club.

The declining number of young people, the still changing face of the parish, the intake of new residents, and my stupidity in not having taken a proper rest after my year as Moderator, all began to point the way to my retirement, to make way for a younger, and more energetic, successor.

When I was a Divinity student "Tubby" Clayton of Toc H had once said to me "You ought never to walk where once you ran", and I certainly felt that I was beginning to "walk" now! Then I saw even more clearly the truth of Archbishop William Temple's words: "What tires me is not so much what I do, but what I don't do." And when, as a student, I first met my predecessor, an old man now (and neither of us, of course, had any idea that I would one day succeed him), who had spent all his ministry in Canongate, as I was to do, he said, "My young friend, don't do what I have done and stay so long in a parish that you haven't the strength to do what you know should be done". . . . He had, remember, been two years assistant in Canongate and forty-eight years Minister before he died and I succeeded him. He had had a much harder time than I had and his had been a wonderful ministry until his latter years when he became old and tired, but always loved.

These considerations along with the changing face of the parish, to which I had come first to an overcrowded "slum" and which was becoming a kind of Edinburgh "Chelsea", made me feel that the time was coming for my retirement.

I had also seen most of my dreams for the parish and Church come true—a Church building beautifully restored both within and without, the restoration of the Church's place in history as it affected both Holyroodhouse and Edinburgh Castle, the acquiring and restoration of the Manse in Reid's Court in the heart of the parish, where a Manse should be, and surely one of the finest Manses in Edinburgh, the acquiring of Russell House, the restoration of Panmure House, and the building of the Harry Younger Hall. In that line there was not really much more to be done by me.

And so in January 1977 I told the Kirk Session that I intended to retire at the end of September, which would have meant that I would have been over forty years as Minister, and, though I kept on the Boys' Club until it closed in March 1978, over fifty years in the Canongate itself.

Now, had I retired from Canongate some years earlier, I should have left my successor at once an easier and yet much more difficult task. Easier, because he would have inherited a much more lively Church with a Boys' choir of over forty boys, an ordained Assistant, a Deaconess and at least one student Assistant, daily prayers in the Memorial Chapel largely taken by the students residing in Russell House and in the Manse, a thriving Boys' Club, and a Youth Fellowship which in Wade Huie's, Bob Henderson's, Hugh Mackay's and Gordon Haggarty's days was quite outstanding. But I should also have left him the later legacy of the depopulation of the parish and the departure of so many of its young people, with no Boys' choir, no Assistant, for John Barclay Burns was to be our last full-time Assistant, no Deaconess and no Youth Fellowship, so that folk might truthfully have said: "It wasn't like that in Dr Wright's time!" But, having stayed on, it was!

The Prince of Wales kindly wrote to me from his ship *H.M.S. Bonnington*:

"How sad to hear you are to retire in the near future—the Canongate will never be really the same without you."

But it was soon to become now better, for fortunately in Charles Robertson an excellent successor was chosen with a new challenge to face, and with the ability, the enthusiasm and determination to face it, and a most capable wife to share it with him.

Before my retirement I had one of the most pleasant of surprises. Harry Richmond told me that three of the old Club boys, Billy Reid, Billy Pinkerton and Stuart McFarlane, wanted me to come with them for a celebration dinner in the Café Royal and asked me to fix a suitable date. So it was that Harry duly called for me in his car on the evening of 25th March 1977 to drive me to the Café Royal for this small dinner party. Judge of my surprise when I got there to find not just these three old Club boys but a group of men representing five decades of membership of the St Giles' Boys' Club, which later became the Canongate Boys' Club, who had met to "honour its founder". Here were men, some of whom I had not seen for years, all gathered together, representing between them the years 1927 to 1977, with a splendid dinner, many speakers and presents, and all so unexpected! It was so good to meet them all and my pleasure was as great as my surprise. I sat between two former Scottish rugger captains—Norman Davidson (back for a few months from New Zealand) and Pringle Fisher—and round the table there were old boys like David Bathgate who had recently been on an Everest Expedition; George Flannigan who had once been "too young to go to Camp"—and was now a grandfather; Richard Long, now a detective; Billy Nicoll, now a policeman; David Croft, a prison officer—and so on—thirty-six of them, with apologies from as far afield as Australia, Canada and South Africa. Even the Menu "To mark the 50th year of the Canongate Boys' Club 1927-77" had a Camp flavour about it—"Skateraw Seafood Cocktail, Cream of Mushroom Soup à la John Sellars, Sirloin Steak Aikengall Style" and so on.

Allan McMillan made a most moving speech, George Cuthbert recited a "poem" he had composed beginning:

> When oft with prolapsed disc I rise
> I lift mine eyes unto the skies
> I think can it have been so long
> Since we in shorts and cassocks long
> Strode down the aisle a-singing.

Billy Reid proposed the toast—to which I, quite unprepared, had to reply, and various other speeches were made and presents given, and Hugh Mackay had prepared in his own inimitable way a Scroll suitably adorned which all present signed and which is now framed:

To The Very Reverend Dr Ronald Selby Wright,
C.V.O., T.D., J.P., F.R.S.E., F.S.A.Scot., etc.
We know that, to you, it is people who matter most, and so we should like to represent the great many whose lives you have so profoundly influenced during fifty years in Our Club.
Thank you, Sir.

Some weeks later I was presented with a bound copy of the proceedings, including the speeches, which I shall always greatly treasure. It was indeed for me a wonderful and memorable night.

Chapter 4

One of the difficulties that faces any Minister of the Church
who is contemplating retirement, is not only where to retire to
but also what to retire with. Throughout his parish ministry
he has had the good fortune to have had a Manse to live in, and
the possession of that should always be set along with the
never very large stipend he receives. When I entered my first
Manse in St John Street my stipend was £350 a year, out of
which had too to come all my expenses. This came entirely out
of endowment paid by the Town and the Crown. A few years
later another £100 was added to the stipend when the Old Kirk
was transferred to Pilton. When I retired in 1977 the stipend
was £2,700 plus expenses; and because the endowment
remained at £450, the rest had to be found by the Church and
congregation, which put an extra burden on them, yet because
of inflation my latter stipend was really less than the former.

Compared with other professions, Ministers' stipends
today are very small; yet it had not always been so. For
example, in 1755 the Ministers of Canongate each received
£102, and had a Manse, while the Headmaster of the High
School received £20; and in 1845 when the Ministers of
Canongate each received £240 and a Manse, the Principal of
the University's salary was £151, the Professor of Divinity
£196, and the Professor of Anatomy's £50!

With little opportunity to save money and with a Manse
that has to be given up on retirement, the prospect of
retirement for most Ministers is indeed a bleak one.
Fortunately in my case my father had taken out two policies
for me when I was at School, and when the first matured I
bought a small flat in Dunbar which I, and also my friends and
relations, could use as a holiday centre; and when the second
matured some years later I was able to sell the Dunbar flat,
which I had greatly enjoyed, and buy a National Trust flat in
The Lodge at North Berwick. I was anxious to have a place in
North Berwick because my brother had retired earlier than I,

and had bought "Farend" in Tantallon Terrace, North Berwick, facing the sea on one side and the green fields on the other, and I looked forward to walking with him and having his good and cheerful company, and also that of his wife Clare, on my visits to North Berwick. Unfortunately my brother died before this could happen, in April 1972, a month before I was to become Moderator of the General Assembly. He had been unwell for a number of years and had suffered at times great pain, and because of that had decided to retire at sixty, and be free to enjoy a more relaxed life in the fresh air. But his pain continued and when his wife took him to be X-rayed she was told that he had so severe an attack of cancer that he would almost certainly be dead within a month. He was taken to the Cottage Hospital at North Berwick where he had a nice room to himself and where his wife and daughter Diana could daily visit him. He had been looking forward so much to coming to the General Assembly and joked to me about having to apologise to the moths for disturbing them from their residence in his morning-coat. He died within the month, on 21st April, my father's birthday, and so I lost from this earth my best friend.

Clare remained on for a time in "Farend" until she got a smaller house in North Berwick. I sold my flat in the Lodge and bought "Farend" from her. Later I sold it to Norman and Elizabeth Drummond whom we have all regarded as "part of the family" and I got a smaller house nearer the shops and station called "Little Court" because I was very anxious to have somewhere in North Berwick to be nearer my sister, who by this time had left her lovely house in Richmond-on-Thames and come with her husband Stanley and her grandchildren Lila and Gina, and was later joined by her daughter Thelma and her baby daughter.

So at least I had somewhere I could live on my retirement (namely at that time "Farend") but was still anxious to have my home still in Edinburgh where I could still continue to take some part in the city I loved so much and retain some of my interests, including my Chaplaincies.

So it was that shortly before my retirement I heard through Miss Helen Nimmo, whose help to me and to the Canongate it would be difficult to exaggerate, that the Queen's House in

Moray Place—the Queen's only Grace and Favour House in Edinburgh—would, she had heard, be shortly vacant. This was confirmed by two other members of the Canongate—Lady Grant and Sir Alastair Blair, and Alastair began to make further discreet enquiries in his ever helpful way.

Now it so happened that when I had been at Crathie in the summer of 1976 Sir Martin Charteris with his wife Gay had joined us when I was having tea with Tommy and Mary Nicol in the garden of Crathie Manse, and the question of my retirement had come up, that Queen's House had been mentioned, and I expressed my interest to Martin who was the Queen's Secretary. Some months later in the course of writing to him I repeated my interest. And so it was that on 16th April 1977 I received the following letter from Windsor Castle:

My dear Ronnie,

Thank you so much for your Easter 1977 letter. It is always a pleasure to get a letter from you and in this case particularly so as I am in the happy position of being able to give you the answer which you would wish to receive.

My colleague, Rennie Maudslay, has spoken to the Queen about the possibility of your being the next occupant of Queen's House, and Her Majesty is delighted that you want to live there and has said that you shall!

Rennie will be writing to you officially about this, but has allowed me the pleasure of being able to give you the news which will, I know, bring happiness not only to you but to your friends.

I am so glad to think that you will be living in the house that Charles Warr occupied, as I know how fond you were of him.

When we last met in Tom's garden at Crathie you cast some seeds which, I am sure you noticed, did not fall on stony ground![1]

Yours ever,

Martin.

When I stayed at Balmoral in the summer I was able to thank the Queen personally for her kindness; and during her

[1] This had nothing to do with Queen's House!

visit in the following year she made a point of asking me how I was enjoying the house. I told her that not only was I enjoying it but also my dog Gen, and she said she knew how much that would matter to me too!

And so it was that at the beginning of October 1977 I left the Canongate Manse which had been such a wonderful home to me, and came to The Queen's House.

My leaving Canongate after all the years there had meant a great upheaval. I had to get rid or dispose of many papers, a large part of my library, much of my furniture and many pictures. . . . Many of the books I gave away, some I sold, and, like some of the furniture, got good prices for them which I was able to invest a little in a Building Society and supplement my pensions; but I was able to take most of my more "precious" things with me, and to find again some of the things I thought I had long lost, and have a new and still comfortable home. I joined St Giles' again, after forty years, now under the enthusiastic ministry of Gilleasbuig Macmillan.

Chapter 5

Queen's House had been given as a Grace and Favour House to the Queen by the Lord Provosts of Edinburgh, Perth, Glasgow, Dundee and Aberdeen, and a number of other people, to be used at the Queen's disposal, and Dr Warr was the first occupant, when the Queen invited him to occupy the House in 1954, when Harry Whitley came as a colleague and successor and occupied the St Giles' Manse.

The House is at 36 Moray Place in a central part of the city, and not too large, and in probably the finest residential square in Edinburgh. It is the first and only Grace and Favour House in Edinburgh.

As Sir Martin Charteris had said in his letter to me, the fact that Dr Warr had been the first Grace and Favour occupant gave me especial pleasure. I was very fond of him and he had always been very kind to me; and when he retired, after being the longest serving Minister ever at St Giles' Cathedral, he joined Canongate. I have written about him elsewhere,[1] and so will add little now except to say that he was one of the kindest and wisest men I have ever met. My father knew and indeed taught him when he was a boy and I knew him from my schooldays and joined St Giles' when he became Minister there in 1926; and when he died in 1969 I took his funeral service in Canongate before a congregation that represented nearly every person or cause that you could think of, from the Sovereign to the humblest subject; nor will I ever forget his funeral procession up the Royal Mile from Canongate when all the traffic was stopped and policemen stood saluting at the crossroads all the way to the private internment at Warriston. He wanted no Memorial and he left me all his papers—most of which are now in the National Library of Scotland—and most of his books. As Lord Charteris said in his letter, it gave me particular pleasure that the Queen should have given me the House she first gave him; and as previously mentioned I was glad too to have followed in his footsteps by becoming Chaplain to the Royal Company of Archers (the Queen's Bodyguard for Scotland), Chaplain to the Merchant Company of Edinburgh, and twice Acting Dean of the Order of the Thistle (once for him and once for John McIntyre), and once Dean of the Chapel Royal in Scotland (when Hugh Douglas was in Australia). But above all I valued his friendship, his wise counsel, and his many kindnesses to me.

The second occupant of the House, Lord Reith, was too, in quite a different way, a remarkable man. You either liked him—or you didn't; he either liked you—or he didn't. Fortunately I got to like him and he seemed to like me. He told me once that if I didn't call him "John" he would cease to call me "Ronnie", and he gave me one of his books inscribed "with immense regard"! Melville Dinwiddie, one of the finest men I have ever known, was very fond of him too, and he knew him better than I did. He greatly enjoyed being Lord High Commissioner, and held that office for two years with great distinction and indeed told me that he would like to have had a third year! But he had his "dislikes" too (he hated Churchill!) and I never felt that he was as kind as he might have

[1] *The Dictionary of National Biography 1960-80*: Oxford University Press.

been to his own family. When I was editing a book for the Oxford University Press called *Fathers of the Kirk* I asked him to write the essay on Thomas Chalmers, since Professor Hugh Watt told me that he was the greatest living authority on Chalmers; but instead of writing 4,000 words he wrote 15,000, and so the essay—and a very fine essay it was—couldn't be included, nor was it long enough to be published separately. With all his faults (and one has only to read his own published Diaries to see some of them) he was a very great man, and his work for the B.B.C. will ever stand as his greatest memorial.

My immediate predecessor in the Queen's House had been Sir Angus Mackintosh, a distinguished Member of the Diplomatic Service who had been British High Commissioner in Sri Lanka and Ambassador to the Republic of Maldives before occupying the House. When he wrote to me about taking over the House I couldn't think how he seemed to know me so well, addressing me as "My dear Ronnie" when I wrote to him as "Sir Angus", until I realised that this was the Innes Mackintosh I had known so well when we were both schoolboys, though I was several years older, before he went to Fettes College. He and his wife found the House very cold, and as a result I was able to inherit a new heating system which has made the house for me much more comfortable.

I was so grateful to the Queen for letting me have such a pleasant house for my retirement, for though I missed the Royal Mile more than I could say, and could obviously not have been able to stay there, I knew the district round Moray Place well from boyhood days, and so was not entirely a stranger to "these parts", and counted myself indeed a lucky man.

I was still able to keep a very small house in North Berwick to be near my dear sister and her family, and though I don't use it often, it is good to know that it is there to visit them, at first with my dog Gen, from time to time, and walk the shores and be refreshed by the sea breezes of North Berwick, which we used to love so much as children on our glorious holidays there, when all the family was so happily together, and when the sea seemed to be always blue and the sun seemed always to shine.

Chapter 6

It has surely been the privilege of the generation to which I belong to have witnessed in our lifetime what must have been the most exciting period in the history of our country. The British Empire, of which our generation was so rightly proud, and which covered almost half of the map of the world in red, changed to the British Commonwealth, and then simply to the Commonwealth. We have witnessed in our time a peaceful social revolution and lived through an age of great discoveries. We have lived through two world wars, in addition to some minor ones, and the reigns of four Kings and of one Queen. It was an age when the North and South Poles were both discovered; the age of the conquest of Everest; the A and H bombs; indeed of the nuclear age itself; of Radar and Wireless and Television, and the first landing on the moon.

Coming nearer home, it was an age when slums were nearly totally abolished and real poverty in our country (though not yet in "the Third World") almost unknown. True, the wars brought their horrors and their cruelty and their tears; but they also brought their heroism and their courage and their laughter.

It is hard for some younger people today to realise how different things were when I was young, when we read *The Boys' Own Paper*, *The Captain*, *Chums* and *The Children's Newspaper*. I remember the first time I listened to the radio. I was a boy of about thirteen or fourteen at the time and heard it in the house of an old Naval Commander in Peeblesshire, himself rather an unpleasant character; but Oh the thrill of hearing 2LO, and from there going on to buy a crystal set complete with cat's whisker and earphones, and being amazed at the miracle of what was then called "wireless". The first time I ever saw television was in 1948 I think. Harry and I were staying with John Williams at St Albans at the time and we trekked across in the snow to see this wonderful new invention at his friend's house, and the small and rather snowy picture. I remember when it first came to Edinburgh in 1953, and how we got all the boys up from Camp at Skateraw by special bus, and spent the whole day watching the Coronation on this new miracle of television. I remember, too, in 1945 hearing, while in hospital at Udine, the news of the first atom bomb which really finished the war in the Far East; and our joy that the war was finished at last outweighed the horror of what atomic warfare really meant. I remember on the morning of the Coronation the excitement of hearing how Everest had been conquered, and how in 1969 the thrill of seeing Neil Armstrong actually walking on the moon, which would have been a most ridiculous idea even a few years before that. And now, too, we have the computer and the silicone chips!

A notable change too in a different sphere can be seen in the happy and friendly relationship between the different branches of the one Holy Catholic and Apostolic Church—so different from my grandmother's days when even the disunited Church of Scotland had a relationship which at times almost amounted to enmity. The friendly meetings, first sponsored by the Abbot of Nunraw (after his gracious approach to Roderick Smith and myself) between ministers and elders of the Church of Scotland with their brethren of the Roman Catholic Church and the Scottish Episcopal Church, received even the blessing of the General Assembly, and it has not been uncommon now for Roman Catholics to address the Assembly and attend various Church of Scotland functions. In 1962 I was indeed the first Church of Scotland minister to preach in St Mary's Episcopal Cathedral in Palmerston Place; United Communion Services and joint Confirmation Services are now held in many of our Boarding Schools. It is good as well to feel that within the lifetime of the generation to which I belong, the various Churches now live together as brothers.

And nearer home how remarkable it was to see the slow departure of the slums I had known, sometimes seven in a room, the poverty I had seen, when few in the old Royal Mile ever knew what it was to wear new clothes, and sometimes even to have a pair of shoes; where now Canongate is a sort of modern Chelsea, where some young men even complain that they haven't enough money, when they have wealth that we never even dreamed of in these earlier days. I remember the excitement when we used to take people to the country for the day for the Sunday School picnic, or later for the week to Camp, when at last they saw the sea and the sand and the waves breaking on the shore—a day in the country or a week

268

at Camp is now for so many people a fortnight or three weeks in Spain. I remember the excitement as a boy when an aeroplane was seen in the sky and people would run out crying "an aeroplane, an aeroplane!" Now for so many it is the ordinary and regular way of travelling and you can get from Edinburgh to London and back in one day, or fly to Cyprus quicker than you can reach London from Edinburgh by train; indeed, as I have mentioned elsewhere, my journey to India in a Jumbo jet, long as it seemed, was shorter than the journey I made from Edinburgh to Thurso by train.

One would like to think that all these changes have brought with them equivalent happiness and contentment; and while of course it is right to be happy that people's conditions are today so much better, it is sad, too, to think that there is still so much discontent. People seem to want more and more for less and less, and greed and covetnousness seem in so many circles to be the order of the day. Once one helped one's neighbour, later one began to try to keep up with him; and now so many want to be "one up" on him. Of course it isn't true of everyone or everything; but there is so much truth in it that it does tend sometimes to make one sad and to wonder really what "progress" is all about. The Old Book tells us that "Godliness with contentment is great gain, for we brought nothing into this world and we take nothing out"—or in that rather delightful translation of the same passage:[1]

> "Do you want to be truly rich? You already are if you are happy and good. After all we didn't bring any money with us when we came into the world and we cannot carry away a single penny when we die. So we should be well-satisfied if we have enough food and clothing. But people who long to be rich soon begin to do all kinds of wrong things to get money, things that hurt them and make them evil-minded and finally send them to Hell itself. For the love of money is the first step towards all kinds of sin. Some people have even turned away from God because of their love for it, and as a result they pierced themselves with many sorrows."

Of course people must have enough but, to coin a phrase, "enough is enough".

[1] I Timothy 6⁶ (*The Living Bible*).

On the other hand this, too, must be acknowledged: I cannot help but feel that, in the words of Anthony Chenevix-Trench "the new generation is morally braver, more truthful, more serious, intelligent, candid, and frank . . .". This generation certainly seems more concerned than we were when we were young to help the old and less privileged, not only here at home but in the so-called "third world" about which my generation knew so little.

I suppose that my philosophy of life can be fairly summed up in the words from Robert Louis Stevenson's *Christmas Sermon*, which, along with Kipling's "If" (that splendid but now, I fear, rather despised poem) used to hang on our nursery wall when we were children, both of which we all got to know by heart but in which I have so often failed.

> "To be honest, to be kind—to earn a little and to spend a little less, to make upon the whole a family happier for his presence, to renounce when that shall be necessary and not be embittered, to keep a few friends but these without capitulation—above all, on the same grim conditions, to keep friends with himself—here is a task for all that a man has of fortitude and delicacy."

And my faith could be summed up in the first fourteen verses of the Gospel according to St John: ". . . and the Word became flesh and dwelt among us and we beheld His glory"; and in the word I chose as my motto: "Confidite"—His Word that has ever comforted and strengthened me in the *Other Home* I have been privileged to enjoy in this world.

For though I know that this world is not our "home" and that we are all "strangers and pilgrims as all our fathers were", I know too that this "other home" which God in his loving-kindness has provided for me in this world, has given me, with at times its sorrows and anxieties, with too my many faults and failings, so much happiness—not least because of the many kindnesses I have received and the many friendships here I have enjoyed—and, knowing that, I realise how even greater must be "the joy and the glory" of our *real* "home".

Kyrie Eleison.

Index

271

Campbell, The Right Hon. Gordon (Lord), 225, 231, 233f
Campbell, Miss Judy, 47
Campbell, Col. J. T., 71, 87
Campbell, Prof. Neil, 25, 207
Campbell, W. W. K., 107, 114f
Campbell of Argyll, 2
Canadian Cemetery, 154
Canadian Forces, 85
Canongate, Edinburgh, 26 *et passim*
Canongate Boys' Club, 22
Canongate Kirk, 26f, 35f
Canterbury, Archbishop of, 226, 231
Cargilfield, 11, 240f
Carpenter, The Very Rev. S. C., 98
Carrington, General Sir Robert, 85
Casa Dusé, 152
Cash, Caleb, 13
Cassels, Field-Marshal Sir James, 107, 114, 181f
Cassillis, Earl of, 33, 174, 207, 257
Caterham, 101
Cerne Abbas, 42
Chalmers, Thomas, 162, 203, 266
Chamberlain, Neville, 39
Chapel Royal, Dean of, 265
Charles, Prince, 33, 177, 183, 188, 191f, 223, 231, 236, 255, 259
Charles, Prince, Edward Stuart, 250
Charteris, Lord, 173, 252f, 263
Charteris, Lady Elizabeth, 189
Charteris Hospital, 228
Chenevix-Trench, Anthony, 18, 172, 202, 206, 252, 270
Chenevix-Trench, Jonathan, 203, 253
Chenevix-Trench, Richard, 203
Chelsea Barracks, 122
Cherbourg, 44f
Chiene, Col. John, 40
Chillon, Castle of, 154
China, 241
"Chips" Mr, 252
Chisholm, Pte. Joe, 58
Chislett, Charles, 141, 149
Christian, King, 160f
Christie, J. T., 73
Christmas 1939, 41
Church, Dr Leslie, 128
Church of Scotland, Union of, 20f
Churchill, Sir Winston, 139, 265
Citadel, Royal Barracks, 95f
Clagenfurt, 150
Clark, Gen. Mark, 137

Clayton, The Rev. T. B. ("Tubby"), 73, 258
Clifton, 98
Clifton Hall, 240f
Clydesdale, Marquis of, 191
Clydesmuir, Lord, 220, 225, 234
Cochrane, Cameron, 203, 219, 254
Cockburn, Lord, 37
Coghill, William, 158
Cole-Hamilton, Richard, 202, 254
Coleridge, F. J. R., 252
Coles, Fr. H. T., 79, 208f
Collins, Canon L. J., 234
Colmer, George, 132ff, 137, 141, 143f, 146, 149f, 152
Colthurst, The Rev. Alan, 56f, 62, 67
Colquhoun, The Rev. James, 32, 166
Commandos, 237
Como, Lake, 152
Connington, 239
Cooper, Alison, 123
Cooper, The Rev. Dr Jack, 166
Coutts, Diana, 173
Coutts, Brigadier Frank, 54f, 179, 182
Craig, The Very Rev. Dr A. C., 241
Craig, John, 35
Craig, Col. Tom, 107, 114, 181
Craigellachie, 89
Craigflower, 18
Cranwell, 238f
Crathie, 192
Crawford, Maj. Ian, 40, 87
Crazy Gang, 47, 92
Crewkerne, 42
Crichton, The Rev. Tom, 166 176
Crichton-Miller, Donald, 201, 254
Cripps, Sir Stafford, 103
Crockatt, Brig. Norman, 123
Crocker, Patrick, 202, 254
Crockett, Major, 84
Croft, David, 207, 260
Croom, Sir John Halliday, 42
Crossman, Gen., 93
Cruden Bay, 77f
Cruickshank, Pte., 54, 70, 87
Crum, Maj. F. M., 30, 66, 102
Cullen, 86
Cumbernauld, 226
Cunningham, Gen. Sir Alan, 13
Cunningham, Admiral Viscount, 13, 150
Curr, Tom, 79
Currie, The Rev. Gordon, 166

278